A Critical History of Television's
The Red Skelton Show, 1951–1971

ALSO BY WESLEY HYATT
AND FROM MCFARLAND

Kicking Off the Week: A History of Monday Night Football *on ABC Television, 1970–2005* (2007)

Emmy Award Winning Nighttime Television Shows, 1948–2004 (2006)

Short-Lived Television Series, 1948–1978: Thirty Years of More Than 1,000 Flops (2003)

A Critical History of Television's *The Red Skelton Show*, 1951–1971

WESLEY HYATT

McFarland & Company, Inc., Publishers
Jefferson, North Carolina, and London

The present work is a reprint of the library bound edition of
A Critical History of Television's *The Red Skelton Show*,
1951–1971, *first published in 2004 by McFarland*.

LIBRARY OF CONGRESS CATALOGUING-IN-PUBLICATION DATA

Hyatt, Wesley.
 A critical history of television's *The Red Skelton Show*,
1951–1971 / Wesley Hyatt.
  p.   cm.
 Includes bibliographical references and index.

ISBN 978-0-7864-4686-5
softcover : 50# alkaline paper ∞

1. Red Skelton show (Television program) I. Title.
PN1992.77.R45H93   2010
791.45'72—dc22   2003027763

British Library cataloguing data are available

©2004 Wesley Hyatt. All rights reserved

*No part of this book may be reproduced or transmitted in any form
or by any means, electronic or mechanical, including photocopying
or recording, or by any information storage and retrieval system,
without permission in writing from the publisher.*

Front cover: *The Red Skelton Show* (CBS) (Photofest)

Manufactured in the United States of America

*McFarland & Company, Inc., Publishers
 Box 611, Jefferson, North Carolina 28640
 www.mcfarlandpub.com*

To Harry Wayne Casey,
whom I consider to be a great entertainer
and am pleased to call a special friend

Acknowledgments

One of the joys of doing this project has been the interviews I conducted among the shrinking number who were connected intimately to *The Red Skelton Show*. Their memories were vivid and lively, their opinions frank and direct. I heard from those who dearly loved the show's star, and those who were less enthusiastic about Red—sometimes much less. With all the information I gleaned from them, viewing some 25 videotapes of the series and reading dozens of articles and books about Red and the show, I believe I've given as fair and wide a portrait of the series and its star as can be done at present.

The interviewees and the dates I talked with them are as follows: Lee Aaker (Oct. 3, 2002); James Bacon (Nov. 8, 2002); George Balzer (Sept. 19, 2002); Lana Cantrell (Nov. 21, 2002); Alan Copeland (Nov. 8, 2002); Ray Erlenborn (Aug. 19, 2002); Benedict Freedman (emailed Sept. 2, 2002); Devery Freeman (Sept. 13, 2002); Stanley Green (Oct. 1, 2002); Chanin Hale (Dec. 9, 2002); Tom Hansen (Sept. 17, 2002); Terry Kyne (Oct. 3, 2002); Perry Lafferty (Aug. 20, 2002); June Lockhart (Dec. 22, 2002); Patrice Munsel (Dec. 4, 2002); Robert Orben (Sept. 26, 2002); Herb Schlosser (Sept. 17, 2002); and Ken Shapiro (Sept. 13, 2002). I particularly want to thank Chanin Hale, who, besides talking to me several times, also supplied the rare photographs of Red and her and his guests on his TV series in this book.

A special mention beyond the call of duty should go to Bets Hobin, whom I first contacted on Sept. 26, 2002. The wife of the show's late director and producer, Bill Hobin, Bets informed me that he had written a massive unpublished autobiography with several chapters about his time on *The Red Skelton Hour*, and she kindly gave me permission to use it and quote from it, for which I am truly thankful. It's the closest equivalent to a Rosetta stone for a series I've ever found when doing research on a project.

Another special note of thanks goes to Mark Quigley, reference and outreach coordinator of the UCLA Film and Television Archive, who generously set up my viewing of 10 hard-to-find tapes of *The Red Skelton Show*, from its premiere in 1951 through a 1969 show with Merv Griffin. Based on my research, UCLA has the most extensive collection of the series' episodes outside of the Skelton estate, and I greatly appreciate Mr. Quigley's assistance in helping an "outsider" view the material.

Other sources for material include Script City of Hollywood, Calif.; several books, articles and websites listed in the Bibliography; and assorted videotape and memorabilia collectors on eBay. Given that people involved on that website use pseudonyms, I'll just have to say thanks to these anonymous helpers collectively.

Outside of research, I'd like to tip my hat once more to my loving parents, Ron and Gayle Hyatt, whose unwavering support of their son's passion for the history of entertainment is an indulgence every child in the world should be fortunate to have. Words of thanks also go out to my sister LuAnn and her husband Skip, for their love as well as their adorable children, my nephew Bennett and my niece Brynn, who can amuse me the same way a great episode of *The Red Skelton Show* can.

Others who put a smile on my face during my efforts on this book include my fellow members of the "Ellis Five"—Renee Duncan, Julie Ellis, Scott Norris and Donna Uguccioni; my office co-workers at Divers Alert Network, Dan Leigh, Steve Mehan and Rick Melvin; another DAN colleague, Steve Barnett, who knows more about photography than I ever will; and my old pals past and present, including Dave Barciz, Bill Cudworth, Tony Cunningham, Jon Dormish, Arthur Jordan, Jimmy Lancaster, Michael Money, Daryl Roth and Carlton Willis.

And I must not forget my pals at Standup Underground, a troupe of hopeful comedians who want to give the world a laugh and were nice enough to include me in the mix when it started in 2002. Watching Red's show not only made me laugh, but realize what could work for me in my stage presence as well, and my fellow jokesters gave me a chance to put my ideas into actual performing, of which I am eternally grateful. So thank you, Carmen Buffington, Art Church, Marshall Henry, Page Lewis, Ann Roy, Kris Snyder, Bruce Sokol, Lawrence "L.T." Tinker, Anne Walker and Roger "Skip" Way.

If there is anybody else I've left out—and I'm sure there is—please be assured that your omission was not intentional, just a lack of ambition and space in trying to name everyone I know.

And to all Red's fans, friends and curiosity seekers reading this book about his show, in the spirit of Red's famous closing words, let me say to you "God bless" from my heart.

Wesley Hyatt
January 2004

Table of Contents

Acknowledgments	vii
Introduction	1
1. Events Leading Up to Red's Television Series	5
2. 1951–1953: You're the Top, Now You're Not	18
3. 1953–1956: From the Bottom to the Top 20	34
4. 1956–1962: "I'm Just Lucky"?	51
5. 1962–1967: The Glory Years	71
6. 1967–1970: "We Had No Concept of That Show Being Cancelled"	100
7. 1970–1971: "It Would Be Presumptuous to Change, Modernize or Innovate Skelton"	122
8. 1971–Present: "It Should Be 'Red Skelton, Red Skelton, Red Skelton'"	140
Appendix A: The Red Skelton Show Cast and Crew Credits	161
Appendix B: The Red Skelton Show Guests by Season	162
Appendix C: Whatever Happened to…? A Select List of *The Red Skeleton Show* Principals	175
Bibliography	177
Index	179

Introduction

The Red Skelton Show ran 20 years, making it still one of the five longest-running network television series of all time seen between 7 and 11 P.M. (*Walt Disney* is first, with 38 years, then *60 Minutes* at 35 years, *Monday Night Football* at 31 years and *The Ed Sullivan Show* at 23 years; *Gunsmoke* ties Red's show at 20 years). It spent nine years as a top 10 series, an accomplishment equaled at this writing by only two other programs, *M*A*S*H* and *Home Improvement*, and surpassed by just two more, *Gunsmoke* (13 years) and *Bonanza* (10 years). It managed the rare feat of peaking at #2 at the end of two non-consecutive seasons, 1962–63 and 1966–67.

The Red Skelton Show has a few unimpressive achievements too, however. After finishing in the top 10 in its debut season on NBC in 1951–52, it became the first top 10 series to drop out of the top 25 its following year. Luckily for Red, his show moved to CBS in the fall of 1953, but it took several seasons for him to regain popularity, finally breaking back into the top 10 in the 1959–60 season—a record nine-year gap between then and the show's last time on the list. Most notoriously, *The Red Skelton Show* was the first top 10 series to be cancelled by a network, CBS, in 1970. Red moved to NBC the next year, but the show's appeal dropped markedly, and he went off after one season.

That cancellation happened in a period when CBS was getting rid of primarily comedies that appealed to elderly and rural viewers in order to please sponsors who wanted to reach younger, more upscale audiences. As a result, most TV historians have lumped Red's show in with the likes of *Petticoat Junction* and *The Jim Nabors Hour* as part of the unsophisticated programming of the period and therefore written off its quality. This is grossly unfair to both Red and his series.

Red didn't help this assessment by doing relatively little TV after the series ended in 1971 until his death in 1997. Absence on television does not make the heart grow fonder—it makes people forget you and your legacy. Even worse, Red grew so upset with CBS's cancellation that to get back at the network, he refused to let reruns appear, thus depriving his fans of the bulk of his best TV work. That tradition carries to this day with his estate, which refuses to license his CBS shows for home viewing on videotapes or DVDs. Only a handful of them exist for sale from other distributors, some in quite poor quality.

All of this has led to *The Red Skelton Show* being rarely seen except among dedicated video enthusiasts. Given that Red is dead, and many of his show's original fans are too by now, that group is very small and nowhere near matches people's familiarity with the other shows previously listed. *Walt Disney*, *60 Minutes*, and *Monday Night Football* are all still on the air at this writing; *M*A*S*H* and *Home Improvement* remain popular in reruns on local TV stations. Even *The Ed Sullivan Show*, *Gunsmoke* and *Bonanza* have dedicated devotees to a certain extent in reruns, and all have multiple episodes on videotapes and DVDs available from reputable companies, thus assuring them of a continuing following among later generations.

But most of Red's material remains unseen, and as the years pass, the demand will continue to decrease unless this situation changes drastically. For anyone who cares about TV history, that's bad.

The Red Skelton Show's years of being TV's most popular comedy variety series and numerous nominations for TV's top award, the Emmy (with admittedly few wins and not as many nominations as years on the air), have been overlooked, replaced instead by remarkably poor and inadequate documentation about it among authors. The inaccuracies are so pervasive, you'd think there's a conspiracy involving a ministry of misinformation about Red Skelton in existence somewhere. Consider these misstatements:

- "Red's show began in 1953"—incredibly, two otherwise very well-researched photo books, Daniel Blum's *Pictorial History of Television* (1959) and Arthur Shulman and Roger Youman's *How Sweet It Was!* (1966), gave this wrong starting year even though they were among the first books covering TV history. (Shulman and Youman kept the mistake in their 1973 update *The Television Years*.) The authors should've recognized better from coverage in the press of the period, if not from their own memories. In its first season on NBC in 1950-51, the series ranked #4 in the ratings and won Red an Emmy—how hard could it have been to overlook *that*?

Additionally, Vincent Terrace followed the same line in his first *Complete Encyclopedia of Television Series 1947–1976*, and worse yet, a contributor to the best seller *The Book of Lists* (1978) used that information to compile a list of the longest-running TV series, thereby perpetuating a myth that Red's show ran two years fewer than *Gunsmoke* when, in fact, they had the same two-decade run—and Red reached that mark first.

- "Red did his show alone almost all the years on TV, except for his last one on NBC"—Tim Brooks and Earle Marsh's *The Complete Directory to Prime Time Network TV Shows 1946–Present* (first printed in 1979) and Alex McNeil's *Total Television* (first printed in 1980) agreed on this general idea in their books and subsequent updates, although McNeil listed Lucille Knoch was a regular in the 1951-53 seasons (that's true). But they differ in listing the personnel that season. Vincent Terrace's *Encyclopedia of Television: Series, Pilots and Specials (1937–1984)* from 1986 listed regulars both in the last NBC run (yet another list of names) and supposed regulars during the CBS years.

There's one thing these books all have in common; they're wrong about the regulars in the last year—and other years too. For example, when the show went to an hour on CBS in 1962, the Tom Hansen Dancers were a regular attraction billed in the introductions and did a production number each week for eight years. Hansen, in fact, had the last Emmy nomination for the show, for Best Choreography in 1970. Yet only Terrace credits the group, even though the show was one of CBS's top audience attractions at the time. Didn't anyone else remember this and tell the other authors during their updates? As for Terrace, his books often commit the sin of listing those who were guest stars as regulars or (in the case of the dancers) not listing the exact years when performers were regulars on a show, and this is the case for many of the people he lists in his *Red Skelton Show* entry.

- "Freddie the Freeloader never spoke"—this chestnut has survived through seven updated editions of *The Complete Directory to Prime Time Network TV Shows 1946–Present* over 20 years. It's become such a prevalent notion that even Robert L. Mott, who wrote for Red in the 1969-70 season, thought it was true. The fact is that Freddie spoke constantly throughout the show's run, from his creation in 1952 until the cancellation in 1971. There were a few sketches where he was mute, but so was everyone else in them too. The majority of the shows where he appeared had him talking, just like Red's other creations.

Other TV history books barely mention Red and his impact. Jeff Kisseloff's *The Box* (1995), an oral history of people involved in TV production from 1920 to 1961, lists Red's name only twice, and one of those was just in an introductory paragraph to one chapter. 1978's *TV Guide: The First 25 Years*, a compilation of the publication's most notable articles, did include one about Red, but not about his performing style, as had articles in the book on Sid Caesar, Jack Benny, Steve Allen, Milton Berle and other comedians. Instead, the book used a 1957 article about his son Richard's battle with leukemia—a touching story, yes, but it tells very little about what Red did on TV. (And oddly, the book had no editorial note about if and when Red's son died.) It just defined Red by his personal rather than professional life—a cheat to him and the reader, especially since *TV Guide* did other, more in-depth articles on the show in later years.

Clearly, *The Red Skelton Show* has been underreported and under-appreciated for far too long.

To get the "inside story" of the program, I have interviewed show personnel on and off stage (see Acknowledgments for a full listing), plus watched dozens of videotapes of the show from its first season to its last, some of which I'll make mention of in the text. Each chapter will cover specific periods of the show based on my judgment of seasons having some elements in common, such as 1951–53, when he was on NBC, and 1962–67, when his show went from a half hour to an hour and received its highest ratings.

There will be some autobiographical details about Red discussed on the way, but the focus here is on the show and what its star did involving it. As you will see, there is enough drama associated with the series that we really do not need to concentrate on a biography of Red, which incidentally already has been done twice. (See a listing of those books and other sources I used for research in the Bibliography.)

Enough with the details. Now let's go on to *The Red Skelton Show*!

1
Events Leading Up to Red's Television Series

Watching *The Red Skelton Show* over its various incarnations from the 1950s through 1970s, one is struck by a variety of contradictory reactions. The show is top-notch inventive comedy at times, then during other periods, its humor is ancient, hackneyed and unfunny. It could be both classy and crass. There are routines in it that virtually no other comedian than Red could handle as well, then there are ones that no other comedian but Red would *want* to handle. Its comedy could be obvious yet touching, and for all of its promises of giving viewers a wildly outrageous, funny show, it remained an essentially conservative program that basically never made fun of any old-fashioned values.

These contrasting elements all are a reflection of its star, Red Skelton. A man who professed to love television and had his biggest professional success there, he turned his back on it in his late fifties and spent a quarter century downplaying or even denying what he had done in the medium. This attitude likewise reflected the opinions of many television critics and historians since that time, who have largely discounted the impact of the man and his series in the history of television.

They're simply wrong. And I will show why, starting off with a look at the man first.

Meet the Mysterious Clown

Red was a friendly, inviting face to viewers who nevertheless felt uncomfortable among his comic peers, even though many of those same people thought he was among the top in their profession. As a man who thought of himself more as a clown than comedian, that feeling is understandable.

What is less comprehensible is why Red felt he needed, at times, to embellish (or as detractors would put it, lie) about his life and career. It could have to do with his insecurities of growing up poor without a father or lacking a formal high school education. Or maybe both of these items, plus others we do not know. What we do know is that for a man who came across so open to the public, he was remarkably mysterious about his own history.

For example, Red's biographers Arthur Marx and Wes D. Gehring wrote at length about the circumstances of Red's birth that fascinated them. Marx heard rumors that Red actually was born on July 18, 1906, seven years earlier than his birth date cited by most sources. Indeed, Red fueled the flame on this rumor to *People* magazine in 1980, when he claimed he was in his seventies at the time.

Yet records from his birthplace of Vincennes, Indiana, plus Red's death record from California and his listing in the Social Security Death Index all agree that Red was born on July 18, 1913. Chances are that he had been using 1906 as a birth year to get work permits when he was underage and on the road and sometimes forgot in interviews that he had done this.

Gehring was more intrigued that the Indiana record listed Red's name as Richard Bernard Eheart. Apparently Red's father, Joseph Skelton, sometimes used the surname of his mother's second husband as his own, and that name, Eheart, was recorded as Red's original surname.

Actually, to the TV historian, the really interesting element surrounding Red's birth is not his surname, nor his real first name. (As you can imagine from seeing him, he got the nickname "Red" for the color of his hair.) It's that middle name, Bernard. You see, Red used to call himself Victor van Bernard on his TV series as his showtime "identity" when he was performing, and his TV show was billed as "A Van Bernard Production." To Red, it wasn't himself who was going out there to face a studio audience, and by extension, millions of fans at home—it was Victor Van Bernard.

A man as big and successful as Red needing an alter ego to survive his stage fright? It may sound strange, but it's true. And it's far from the only oddity that cropped up as Red Skelton grew up from a nobody to a top TV attraction.

Born in a Trunk?

For years Red claimed that Joseph Skelton, his father who died tragically two months before Red was born, had been a clown, and that his profession inspired Red. It's a nice story, but Gehring found little evidence of that being Joseph's job, at least not in the few years before Red was born. By the time of the birth of Joseph's second son Chris on July 15, 1907 (his first was Joseph Ishmal on Sept. 29, 1905), Red's father had a job listed as a lineman in the Vincennes city directory. The next year, when another boy, Paul, was born to the family on July 10, 1908, Joseph was listed as a grocer, the same job his local obituary said he had when he died in 1913.

Joseph may have indeed been a clown before the boys were born; Red did say his dad was with a circus in the 1890s. Whatever the case, show business was hardly on the minds of any of the boys as they eked out a life to support themselves and their widowed mom in Vincennes in the 1910s and 1920s. Red did his part by selling newspapers, racking up billiard balls at a local pool hall, and other doing chores that paid him some money.

For years Red claimed that his turning point came from a chance meeting with comic Ed Wynn when the latter came to perform in Vincennes when Red was a youngster. Supposedly Ed bought a paper from Red while in town, then was beguiled or took pity on Red and bought him a ticket for his show in town that night. Again, as with the "my father was a clown" claim, there is little in contemporary accounts to verify that Wynn even visited the town, and Red's recollection of how old he was when it happened varied from 7 to 10 years old, depending on the interview. Some think that Red's fondness for Wynn's performing style in vaudeville and/or radio led him to make this claim as one of fact. It can at least be said that Skelton remained an eternal fan of Wynn's, having the comedian on his show several times through 1966, the year he died at age 80.

Red's real induction into show business supposedly came in his teens, when he left school to perform in various venues in the entertainment field, including a touring acting group, a river showboat, and a touring circus. Yet here again, what he said in interviews does not match up well with what supporting documents can be found in his favor. Papers show he was billed as a performer in minstrel shows produced by Clarence Stout, a music impresario based in Vincennes, in 1929, when he was 15.

Fact and lore from Red finally combine the following year, as it is confirmed that he toured Kansas City as a comic in 1930 and while there met 15-year-old Edna Stilwell. She didn't care for him at the time. But the next year, when he returned to emcee a Walkathon (a sad sport in the early days of the Depression whereby couples competed to stay on their feet the longest to win a sizable amount of money; Red had to keep them and spectators amused during the proceedings, a tough enough job in itself), she found him more amusing.

As luck would have it, Edna competed in the contest and actually won after more than two months. She celebrated her win with Red, and they were married on June 1, 1931, four days after she turned 16. Though the marriage would not last (they filed for divorce in 1943 and had it finalized a year later), Edna would prove to be excellent for Red as a business and professional manager. She knew what he deserved in terms of his salary and his bookings, and as such she would be his woman in charge until around 1952, when it was said Red stopped dealing with her on any level due to jealousy from his second wife. She died in 1982.

Getting into Radio and Movies

For three years after he wed Edna, Red basically played the "Walkathon circuit" across America. Then in 1934, his performance in a Walkathon in Atlanta caught the attention of vaudeville comic "Uncle Jim" Harkins, who suggested Red contact a New York agent named Tom Kennedy to start working in Harkins' field. Kennedy booked Red in several venues, including the Lido Club in Montreal, Canada, where, despite the challenges thrown by hecklers in his first few shows, Red succeeded and became a hit.

His act basically consisted of jokes and mimicry, with none of his characters he later did on TV in place. He became familiar with the routines of other vaudevillians, including Milton Berle, one of the few in his profession with whom Red felt comfortable in socializing due to their somewhat similar backgrounds and unsubtle comic styles. The only problem for Red was that vaudeville was slowly dying in the 1930s, as radio and movies easily held more attention for the masses across America. But Red, unlike some vaudevillians, would be able to make it in both media.

He went for a time alternating between clubs in Montreal and Toronto before finally getting back to the States and making his belated New York City debut in June 1937. Red by that time had refined his routine to include brilliant pantomiming of various types of people, including the different ways people dunked their donuts, which he had to end once his props started costing him his waistline. His reviews were solid and led to him making his radio debut on *The Rudy Vallee Show* on Aug. 12 that year.

Rudy Vallee was the radio matinee idol of the 1930s whose professional talent show outshone all his competitors, making it the *Star Search* of its day for those who wanted to make it big. Red was a hit on the show and fan mail demanded that he return, which he did two weeks later, followed by another go in November. But he learned, as did many other vaudeville comics, that radio ate up your material fast, and you could not rely on the same routine over and over again to win audiences, so he looked to keep updating his routines accordingly.

Meanwhile, film producer Pancho Berman saw Red performing on stage in New York and signed him in August 1937 to make his film debut in *Having Wonderful Time*, a hit Broadway comedy about a summer camp catering largely to Jews in the Catskills of New York. With anti–Semitism unfortunately a consideration for the movie version to succeed, Red and other non–Jewish actors starred in the film. When it came out a year later, it flopped, and Red's primary mode of work in 1938 remained in vaudeville.

But by that year, Red and Edna had switched agents from Tom Kennedy to advertising executive Freeman Keyes, who managed to get Red into his own radio show. *Avalon Time* had been running on NBC radio Saturdays 7–7:30 P.M. on the East Coast since Oct. 1, 1938, hosted by country singer Red Foley. The show was not exactly a ratings grabber, so effective Jan. 1, 1939, Red became its new host. His wife Edna could be heard on the show as well as a mock heckler, and Foley stayed as a regular until he left after a few months. Curt Massey took his place, but nobody cared or made much notice of the show. Red last did it on Dec. 20, 1939; *Avalon Time* limped along with Cliff Arquette (later to gain fame as his rustic character Charley Weaver) and Don McNeill until it ended on May 1, 1940. The most interesting element about the series was that it marked the first time Red used a writer, Jack Douglas, who would continue to work with Red into his early TV days.

Red didn't have to worry about losing the radio show. There were other club gigs awaiting him, and most importantly, on Jan. 29, 1940, he earned the prestigious honor of entertaining President Franklin D. Roosevelt at the latter's birthday luncheon. Another entertainer on the bill, actor Mickey Rooney, saw Red's jokes decimate the audience and came back to his movie studio MGM, where Rooney then reigned as the #1 box office attraction, to tell his boss Louis B. Mayer that he ought to sign the comic. (Red may have been grateful for this move, for Rooney would become one of Red's most frequent guest stars on his TV series.) After some prodding, Mayer tested Red on film, and after some initial fumbling and stumbling, Red came up with a bit of physical comedy that cracked up all who saw it. Red got a movie contract for his troubles.

There was an interesting clause in that contract. It allowed Red to work on television as well as radio. "They all thought I was nuts," Red recalled in 1970 about MGM executives' reaction to the provision. Television was nowhere as developed and explored in Hollywood in 1940 the way it had been in New York City, where Red principally worked in the last few years, and though it still remained largely experimental, Red realized that with his physical humor, he could be a bigger star on it than radio or even movies ever would allow him.

He sure was right about that one.

Red's Rise in the Movies

The first role MGM gave Red was in 1940's *Flight Command*, as supporting comic relief to Robert Taylor in a war melodrama. He performed the same task in his next film, *The People vs. Dr. Kildare* in 1941, where he played an intern. It took his third film, 1941's *Whistling in the Dark*, to give Red a lead role in a comedy that became a hit.

In *Whistling in the Dark*, Red played radio actor Wally Benton, whose detective character, the Fox, is much more calm and clever than the actor. When gangsters kidnap Wally to give them advice on how to carry out the perfect murder, he finds himself having to do their bidding to stay alive, and then tries to undo his own plan before an innocent man is killed. Red's great delivery of lines and body language won him plaudits, and the comic soon became MGM's leading humor star.

Unfortunately, MGM's forte was not comedy by any means, and Red frequently saw himself having to do supporting roles in several musicals, ranging from 1942's *Panama Hattie* through 1952's *Lovely to Look At* between his leading comedy movies. Though no one would argue any of Red's film comedies were classics, he did have several amusing moments in features like *The Fuller Brush Man* (where he was loaned out to Columbia Pictures) and *A Southern Yankee*, both in 1948.

Helping Red polish his comedy on the later films was silent movie comedian Buster Keaton, who found himself needing work in the 1940s and signed with MGM as a consultant. Keaton praised Red's talents over the years in several interviews, even saying the comedian was so expressive he was one of the few of his generation who could have made it big in silent pictures. But strangely, Red was far less appreciative in returning the compliments. He did drop by and offer words of praise when the TV series *This Is Your Life* surprised Buster Keaton by recounting his life story on April 3, 1957, and in 1987, he gave his memories of the comedian for the PBS series *American Masters*. But Red never had Buster as a guest on his TV series, even though that comedian had a celebrated comeback in TV and movies through his death in 1966, an oddity indeed given their relationship and Keaton's perfect suitability to do pantomime with Red.

Red's film career on MGM petered out after a mixed bag of credits in 1953. But if nothing else, the success of *Whistling in the Dark* paved the way for Red to get a new radio show, and that development, more than his movies, made him a household name.

The Raleigh Cigarette Program

As was often the custom of the time, Red's radio show, which debuted on Oct. 7, 1941, did not bear his name in the title but rather that of its sponsor. *The Raleigh Cigarette Program* had Red starring in a half-hour variety package for Raleigh Cigarettes (of course!) with Ozzie Nelson as Red's bandleader and his wife Harriet as vocalist and occasional foil for Red in sketches. A topical monologue kicked off each show, followed by a band number and then a main sketch. Slotted at Tuesdays 10:30–11 P.M. on the East Coast, it followed the popular *Bob Hope Show*, and like that comedian, Red's radio show was also a top hit.

Red unveiled two long-running characters that first season on the air, Clem Kadiddlehopper and Junior, "the mean widdle kid." Clem Kadiddlehopper was the quintessential lamebrained country bumpkin. The character had his roots in Carl Hopper, a neighbor of Red's in Vincennes—well, not the stupidity, but other traits. Carl Hopper's poor hearing led him to misconstrue hearing and speaking words, yet he nonetheless had a cheerful exterior. Carl later got a hearing aid and fared better as an adult, but his attitude, and the fact that Red had nicknamed him "Kadiddle," obviously stuck with the comedian in creating Clem. Harriet Nelson played his girlfriend Daisy in the sketches involving Clem, and at first he was said to be a cab driver, but later his employment was varied and unspecified.

To do Clem, Red typically drew in his lower lip, sported a somewhat bewildered look and wore a hat whose brim was turned up. (Hats were important for every character of Red's, even on radio, as he felt they helped him get into character.) For an idea of how dumb sounding Clem was, just listen to the voice of Bullwinkle on any episode of the cartoon *The Bullwinkle Show* (a/k/a *Rocky and His Friends*), which ran on the networks in 1959–73 and 1981–82. The dull vocal with occasional inflections by Bullwinkle is a match for Clem's, so much so that Red threatened to file a lawsuit for copyright infringement by the character.

But the breakout character was Junior, a troublesome lad who liked to do things his parents told him not to do. "If I dood it, I gets a whipping," he'd tell the amused audience, after which he proceeded to break something or cause trouble and announce, "I dood it!" The catchphrase was so ingrained in the early 1940s that a 1943 film starring Red was titled *I Dood It*, even though Red did not play Junior in it. The limitations of the character being done as an adult in full view of a home audience made it seem unlikely that Red would reprise it on TV, and he did not—for a while, that is.

The show's chief writer, as with *Avalon Time*, remained Red's wife

Edna, even after she and Red divorced on Feb. 17, 1944. (He married the former Georgia Davis on March 9, 1945.) She and Red devised a system of cataloging jokes for later use and reference that proved invaluable to Red. He grouped his jokes on 3-by-5 index cards under one-word categories—"Birds," "Hotels," "Tennis," and so forth—and updated some over the years to make references more contemporary, like replacing "Hedy Lamarr" with a current sexpot.

Red's estate sold the catalog after his death, and I managed to purchase a lot of 40 of them. Here are samples of some of the gags that he used in his routines, possibly although not assuredly, on his 1940s radio show:

> No one ever got rich being nosey, except maybe Jimmy Durante.
>
> I went for a long walk in the woods and stepped on a skunk in the dark, and was he surprised. The second surprise was on me.
>
> The craziest things happen when you're jogging. There was a guy up ahead of me running along, so I caught up to him and said: "Jogging? Health?" He said: "Prison—escape."

Red's joke file grew so much that by the 1960s, it took up some 250 foot-long boxes in his house in Cathedral City, Calif. It was so extensive that when comic Jack Kirkwood offered Red his file, only 20 percent of the jokes contained within it were ones Red did not have. Red told Dwight Whitney of *TV Guide* in 1963 that outside of Milton Berle, he thought he had the biggest file of gags in the world—"maybe a half million jokes."

Yet a joke file and one writer can go only so far in crafting comic playlets for a radio show. There were other writers for the show in the early 1940s, but they got neither much credit nor much consideration from Red, a pattern that unfortunately would characterize his views of comedy writers the rest of his life. And already in radio, Red did not like to see his writers in person or in the audience, the same attitude he held on TV.

Working the longest with Red as writers in this period were Jack Douglas (from *Avalon Time*), Benedict Freedman, who was hired onto the show when he was just 19, and John Fenton Murray. All these men would continue to work with Red through his TV show years in 1953. They and any other writers had to write an entire script individually around premises outlined by Edna Skelton, then she and Red would select the best parts of each for a master script for him to use that week. Some of the unused material later went into the joke file where Red could use it in the future, should he feel comfortable with it. This setup might have made the show a top comedy draw, but for comedy writers in the know, it became one series to avoid if you wanted to feel appreciated for your work.

Veteran comedy writer Sol Saks (who created the TV series *Bewitched*, among other hits, in a lengthy career) quit writing for Red's show after just two weeks. As he told Jordan R. Young in *The Laugh Crafters*, "You didn't work with him; his wife Edna was then doing his writing, and it was a curious way of writing. She gave you a script, and you went home and rewrote the script with your lines—the same story with your lines—and handed it in. And then in two weeks you might hear your lines."

Saks didn't get to work with any of his fellow writers, including Mrs. Skelton. He did get to see Red in a dress rehearsal, but after the show was over, he passed by Saks without recognizing him. Ironically, Saks later would write for *The Adventures of Ozzie and Harriet*, a sitcom starring Red's old bandleader Ozzie Nelson and his wife, which ran on radio through 1954 and had an even longer run on TV, from 1952 to 1966. (It's still the longest-running network TV sitcom, although the current contract for *The Simpsons* will make it pass that mark by the end of 2004.) *The Adventures of Ozzie and Harriet* debuted on Oct. 8, 1944, a few months after the Nelsons were free to work because Red's show ended temporarily.

You see, Red, like millions of other American men, found himself drafted to serve in World War II. Surprisingly, he was not called to serve in the USO entertainment branch, but actually had to be a private in the Army, even though he had performed thousands of times for military bases across America from 1941 to 1944. He did his last radio show June 6, 1944, and was inducted into service the following day.

Red's stint in the Army ran beyond the end of the war. He suffered a nervous breakdown during his service in Italy and recuperated for several months in an Army hospital in Virginia before being dismissed on Sept. 18, 1945. Less than three months later, he was back on the air, and luckily for him, it was the same network, time slot, sponsor—and high ratings.

The Raleigh Cigarette Program, *Take Two*

Red's return to radio on Dec. 4, 1945, did have a few new twists. David Forrester assumed Ozzie Nelson's position as bandleader. Character actresses Lurene Tuttle, Verna Felton and GeGe Pearson took regular roles on the show, the latter playing Clem Kadiddlehopper's new girlfriend Sarah Dew.

There now was a wider array of regular characters too—Willie Lump Lump, the sot, seen on TV wearing a rumpled outfit; Cauliflower McPugg, the punch-drunk boxer to end all punch-drunk boxers, seen on TV in the early years wearing a sweatshirt with his last name that underlined the "PU" in it (get it?); and Deadeye, "the scourge of the West," an inept cowboy who couldn't control his horse or sometimes even himself as he attempted to make good in the frontier days of America. Some sources list the character as "Sheriff Deadeye," but, in fact, this western figure did not always hold that rank.

The best of the bunch may have been San Fernando Red, a scam artist and erstwhile politician whose approach was similar to that of W.C. Fields. (Fields was so impressed with Red that he considered him the perfect person to play him in the movies.) San Fernando sported a trim white mustache, fancy hat and a vest whereby Red could place his thumbs to look authoritative in his self-serving pronouncements. San Fernando's philosophy was perhaps best summed up by a line he spoke on TV in 1962: "You show me a man who makes an honest buck, and I'll show you a man who's broke!" He sometimes had a secretary (maybe more than that?) assist him in his cons, played a few times in the late 1950s and early 1960s by Amanda Blake, who seemed to welcome the chance to belly laugh freely away from the confines of her role as Miss Kitty on the CBS western *Gunsmoke* from 1955 to 1974.

Another concoction was Bolivar (rhymed with "Oliver") Shagnasty, who a *Newsweek* reporter in 1959 described as a "loudmouthed braggart." It's a good thing the reporter did so, since no other reference book I've seen even tries to discuss the characterization at all, and watching Bolivar on the few videotapes he does appear provides little clue as to his attitude and behavior being distinctive in any manner. It just comes across as Red cracking wise on a cast member. Indeed, Bolivar did not pop up on TV as much as the other characters that survived the transition to video.

Red often played those roles in dress after his radio show to delight his studio audience—and perhaps to show how ready he was to go into TV. Indeed, by 1947 he supposedly already pointed out to Louis B. Mayer that he could and did want to do TV because of his lack of satisfaction with his movie roles and the growing expansion of the medium. (Commercial television had begun in Los Angeles with the debut of station KTLA on Jan. 22, 1947.) Mayer managed to convince Red to put that idea on hold for a few years with better film offers. Meanwhile, that same year, Red added a new element to his radio show that would serve him well on TV too.

David Rose and "Holiday for Strings"

In 1947 David Rose replaced David Forrester as Red's conductor. Red actually had wanted Rose to do the music when the show began after the war in 1945, having enjoyed working with him at a few military base performances in the early 1940s, but Rose could not join Red at that time. Rose provided music for Red for nearly 25 years on radio and TV and would have the longest on-air relationship with Red as anyone.

Born in London on June 15, 1910, Rose came to America with his family seven years later. He made his initial mark in the music world as an arranger and pianist with 1930s hitmakers Ted Fio Rito and His Orchestra. He also wrote the 1936 Benny Goodman hit "It's Been So Long."

But Rose's real claim to fame came on his own in 1943, when his instrumental "Holiday for Strings" became a million-seller and stayed on the music charts for nearly half the year. A bouncy concoction featuring rapid-fire plucking by violins, "Holiday for Strings" became his theme song, and when he joined the Skelton show four years later, the song likewise became part of the show. In the 1960s Rose orchestrated it with a modified interlude featuring a horn section as the TV show's opening and closing theme, but otherwise it stayed fairly close to what it sounded like in the original recording.

Most comedians had long runs on radio with their orchestra leaders supplying them background music, the best example being Bob Hope working with Les Brown and His Band of Renown from 1947 through the 1990s. In Rose's case, he became a personal friend of Red's and often socialized with him away from work until the show ended. He also was once married to Red's frequent guest Martha Raye, and the two got along cordially during her visits, according to reports.

Rose also moonlighted over the years with Red. Among the highlights, from September 1955 through February 1956, he was the orchestra leader for *The Tony Martin Show* on NBC TV on Monday nights while also doing *The Red Skelton Show*. He received an Emmy nomination in 1966 for Individual Achievement in Music Composition for the western series *Bonanza* and an Emmy Award in the same category for the special *An Evening with Fred Astaire* in 1959. In 1958 he earned a Grammy nomination for Best Orchestra for the album *Young Man's Lament*, joined by Andre Previn, and Previn joined Rose again the next year when Rose won a Grammy in the same category for the album *Like Young*.

Prior to joining Red, Rose had Oscar nominations in 1944 for Best Scoring of a Dramatic or Comedy Picture for *The Princess and the Pirate* and in 1945 for Best Song for writing the music for "So in Love" from

Wonder Man. After Red's show ended, Rose remained active on scoring TV series into his seventies, winning Emmys in 1979 and 1982 for Outstanding Music for a Series for *Little House on the Prairie*. He, in fact, provided music for all of Michael Landon's series, from *Bonanza* (where he won another Emmy in 1971 for Best Music for a Series) through *Father Murphy* and *Highway to Heaven*.

Through all his triumphs, Rose had only nice things to say about Red Skelton, even though Skelton stopped talking to him (as he did with many other people) after Red's show ended in 1971. "I have worked with Red 12 years and have never seen him angry with the people he works with," Rose told *TV Guide* in 1961. Apparently that trait rubbed off on his bandleader too, for if Rose ever got that angry, no one I interviewed recalled him doing so.

Finally Going to TV

On Sept. 3, 1948, Red started his new season on radio with a new time slot (Fridays at 9:30 P.M. on the East Coast) and a new sponsor, Proctor and Gamble, the giant soap and home products company. The rising production costs for Red's show scared off previous sponsor Raleigh Cigarettes. Proctor and Gamble would remain Red's sponsor into TV, with Red promoting Tide, the company's top laundry detergent.

At the same time, CBS Chairman William S. Paley launched a plan to recruit much of the talent on NBC radio for his network. He found out from an accountant that performers could keep more of their money after capital gains taxes if they incorporated themselves as businesses and sold their shows to CBS. The plan would save them 50 percent more than in previous years. Not surprisingly, without NBC offering them the same deal, many stars jumped to Paley's network.

After CBS made a deal with Bing Crosby, Red was the second major star to jump ship from NBC, signing with CBS radio in January 1949. He finished his NBC run on May 20, 1949, and went to CBS radio on Sundays at 8:30 P.M. on the East Coast, starting Oct. 2, 1949.

But significantly, the CBS deal did not include television. Therefore, he was able to negotiate the best deal with any network for a series, and he wound up choosing NBC in 1951. Although it's unclear why Red, whom everyone felt would be a natural, did not do TV before then, it can be presumed that his heavy radio and film schedule (he did five movies in 1950 alone) held him back from getting into the medium, and there was also the logistics problem of doing a live TV show from Los Angeles that could be seen at the same time on the East Coast. The latter ended with the connection of the coaxial cable to both coasts in 1951, allowing live transmissions across continental America.

So Red finally got onto television. And as successful as Red was on radio in the 1940s, he would find even greater fame and fortune on TV for the next two decades.

2
1951–1953: You're the Top, Now You're Not

After NBC finalized their contract with Red, it was announced that he would be airing on the network live Sunday nights 10–10:30 P.M. on the East Coast, and 7–7:30 P.M. on the West Coast, with his show originating from Los Angeles. It would run an hour after NBC's biggest Sunday attraction from the previous year, *The Colgate Comedy Hour*, which finished #5 for the 1950–51 season versus the #15 rating for its direct competition on CBS, *The Ed Sullivan Show* (then titled *The Toast of the Town*).

But why start Red at the rather late hour of 10 P.M.? If he already was a proven audience grabber on radio, why not make him a headliner at 8 or 9 instead? Pat Weaver, who was in charge of NBC television programming at the time and will be remembered eternally for creating two of the longest-running signature series for the network, *The Today Show* and *The Tonight Show*, explained his thinking to Irv Broughton in the latter's 1986 book *Producers on Producing* by saying it was an effort to create as many hits as possible for NBC on Sunday nights:

"So the obvious thing, once we had a runaway hit, was to put, say, Red Skelton, whom we also had, on at 9, or put him on at 7:30. We put him on at 10 because we wanted *Television Playhouse* [actually, it was *Philco Television Playhouse* alternating weekly with *Goodyear Television Playhouse*; the different titles were due to having two rotating sponsors], which was our best drama, to get the inheritance of this huge top five *Comedy Hour* audience with the enticement of Red Skelton to come after the drama, and maybe they would sit through the drama when normally they wouldn't."

The plan worked brilliantly. All three series wound up in the top 15 for the 1951–52 season, with Red at #4 in the ratings, *The Colgate Comedy Hour* at #5 and *The Philco Television Playhouse* at #12. By the middle of the season CBS cut back Philco's competition, *The Fred Waring Show*, from an hour to a half hour and imported the big money game show *Break the Bank* from NBC to fill the 9:30–10 P.M. slot in a losing attempt to gain an audience against the anthology.

NBC had won Sunday nights on television, due in no small part to Red. Much was expected of him when he entered the new medium, and he paid off handsomely.

The Video Buildup

Red was rehearsing for television as early as 1948, if an article by Noel Busch for *Television Age* magazine in 1965 titled "Television Crown Prince" is to be believed. Skelton realized that he had performed for virtually all sorts of audiences except the ones found in people's living rooms, and since television's main audience would be in this form, Red realized he had to bone up on his knowledge of what people in these venues found funny. (The fact that Red's radio show audience was primarily in living rooms too apparently escaped notice by the comedian.)

At any rate, Busch reported, "Though normally a social recluse, he now began going to every dinner, cocktail party or other gathering to which he could gain access, researching what makes people laugh when they are not in a theater." After this, Red went back to touring in theaters to try out his material for television—and not just in America either.

The Sept. 29, 1951, edition of *TV Digest* (a forerunner of *TV Guide* published for the Philadelphia viewing area) boasted that "Red Skelton returned from Europe again just last month, this time to 'go into training for his television show.' His comedy took Europe by storm and in many a theater in which he appeared, attendance records were broken. At the Palladium in London, audience applause forced him to keep his performance going for 81 minutes."

The periodical also indicated that Red would present Strike-Out McGonigle, "devil of the diamond," as one of his regular characters, but if he was, he certainly didn't make the grade to last on television. Wearing an old-time baseball cap and sporting a walrus mustache, McGonigle struck out as being part of Red's television entourage on the debut, and though a few other references were made to the character in print, I have yet to view any evidence he was on the television series.

What and who did make it to television? Well, let's travel back in time to Sunday, Sept. 30, 1951, at 10 P.M. Eastern time for the debut of *Red Skelton* (the show's actual title on the air, although most publications referred to it as *The Red Skelton Show*). And here's what happened…

George Appleby reacts to the shenanigans of nurse Chanin Hale and doctor Robert Morse in a sketch on the show telecast Nov. 30, 1965.

The First Show

It looked like a typical television station sign-on title card of the time. Wait a minute, the guy in the Indian headdress in the middle. Is that...? Yes, it's Red Skelton, the announcer said.

Red then strode on view from stage left, as he always would for his show's beginning over the next 20 years, amid a huge round of applause. "It's always quite flattering to get a reception without doing anything," he said with a smile. "This, as you know, is my first televised broadcast. I have worked in every branch of show business but grand opera, carnivals and television, and tonight opens that for me."

After mentioning how he did a lot of nightclubs, Red fiddled with his hat to do a drunk routine. An insect flew near him during the act, and he cracked, "A fly from CBS!" Next came humorous personality routines involving an overly eager doorman, people looking for seats in an aisle and a head usher at a theater who is a "personality kid" (as Red described him, "He has starched underwear"). Topping them all off was his pantomime of the different ways people eat popcorn in the theater, especially one involving Red trying to eat while crying at the show he's watching.

After introducing the show's sponsor Tide and its commercial, Red then performed a bit about being in Europe with an ill-fitting suit. That led to him introducing the Skylarks, a three-man, two-women singing and dancing troupe popular on television in the 1950s, though not that much on records. After their number, Red came out twirling his hat and announced what many people in the audience were wondering: Would Red be doing any of his radio characters? "Some of them, yes," he said.

Red proceeded to go through each one. The first up was Deadeye, with a prop cactus installed near Red by Lucy Knoch with a slight leer from Red. (There will be more on this actress in the "Meet Lucy Knoch" section.) As Red shot his gun, the sound effects man missed the cue the first time, then came in too early on the second try. "Wait till I shot it!" Red laughed. "There's a boy, he's got possibilities of developing into a total stranger."

(Red had used that joke earlier on stage, thus showing even here he was recycling old jokes as he would throughout his television career. In fact, Red repeated several jokes from this season in later shows, sometimes much later. For example, Cauliflower McPugg in one show told a reporter regarding one of his boxing matches that "I threw a right cross, then a left cross, and then a Blue Cross came in." That showed up again in 1958. And in a show where he was stuck in a snowbound cabin with two other men looking over their supplies, he quipped, "Twelve bottles of liquor and a loaf of bread? What are we gonna do with a loaf of bread?!" That one reappeared in 1966, believe it or not.)

A still photo of Red in Deadeye makeup then appeared to let people know what the character would look like— Red was not getting into other makeup or costumes for this show. A similar setup had Red say that San Fernando Red, the "crooked politician," as he put it, would be on television, albeit with more of a Southern accent.

For fans of his "mean widdle kid," Red informed them he would not be doing Junior on television because "I think it would look kind of ridiculous for a guy 6-foot-3 to run around with short pants on, see?" He later quipped that "My boy Richard has turned out to be a real Junior" and flipped his hat upside down to approximate a sailor's hat and did child talk in a solid routine.

After all that came a sketch where Red shot a piano player for doing too many trills while Red attempted to sign along, and finally the end of the show. Red told his audience "Gee, I like television. On radio you're cut right off, but I could stay out here as long as I want to." Just after that, two stagehands grabbed Red's ankles from behind the stage curtain and yanked him back, pulling him down face forward. It was an expected and delightful ending that would be used too often by the second season and lose much of its appeal (not to mention the danger it posed to Red in doing the pratfall).

That was the show. Admittedly it was not much to watch on screen, with most of the visuals being Red in front of a curtain except for the Skylarks' number, when the curtain was opened and closed. But to most viewers and critics, that was enough. It earned near-universal hosannas, and success for the television *Red Skelton Show* was on its way.

Putting the Series Together

Like most radio comics venturing into television, Red decided to have different scripts for the latter medium, although unlike some, he used the same writers for both. His four writers—John Fenton Murray, Benedict Freedman, Will Fowler and Jack Douglas—would meet at Red's house Tuesday nights to test run television ideas and rehearse them in his living room. Even with this process, according to *Newsweek* magazine in 1952, Red supposedly "contributes at least 50 percent of each show himself," and "about 80 percent of the show is never written down."

The *TV Guide* of Washington, D.C., a predecessor to the national edition begun in 1953, elaborated in its May 16, 1952, feature story on Red that he "doesn't believe in scripts. He plots an approximate course with the writers and the director, but puts no dialogue in writing. The actors memorize their 'lines' from the situations arising out of rehearsals."

Rehearsals with no cameras, just a boom microphone, took place Saturday nights in front of a studio audience of 470 people. Red took the tape of the show home with him that night and reviewed it until as late as 4 A.M., looking for dead spots, ad-libs that worked, and whatever else on the recording that interested him.

On Sundays at noon, Red would enjoy a "real Indiana breakfast" of potatoes, ham, eggs and chocolate milk before going over changes for his show in the afternoon. A dress rehearsal at the studio took place at 5 P.M. along with David Rose and his orchestra, with Red keeping the punchlines a secret to get the musicians to laugh on air with him. Show time would be at 7 P.M., of course, for airing live at 10 P.M. on the East Coast. Then Red would go home and get to enjoy Monday, his only day off from working in radio or television. Believe it or not, this schedule of Red basically doing his show from rehearsal to actual airing (or later filming and taping) in just two days would be the standard operating procedure for the comedian for most of his television run, even when he went to an hour in the 1960s, although that required a different setup, as we will examine later.

Although a considerable amount of what Red did in his first season was visual routines from his touring days, several of his favorite characters from radio popped up on television too. Beside the aforementioned Deadeye and San Fernando Red, Clem Kadiddlehopper, Cauliflower McPugg, and Willie Lump Lump appeared in Red's first season on the tube, usually in the main sketch. But it was not unusual to have Red just play Red or an unnamed character, usually someone whose foibles were easily recognized and appreciated by the audience.

Before the main sketches, the standard show had him do an opening monologue, usually dealing with his family and friends but sometimes topical political material as well. Generally, however, the latter did not go over too well, although some contemporary references were pretty good. Referring to the emotional Johnnie Ray, who had an early 1950s hit called "Cry," Red said, "Johnnie Ray, that's the guy who cries between songs." Always mixed in with these jokes would be a routine by the seagulls Gertrude and Heathcliff, where, using a "dumb" voice with thumbs propped underneath his armpits, Red would deliver the birds' lines and jokes to save him in case the others died on him. ("Boys, get the car ready!" he announced to the stagehands after one received a poor reaction.)

The Red Skelton Show also had a few people show up along with Red to help him out, though none of the supporting cast ever received much work nor credit on the show, taking a back seat to Red's antics in most cases. The only one of these to be a regular was Lucy Knoch.

Meet Lucy Knoch

Lucy (sometimes billed as Lucille) Knoch was a blonde ingénue who resembled a cross between Ginger Rogers and Doris Day. A native of Nashville, Tenn., Knoch came to Hollywood in the 1940s and made several minor movie appearances. Her first films were uncredited bit parts in 1945 (*Incendiary Blonde, The Affairs of Susan, You Came Along*), 1946 (*The Blue Dahlia, Blue Skies, Cross My Heart, To Each His Own*) and 1948 (*The Big Clock*). For a time, she was under contract with Paramount Pictures.

According to the publicity of the time, Knoch came to the attention of Red and his business manager Bo Roos when they were having lunch at a restaurant while looking for an actress to do Red's new television show. They offered Knoch a chance to test for the small role, and she did it and won the part.

Knoch found herself doing mostly small bits on Red's show, often there just to be a pretty woman for his characters to flirt with, though she did display a flair for telling jokes and holding her own as best she could with his efforts to crack her up. She never knew exactly what she was to say to Red for that week's show until the Saturday rehearsal, and even then had to be prepared for his ad-libs on the live show the following day. After Red's run on NBC ended, so did her association with the series, though she did show up in Red's 1953 movie *The Clown* in another unbilled brief role.

Her career thereafter did not amount to much. She did do a few movies during her tenure with Red, including her first billed film role in *Two Tickets to Broadway* in 1951 as "Girl," and other unbilled bits in *The Bad and the Beautiful* in 1952 and *Sabre Jet* in 1953. Undoubtedly her best role came in 1954, when she was 13th billed in the hit corporate drama *Executive Suite* playing Louis Calhern's wife.

Knoch's last major movie role was in *Pal Joey* in 1957 as yet another unnamed "Girl," according to the credits. She is so obscure she is not listed in most entertainment reference books. I could not find any information about her current whereabouts.

Also Appearing

Other actors showed up in recurring parts. Chief among these was Benny Rubin, a star in vaudeville in the 1920s and 1930s, who found himself having to make do with supporting roles in films of the 1940s. He entered the fledgling New York television scene in the late 1940s as a regular joke teller on the video adaptation of the radio hit *Stop Me If You've*

Heard This One, which ran from March 4, 1948, through April 22, 1949. Replacing it was his own talent variety series on NBC Friday nights from April 29 through June 24, 1949. He told Richard Lamparski in *Whatever Became Of...? Tenth Series* that *The Benny Rubin Show* went off the air because of "this foul temper of mine. I did myself in and ended up doing bit parts when I should have been really making a contribution in a very creative capacity."

Rubin went back to Hollywood and found himself doing *The Red Skelton Show* quite often during the 1951–52 season and occasionally thereafter through the 1960s, as well as many other comedy shows. In his 1973 autobiography *Come Backstage With Me*, Rubin wrote, "When you're called for a Jack Benny show, you never say 'I'm going to work,' it's like the Lucy show, or Red Skelton's frolics, no pressure. On most shows a bit player is hardly more than a prop you bounce a gag off."

Sometimes Rubin was the one bouncing the gag off Skelton, however. In one sketch in 1952, he blew the commercial he was doing for Tide detergent within the show by telling viewers, "Now just remember this—T-E-D-I!" Skelton nearly busted a gut over the misspelling, which Rubin did not realize immediately, and quipped to him, "Oh, you're back to vaudeville!"

Proctor and Gamble, the sponsor who sold Tide as part of its wares, didn't mind the gaffe and let Rubin come back to do the show. The company didn't need to worry about some minor mistake anyway, as it was plugged nicely on the hottest new series on NBC that season. (In fact, one sketch at a hospital even had a clock with a "PG" lettering on it prominent in the background, no doubt pleasing the advertiser.)

A Commercial and Critical Success

Looking back at the press clippings of the period, it's well nigh impossible to find anyone with anything bad to say about Red and his series. About the only quibble anyone had following the opening of *The Red Skelton Show* was its lack of sets and costuming, and that was addressed quickly. Reviewing his Oct. 21, 1951, show, *Variety* noted that "Red Skelton and his writing stable, whether taking their cues from critics or not, have apparently decided it's time to invest the package with more production values than were evident on the first few stanzas.... Because of the added sight values, it was Skelton at his best, and that's among the best comedy to be seen."

Red easily blew past his competition in his inaugural season. ABC offered evangelist Billy Graham the *Hour of Decision* as part of a Sunday night lineup that aired just documentaries and religious programs from

9–11 P.M. *Celebrity Time* on CBS offered Conrad Nagel hosting a quiz show, which began in 1949 and mutated into a variety program in a last-ditch effort to get some of Red's audience. And DuMont, a struggling fourth network that went out of business in 1955, offered the hour-long courtroom drama from Chicago *They Stand Accused*. None of the shows came anywhere near Red's ratings.

Soon the awards were coming Red's way. The Dec. 21, 1951, issue of the New York edition of *TV Guide* gave Red its Gold Medal Award in the Comedian of the Year category. The magazine wrote, "Big things were expected of this major radio and movie star as he made his television debut this fall. And big things were forthcoming. In a few short weeks, he has zoomed from nowhere in television to second place among all national programs in [the] Nielsen ratings. Featuring a remarkably large gallery of rounded comic characters, he has put on a show of continuous laughter."

In the same issue, Leonard Resnick of Brooklyn, N.Y., wrote to the magazine the following: "Send Milton Berle back to his mother. The bobbysoxers can have Martin & Lewis, and the beanbaggers can have Jerry Lester. Durante can return to Mrs. Calabash and Cantor to his five daughters. There's a great new television comedian, Red Skelton, who outdoes all his own movie hilarity. The other 'comics' should take lessons from him, and I'm sure if you ask, most of your readers will agree with me." The editor responded by defending the other comics mentioned and their fans, but there was no denying Red was a top draw to many on television.

Red's biggest win came a month later, at the fourth annual Emmy awards presentation on Feb. 18, 1952. Red won two statuettes: for Best Comedy Show, beating out *The George Burns and Grace Allen Show*, *The Herb Shriner Show*, *I Love Lucy* and *You Bet Your Life*; and Best Comedian or Comedienne, competing against Lucille Ball, Sid Caesar, Imogene Coca, Jimmy Durante, Dean Martin and Jerry Lewis (listed oddly as one entry) and Herb Shriner. One could argue about the odd placement of *The Red Skelton Show* in the Best Comedy Show category while there was a Best Variety Show category that contained more similar shows to Red's like *The Colgate Comedy Hour* and *Your Show of Shows* (1952's winner in the category), but the Emmys have been shown generation after generation to have weird nominating criteria, so let's not belabor that.

Red's win marked the third time both a performer and his comedy series won in both categories the same year. Ed Wynn did it with *The Ed Wynn Show* in 1949, as did Milton Berle with *Texaco Star Theater* (another case of Emmy category curiosity; Ed's was for Best Live Show, while Milton's was for Best Kinescope Show, since that was the only way viewers in Los Angeles, where the Emmys originated, could see the series in 1949), followed in 1950 by Alan Young and *The Alan Young Show*. The significance should not be lost here; Ed was one of Red's idols, while Berle was one of the few comedians Red appreciated and felt unintimidated enough by him to later work with him on his show.

In his acceptance speech, Red humbly said, "I think this should have gone to Lucille Ball." Reportedly the comedienne cried upon hearing his words. That situation was rectified the following year, when *I Love Lucy* won for Best Situation Comedy and Ball for Best Comedienne. (They split up the Best Comedian and Best Comedienne categories, those wacky Emmy folk.)

After winning the trophies, Red displayed them at the top of his show a few days later, on Feb. 24, 1952. Little did he or the audience realize it would be another eight long years before Red would see his next Emmy, as everything that went so well in 1951–52 virtually fell apart in 1952–53.

From Being Live to Taking a Dive

Red decided around the time of the last show of his first television season, on June 10, 1952, to make two changes on the series that would backfire on him. He decided to have the next season on film rather than live from Hollywood, and to have it air on Sundays at 7 P.M. Eastern time, the same time it had in the Pacific time zone covering Red's adopted home state of California.

When speaking Red possessed a, shall we say, selective memory of the reason for the 1952 time change to Dwight Whitney for *TV Guide* in 1959. "The sponsor thought he could get the kiddie audience too, and moved me to an earlier time slot," Red claimed. But contemporary reports specified it was Red, not Proctor and Gamble, who wanted him on three hours earlier than before in the East. For example, *Newsweek* claimed that Red wanted his show in an earlier time slot so that children on the East Coast could watch him. Whoever made the call, NBC replaced Red at 10 P.M. on Sundays in the fall of 1952 with a loser anthology called *The Doctor* starring Warner Anderson. It ran one year, beaten in head-to-head competition against the action anthology *The Web* on CBS.

There was no confusion over the issue of filming the show. Red found it grueling to do both a half-hour television show and half-hour radio show live each week with different routines for 39 weeks a year. (His radio show on CBS began airing on Wednesdays at 9 P.M. from the start of the 1951 season through June 25, 1952, then he went to back to

NBC on radio Tuesdays at 8:30 P.M. starting Sept. 16, 1952.) Especially burdensome to him for live television was having to make costume and makeup changes for his characters. Seeing the time advantages that filming gave *I Love Lucy*, among other filmed comedies, Red and his producers told NBC they would go to CBS unless he could do the next season filmed. Naturally, the network acquiesced to its hot property.

As with *I Love Lucy*, *The Red Skelton Show* was filmed by three cameras simultaneously, allowing the director to pick which shots he wanted to use as the show went along, typically with one for close-ups, one for medium shots and one for long shots. But the filming took place at Eagle Lion Studios, a production outfit not designed to have a studio where the audience could sit and watch the show.

So, with no studio audience, the series had to rely on a "laugh track," prerecorded giggles and chuckles that critics and sophisticated audiences hated even as early as 1952 due to its artificial nature of making huge laughs out of lousy jokes. (See the bad reviews or even watch a video of *My Little Margie*, which ran from 1952 to 1955, if you need to be convinced of that.) That definitely hurt the show, plus the lack of a studio audience meant Red had no one but the crew and maybe some visitors to the set to play off his monologue and routines, thus giving him no sense of when an ad-lib or change in line might work. As a result of all this, Red's sprightly comedy of 1951–52 became a deadly, plodding affair in much of 1952–53.

Reviewing the Sept. 28, 1952, season opener, *Variety* razzed Red almost inversely to the proportion they praised him the previous year. "Stal." wrote that Red "flubbed badly in his first time out" and suggested that Red switch his format and even his writers. (He had the same four he'd used in 1951–52.) The reviewer said viewers "could call each turn, from his opening monologue, complete with his stories of his son and daughter ... and reliance on his now-stock characters," referring specifically to Cauliflower McPugg and Willie Lump Lump.

But it wasn't just Red that had "Stal." seeing, uh, red. The visual presentation received a fair amount of catcalls as well. "Film itself was fuzzy and displayed poor lighting. In addition, the editing was spotty, with the camera cuts too often jarring."

Other critics heaped on the scorn for the debut as well. *TV Guide* called it "no great shakes as entertainment." And while the critics can blast a show the public loves, home viewers did not enjoy the second season of *The Red Skelton Show* either. It fell almost immediately out of the top 10 and was no longer "must see TV," as NBC promoted its Thursday night lineup in the 1990s, of its era.

Even a cameo by movie superstar and television holdout John Wayne that fall in a sketch (he had no lines, just appeared as a vision in a lame routine) went largely unnoticed, even though it quite possibly was his first network television appearance. As in the previous season, there were no major guest stars on the series, just bit roles by character actors like Ned Glass, and that did not help its appeal either.

There were talks about changing the format of the show as early as November, but it didn't happen. Reports later revealed Red was drinking heavily in this period in response to the stress of the show, among other factors, so to have him switch his established working setup before the end of the season was not thought to be wise. He and his crew slogged through the rest of the year, realizing the show was not as warmly received by anyone as it had been in its debut season.

Even worse, Red had surgery on a herniated diaphragm in December 1952 that knocked him out of filming for a few weeks. At that time there was no problem, since he already had done six films for the series prior to his operation and would be able to recuperate in time to do the show without any repeats. But a viral infection followed in February 1953, forcing Red out of action again, and NBC unwisely decided to repeat for a few weeks some of Red's more recent shows rather than ones from the start of the season. Viewers stayed away in droves. Nothing seemed to go right for either Red or his series that season.

A Few Bright Spots

Despite all the negative press it received, there were some nice moments contained in the 1952–53 season. The biggest of them had to be the debut of Freddie the Freeloader, a character who was Red's personal favorite, as well as for the majority of his fans. A hobo who lived in a shack near a garbage dump, Freddie was an adorable innocent in tattered clothes who refused to let the world get him down in the face of his downtrodden existence. The character's greatest appeal to Red was obvious—it allowed him to put on greasepaint to make Freddie's eyes and mouth exaggerated, just like a clown. And just like Red's other characters, he was recognizable by his head gear, in this case, a battered top hat.

Freddie's appearances then were not as elaborate as they would be in later seasons, when prominent guest stars such as Edward Everett Horton would play his pal and fellow bum Muggsy; but in general, they always had a few good chuckles to them, especially in comparison to other sketches. Commenting about a horse race in one playlet, Freddie argued that Lady Godiva was the world's best gambler because "She put everything she had on one horse."

Red explained Freddie's origins to Dora Albert in the May 1959 issue of *TV Radio Mirror*. "Why, I got that idea from my father, who used to play a tramp clown in the circus. He played a sad clown, and had a special makeup of his own—white on his eyelids, white on his mouth, absolutely no red on the nose—I wear identically that makeup." Remember that Red's father died before he was born, and thus the idea that he created Freddy from how people described his dad makes it more touching—if indeed the tale is true.

Another good moment came when radio sound effects veteran Ray Erlenborn did a guest shot showing the mechanics of his job with a perfect deadpan expression on his face. "I had done this sound effects act," Erlenborn told me. "It started with this tour of a studio, and everyone in Hollywood was familiar with it." Erlenborn's low-key or blank expressions stood in contrast to Red's amazed look at the noises Erlenborn produced, making a fine bit of TV comedy at a time when the show needed it. Neither man knew it, but Erlenborn would be working for Red a few years later.

Other than these moments, however, much of the 1952–53 season was lackluster. Nevertheless, in 2001, Red's third wife and widow Lothian Skelton packaged sketches from those shows together with ones from 1951–52 in a three-volume home video set and for a series of shows aired mainly on public television stations called *The Red Skelton Scrapbook*. The dubious result is an extremely spotty viewing session, as one sketch from the generally top-quality first season precedes or follows a lesser one from the second season. Lothian probably could not include sketches from the first year that revolved around the show's commercials for Tide, but still, there had to have been enough from those 39 shows to prevent her from needing to recycle the often drawn-out, slow-moving 1952–53 offerings in the package.

Erlenborn agreed with my assessment of those re-edited shows, having viewed them himself and feeling that they are a bad way for newcomers to be introduced to Red, even though they are offered by his estate through Red's official website. "They're so old and worn out," he said. "People get the wrong impression of him."

The "Sophomore Slump"

In 1953, unlike the previous year, Red didn't have to worry about attending the Emmy awards. He and his show received no nominations. It wasn't the first time this event had happened, but still it was a humiliating blow to his prestige. He would not get another nomination until four years later, and that did not involve his program either.

Red had his own opinion about the reasons for his 1952–53 "sophomore slump" on television. Unfortunately, his reasons varied from story to story and made little if any sense.

He told *TV Guide* in 1956 it was because the public didn't like hearing about how much money he had in his contract to do the show. Did Red seriously think everyone heard only about his financial success on television and not other stars'? Or that the idea of a star being well paid for having a hit show was something the masses could not appreciate? Really, now.

Three years later in the same publication, Red gave Dwight Whitney this explanation: "I got sick, and they started substituting kinescopes. That did it. The third year I threw everybody out and went back to the way things were the first year." Well, NBC actually substituted his films, not kinescopes; not everything went back the same way in the third season; and the show already was tanking before the repeats happened.

Actually, one valid excuse Red could've given for doing worse his second year in terms of audience size was tougher competition in his new time slot—but not from television. As any fan of the "golden age" of radio can tell you, Sunday nights at 7 P.M. had been the longtime home slot for *The Jack Benny Program* on radio since 1934. And though nighttime television now was drawing larger audiences than nighttime radio, there still remained enough diehard enthusiasts for the latter medium who kept *The Jack Benny Program* at the top of the radio ratings even as late as 1952–53. It was several million people less than had listened to the show in the 1930s and 1940s, but it was still large enough that it probably drew away potential viewers to Red's television show.

As for Red's network TV opposition, kids were the primary audience of *The Gene Autry Show* on CBS, so it really posed no threat for the mostly adult fans of Red's show. On DuMont, *Georgetown University Forum* was a stodgy "talking heads" public affairs program probably watched by just family and friends of faculty members of Georgetown University in Washington, D.C. The best network competition for Red came on ABC via *You Asked for It*, a viewer participation series hosted by Art Baker; but like the other network series, it finished behind *The Red Skelton Show* in the ratings.

By the end of the season, *The Red Skelton Show* finished at #28, tied with ABC's highest-rated show that season, *The Lone Ranger*. It was not a bad average and one that other shows would've loved to have had, but for a show that had been near the top the previous season, it was a definitely disappointing result, especially since seven of the top 10 series for 1951–52 returned to the same top 10 list in 1952–53. In fact, no other top 10 series in one season would fall so drastically the following season until the 1958–59 season, when *The Restless Gun* and *December Bride*, #8 and #9 respectively in the 1957–58 season, failed to make the top 30 a year later. It was an embarrassing distinction for *The Red Skelton Show* to have within the industry at the time.

At the same time, the show's sponsor, Proctor and Gamble, announced it would not renew a contract to advertise on the program given this considerable downturn in popularity. Without the sponsor, NBC looked for other shows to put in the slot. Despite having a top 30 show, Red's reputation in the industry as being unreliable and no longer able to deliver top comedy made the network unwilling to try to sell him to another sponsor.

If that was not enough, his radio series ended on NBC May 26, 1953, just a few weeks before his television series concluded its run on the network on June 21, 1953. The final insult to injury came when MGM dropped his movie contract and no other studio indicated they wanted to sign him. All of these events fell on Red prior to his 40th birthday and would've provided the perfect formula for middle-age depression for any performer thinking he or she was washed up in show business. Luckily, that was not the end of the story for Red.

Saved by CBS

At first, things seemed hopeless to Red's business manager Bo Roos. He tried to get a series deal with CBS and then even struggling ABC, which could've used a "name" performer at the time, but both passed. Then Red's director from 1952–53, Marty Rackin, who took over the spot from John Gaunt after Red's first season, suggested the comic play Las Vegas and show the network brass he could still deliver a top-notch show. His engagement at the Sahara Hotel in July 1953 was a smash, and CBS executives who saw him rewarded Red with a contract with the network. (The fact that they had just opened up their Television City studio operations in Hollywood in 1952 and could use productions at the facility did not hurt Red's cause either.) However, they did require that Red hire new writers and go back to doing a live show.

As for NBC, it installed *The Paul Winchell-Jerry Mahoney Show* into Red's previous Sunday at 7 P.M. time slot. It proved to be much less of a draw than Red's show and went off a year later, ending a four-year nighttime run for ventriloquist Paul Winchell. (He then went into doing daytime series on the networks for the rest of the 1950s.) The time slot became somewhat of a "black hole" for series on the network, with no NBC program lasting more than a year there until the second half hour of *The Bell Telephone Hour* ran in it in 1965–67. (In contrast, CBS had a winner with *Lassie* occupying the 7–7:30 slot on Sundays from 1954 to 1971.) As for the network's dismissal of Red, former NBC President Pat Weaver told author Irv Broughton, in retrospect, "It was a great loss, but you win some and you lose some."

But NBC did not see the disappearance of *The Red Skelton Show* as a loser at the time. Indeed, Red's show would undergo its worst ratings and reviews over the next few years on CBS, and in his early forties, Red almost became a has-been on the medium. Almost, that is.

3
1953–1956: From the Bottom to the Top 20

To get an idea of how lowly regarded *The Red Skelton Show* was on CBS during its first few years there, consider this: The most-publicized incident regarding the show in 1954 was that it gave Johnny Carson his first network variety show.

Carson had been doing a local Los Angeles television variety show on Sunday afternoons called *Carson's Cellar* in 1951 when he ended one show by having a man run quickly past the camera and said that person was his special guest star, Red Skelton. Luckily for Carson, Skelton saw the show, laughed and agreed to do the show as a guest with a one-line bit joking with Carson afterward. Later, Carson's television fortunes sank following his ill-fated hosting of the CBS game show *Earn Your Vacation* in 1953, so he joined Skelton's staff to write jokes for the seagull characters Gertrude and Heathcliff.

Then, on Aug. 18, 1954, Red broke his leg falling through a prop door in rehearsal for that night's show, and—in the time-honored tradition of "You're gonna go out there a nobody and finish as a star!"—Carson became the de facto understudy for Red and substituted for him. The 29-year-old wrote a monologue for himself, did so well that Jack Benny, among others, singled him out for praise, and within a year, Carson had his own CBS nighttime variety show. It lasted just a year, but it was enough to get him going back as an on-air talent on the networks, leading eventually to his 30-year stint as host of *The Tonight Show* starting in 1962.

There was nothing nearly so entertaining about the rest of *The Red Skelton Show* the first two seasons it was on the air, however. Reviews were poor, ratings sagged, and backstage personnel came and went frequently like characters on a soap opera. Had it not been that CBS and Red had signed a three-year contract, we would be talking instead about what a huge flop the comedian had been on the medium, for it was not until the last year of the contract that the show finally jelled into something that, if not a critical favorite, nevertheless appealed to viewers close to the same scale of his first year on television. But it was a messy climb to get there.

The Dead Sea(sons)

The first obstacle Red faced on CBS was horrible scheduling. The network installed his half-hour show on Tuesdays at 8:30 P.M. from Sept. 22, 1953, through June 1954, running opposite television's #1 comedy variety star Milton Berle on NBC, a man whom Red admired and had somewhat similar taste and appeal in broad comedy. Berle had owned Tuesdays 8–9 P.M. since he became the regular host on *The Texaco Star Theater* in the fall of 1948, and like all previous CBS competition, Red and his show did not faze Berle, as the latter comic finished #6 in the ratings for the 1953–54 season.

Even worse, *The Red Skelton Show* came on midway opposite Berle, with its lead-in being none other than *The Gene Autry Show*, the western that Red beat on NBC in 1952–53. What kind of boneheaded thinking allowed that to happen?

Perhaps seeing the errors of their ways, CBS moved *The Gene Autry Show* to Saturdays at 7 P.M. in 1954, where it ran for two more years, and gave Red a fighting chance to compete head on against Berle at 8 P.M. on Tuesdays on Sept. 23, 1954. To entice viewers to try Red, or maybe even return to him, the network made the unusual decision to have *The Red Skelton Show* continue production for a full year and serve as the summer replacement for the popular *Arthur Godfrey and His Friends* variety series (the #7 series for the 1953–54 season). Red's show expanded to an hour to fill the time slot and became known as *The Red Skelton Revue* during this period, then shrunk back to a half hour in the fall of 1954. It was not a problem for him to do the summer show, since he had no movie roles following his release from MGM.

Unfortunately, Red's summer activity did not increase noticeably his viewership opposite Berle, whose show finished at #13 for the 1954–55 season. In fact, everything on CBS Tuesday nights in 1954–55 had a lackluster performance, but the best the network could do at the start of January 1955 was to shuffle the order the shows ran and hope for something to click. *The Red Skelton Show* now went to Tuesdays 9:30–10 P.M., replacing the drama anthology *Danger*, which moved back a half hour to start at 10 P.M. and bumped the sitcom *Life with Father* from its 10–10:30 slot to Red's former 8–8:30 P.M. airing time. None of this switching made any of the shows into hits, and *The Red Skelton Show* looked like a lost cause, a program designed to fill time simply because nothing else was available to put on the air.

There also was the nagging issue of Red's supporting players. He had no other regulars in his cast other than the ever-reliable David Rose and his orchestra, and Red's guest stars tended to be minor ones, not really household names, probably because the budget for a half-hour variety series did not allow for salaries as high as those for hour-long shows. The biggest name on the CBS debut, for example, was Phyllis Coates, whose claim to fame then was being the original Lois Lane on the syndicated action hit *The Adventures of Superman.*

The show did bring out the "big names" in the hour format in the summer of 1954, with its debut guests including flamboyant pianist Liberace (then at the peak of his television popularity) and movie star Tony Curtis (promoting his film *Black Shield of Falworth*), followed by Burt Lancaster, Frank Sinatra and Rosemary Clooney. But when it went back to a half hour that fall, the unspectacular likes of Ella Logan, Barbara Ruick, Reginald Denny and Mary McCarty were the usual types of none-too-special guests on Red's show—hardly an inducement to watch him over "Uncle Miltie" Berle. The show did add a dancing troupe known as the Redettes in 1954 for a few years, apparently to show it could have the same sort of talent the hour variety shows had; but in general, the choreography on display by the group was perfunctory at best and did not involve Red.

As for the show's overall quality in this period, the 1953–54 and 1954–55 seasons of *The Red Skelton Show* are among the hardest ones to find copies to watch, but the few that do exist amply point out the problems that critics observed about the program—if they examined it at all, that is. The show's status in the industry was so marginal that *Variety* did not even review its 1954 fall preview, a courtesy it extended to almost every other show on the air, including non-entertainment ones. In fact, *The Red Skelton Show* had no reviews in *Variety* from July 1954 until September 1955, a rare relatively long span between critiques for a nighttime network entertainment series.

That July 1954 review indicated the publication pretty much had given up hope on the whole enterprise. Eyeing the expanded hour-long summer show, a *Variety* scribe wrote, "It shapes up as a fairish variety show, but it's doubtful whether it's going to make much of an impact against Berle." Additionally, "Chan." pointed out that "CBS' sagacity of giving Skelton 60 minutes with the same kind of format that gives him trouble in 30 is highly questionable."

The publication's Hollywood counterpart, *Daily Variety*, was similarly not impressed by him when it reviewed his show in October 1954.

"Helm." commented that "It seemed pretty much a slapdash effort" and singled out one joke where a motorist asked for ethyl for his car and Red brought him some women, apparently named Ethel, as an example of the weak writing for the show.

A rare video of a show from this period confirms the critical belief that *The Red Skelton Show* from the fall of 1953 through 1954 was mediocre at best. The Feb. 9, 1954, edition had Ed Sullivan, as stiff as he ever was during his early years as a television host, coming out at the start of the show to drop names of stars who had told him to say "Hi" to Red, a bit that came across as artificial. Then Ed did his typical shtick of introducing notable people sitting in the audience before Red came back in costume as Cauliflower McPugg and did a lame "interview" with Ed. Sullivan disappeared the rest of the show, which probably was a blessing given his robotic delivery and the weak quality of the main sketch.

The meat of the show had Red as Deadeye in a saloon hall where guests the King Sisters, as chorus girls, performed a number and dropped out of sight the way Sullivan had done for the rest of the show. Amid stock cowboy and Indian gags, Red attempted to inject life into the proceedings,

Red (left) and Chanin Hale listen to Red's producer Seymour Berns in this offstage photograph, taken sometime in the mid-1960s.

but a sluggish pace and uninspired dialogue made it an uphill battle. It's hard for a television historian watching it not to wonder how many people changed the channel to watch Milton Berle or even turned off the set, given the show's quality, or lack thereof.

The Backstage Merry-Go-Round

Whenever a comedy show flails the way Red's did in the early CBS years, the answer is always to replace the writers, and so it was here. His new quartet in 1953 to replace his four writers from the NBC days consisted of Howard Leeds, Arthur Julian, Arthur Ross and Arthur Stander. It sounds like a bad joke that Red had three writers with the same first name, but with their dismissal at the end of the first season came an even more improbable replacement coincidence. Red was getting rid of Arthur Ross in his foursome and replacing him and the others with the unrelated David Ross and Bob Ross.

Readers should not get the wrong impression that these scribes were the fault for why *The Red Skelton Show* stumbled on CBS from 1953 to 1955; it's just that somehow their abilities did not mesh with what Red and his show needed in this period. Howard Leeds went on to get an Emmy nomination for his writing on *The George Gobel Show* in 1955. Arthur Julian carried on in his profession as well and received an Emmy nomination for *The Carol Burnett Show* in 1971. Both Leeds and Julian had worked together on *The Beulah Show* on radio in the late 1940s and early 1950s prior to writing for Red. And Artie Stander wrote for *Amos 'n' Andy* on radio and went on to write for *The Andy Griffith Show* on television in the 1960s before his untimely death in 1963.

As for the two Rosses in 1954, Bob Ross, like Artie Stander, wrote for *Amos 'n' Andy* on radio, with Ross being the head writer, and worked on *The Andy Griffith Show* on television in the 1960s. But Ross was the show's producer, not writer, from 1965 to 1968, and received an Emmy nomination for his work in 1967.

Once the Rosses' stint ended in the summer of 1954, the new writing lineup that fall was Hal Goodman, Larry Klein, Al Gordon and Martin Ragaway. These four also had impressive comedy credits like their predecessors. For example, Gordon had been writing for *The Jack Benny Program* since 1950, and Ragaway had written for *The Abbott and Costello Show* on radio in the 1940s.

But as with the 1953–54 writers, they lasted only one season, although Ragaway would return to write for Red in 1960. Goodman and Klein would go on to earn Emmy nominations for writing *The Steve Allen Show* in 1959, *The Flip Wilson Show* in 1972 and 1973 and *The Tonight*

Show Starring Johnny Carson in 1980, among other credits, and actually won Emmys in 1971 for *The Flip Wilson Show*. Gordon received 10 Emmy nominations from 1955 to 1970, including six nominations with two of them being wins for *The Jack Benny Program*, and one nomination apiece for *The Smothers Brothers Comedy Hour* in 1968 and *The Carol Burnett Show* in 1969.

Writers were not only ones altered in the "backstage merry-go-round" that was Red's show from 1953 to 1955. When the 1953–54 season started, unlike the NBC television years, Red no longer was his show's producer. That duty fell to Ben Brady. The show also employed Cecil Barker as its first executive producer. And Seymour Berns assumed Marty Rackin's former role as director. As with the writing teams, all men were ousted by Red in 1954, although only temporarily in the case of Barker and Berns.

Berns went on to direct *Shower of Stars*, a successful monthly CBS variety show that started in the fall of 1954 and had Red on several times as a major guest (more on that later). Replacing him on Red's series was Jack Donohue, who also served as co-producer along with Douglas Whitney. The new executive producer was Nat Perrin, who didn't like Whitney and Donohue's work with Red, so in 1955, he brought back the man he replaced as executive producer, Cecil Barker, to be Red's producer, and Donohue wound up being replaced by the man whose job he assumed, Seymour Berns. To complete this clunky hiring-firing-rehiring pattern, someone decided the show needed no executive producer by 1955, and so Perrin left. Berns later would assume Barker's job of producer when the latter left the show in 1964.

All of these personnel shifts occurred under the watch of Hubbell Robinson, the CBS executive vice president in charge of network programs. He suggested some of the changes in staff to Red, which the comedian interpreted more as interference than help, as Red recalled his early CBS years to Dan Jenkins in *TV Guide* in 1960. "Hubbell Robinson hated me," Red said. "Every year he tried to get CBS to fire me. He talked to my sponsors. He said I wasn't what the people wanted, that I was too corny."

Jenkins asked Robinson for his response to Red's statements. "I would call this a monumental inaccuracy. After Red's first year with CBS, which was a pretty rocky one, I worked closely with him and even put together the production team that is with him today—producer Cecil Barker and director Seymour Berns. I tried for three years to get him an hour show because I thought he was big enough and important enough. I always did have a running fight with him, however, over his ad libs."

So given his low critical and public appeal and backstage troubles, how did Red manage to stay on the air from 1953 to 1955 on CBS? Well, the network realized his competition was tough, he had an established name and an acknowledged degree of talent as a comic, and they had spent a good deal of money on him as a television personality and wanted to see it pay off. Still, Red knew he had to show the network his desire to be on the air, so he started making more guest appearances on other CBS productions.

Doing Outside Shows

Red had pretty much confined himself to his television and radio series when he was on NBC from 1951–53. About all he did were guest shots on the NBC comedy variety programs *The Colgate Comedy Hour* on March 30, 1952, and *All Star Revue* on Oct. 4, 1952.

But with his CBS incarnation floundering, Red took time out in the 1954–55 season to moonlight as a virtual semi-regular on his network's hour-long musical variety series *Shower of Stars*, which debuted on Sept. 30, 1954, and ran monthly through April 17, 1958. These appearances presented Red strikingly in the same manner he had functioned in the MGM musicals of the 1940s, as a top-billed performer with actually little to do in terms of comedy, mostly just to introduce performers and maybe croon a number or two.

For example, Red turned up with his familiar crew of David Rose conducting and Seymour Berns directing in the Jan. 20, 1955, edition of *Shower of Stars* titled "Show Stoppers," featuring Ethel Merman and Bobby Van and the sister act of Betty and Jane Kean. Red and Merman teamed up again on June 9, 1955, for the "All Star Show" along with Edgar Bergen and his dummy Charlie McCarthy, Dan Dailey, Betty Grable and her conductor husband Harry James, Tony Martin, Marilyn Maxwell and others. "Ethel Merman's Show Stoppers" on Nov. 14, 1955, included the title Broadway belter, Red, Peter Lind Hayes and his wife Mary Healy, and dancer Harold Lang in the mix.

Red finally escaped being with Ethel Merman on a Feb. 16, 1956, show titled "The Golden Records," introducing the Andrews Sisters (Patty, Maxine and Laverne), Frankie Laine, Georgia Gibbs and others singing their hits. If being upstaged by singers wasn't enough for Red, Jack Benny made a cameo at the start of the show and got probably the largest laughs on it. As Red told him, he wasn't supposed to be on the show because it involved artists who sold a million. Jack apologized and said, "Oh, I thought it was *saved* a million!" and walked off to applause.

Red made a few other visits to other shows in this era. He was the Mystery Guest on the game show *What's My Line?* on Sept. 26, 1954. He turned up several times to do his routines on *The Ed Sullivan Show* from 1953 to 1956, with Ed being a big booster of Red's talent and Red likewise admiring Ed and his show. Red even served as guest host for the show one night in the summer of 1956 when Ed was hospitalized. And Red did CBS's other big monthly variety series *Ford Star Jubilee* on Dec. 17, 1955, in "I Hear America Singing," with Eddie Fisher, Debbie Reynolds, Nat "King" Cole, Ella Fitzgerald and Bobby Van.

All of these kept his face familiar with the television public, but none came close to boosting him as much as an acting role he did on Sept. 8, 1955, on *Climax!*, the show that was interrupted once a month by *Shower of Stars*. It was a comedy written especially for Red, and unlike much of his previous work on his series, he soared in the role.

Public Pigeon Number One

For his *Climax!* appearance, Red got an assist from Devery Freeman, who had penned the scripts of several of Red's biggest movie hits, including *The Fuller Brush Man* in 1948 and *Watch the Birdie* in 1950. Freeman wrote another story tailored for Red, only this time it was to be a live one-hour television comedy.

Recalling his role nearly 50 years later, Freeman said he had little involvement with the show after writing it. "The nature of writers at that time, you were on your next assignment when they were shooting your script. I was never on the set."

The plot had Red playing Rusty Morgan, a counter employee (with a history of bad investments) at a diner dating cashier Edith Enders (played by Ann Rutherford). His worst comes when he unwittingly becoming the dupe in a con operation and purchases $1,500 in phony uranium stocks from White Eagle Mines while working with the criminals. When he realizes he's been taken, Rusty then tries to capture the crooks who sold him the stocks but winds up getting arrested instead.

The authorities then realize Rusty's innocence and that he could lead them to the real thieves, so in some hilarious scenes in the second half hour, all the prison officials pretend not to observe Rusty breaking out and even try to help him by such means as dropping him a rope ladder alongside the prison wall. All ends well eventually, of course, with the baddies nabbed by the cops and Rusty and Edith reunited and planning to get wed.

Public Pigeon Number One was a perfect vehicle for Red because even though it left no room for him to ad lib despite being a live show, it displayed his talents as an actor and comedian splendidly within that limitation. He played it virtually in character until the end, when he bobbled a few final words of dialogue and giggled, and managed to prove he could be endearing and flat-out funny given the right material.

More importantly, *Climax!* was a hit at the time (it ranked #22 for the 1955–56 season), and very likely the exposure from the show helped to convince some viewers to give Red's show a chance for the upcoming 1955–56 season. There were other factors that probably worked for Red as well, which we will examine soon, but this one has been neglected by Red's biographers, especially given the fact that the property was thought strong enough to become a motion picture—the last movie starring Red, in fact. (He popped up in only two more movies in small roles— 1961's *Ocean's Eleven*, playing himself in the Las Vegas caper flick, and 1965's *Those Magnificent Men in Their Flying Machines*. On his April 3, 1962, show, Red claimed in his monologue that producer Joe Pasternak wanted him to do the movie *Jumbo*; if that was the case, one can assume that Jimmy Durante played the character Red was offered in the final product.)

"This one, they said they were allowed to do as a picture," Freeman said, without exactly clarifying who "they" were, presumably the owners of the copyright. "That got out of my control." He didn't fight for the property rights because "I didn't care. I was happy. I never saw the movie version."

Neither did many viewers, for that matter. Red filmed the movie in color following his 1955–56 season's shows in the summer of 1956. After a test showing to movie audiences in late 1956 ("It was a sneak preview. They got a lot of sneaks in," Red joked on his Dec. 4, 1956, show), *Public Pigeon Number One* came out in early 1957 to reviews ranging from so-so to poor. A box office flop, it also was one of the last releases by the struggling RKO film company, which was sold to Desilu (Lucille Ball's production company) a year later. As of this writing, it has not been released on home video, not that there has been much demand for it anyway. The *Climax!* version, on the other hand, has been available for sale for at least a decade.

Yet the "coming attractions" preview for the *Public Pigeon Number One* film does exist, and having seen it, I can safely guess what the problems were in the film. Specifically, the script expanded the story into tired set pieces, including the inevitable clichéd car chase, and veteran comedy movie director Norman Z. McLeod paced the material slower than desired. (He would direct just one more picture after this, 1959's *Alias Jesse James*, before dying in 1961.) A telling comparison between the television and movie incarnations can be seen via the preview: As the stock swindlers try to convince Red's character that he's being sworn into the FBI by them, part of his recitation includes after "I solemnly swear" the phrase "Through rain and sleet." On television Red breezed through it and got to the real punch line quickly; in the film, Red says it quizzically with a pause for a laugh that does not occur. Incidentally, the only actor from the television version to do the movie was Red; Janet Blair assumed Ann Rutherford's role as Red's girlfriend.

The television *Public Pigeon Number One* was the last time Freeman worked with Skelton. He said his relationship to Red was never more than purely professional. "I never met him. I never even spoke on the phone. He never had the courtesy to thank me."

But don't think that lack of respect bothered Freeman, for he felt a similar disdain toward Skelton despite how often the two collaborated on entertaining the public. "I never thought he was as good as some people," Freeman said. "I don't like people who make funny faces when they're trying to tell stories. That has nothing to do with humor."

Luckily for Red, a majority of television viewers were disagreeing with Freeman's opinion.

Turning the Tide in Red's Favor in 1955

Though the majority of the television audience did not realize it at the time, a renaissance of Red's television show was taking place a few months prior to his role on *Public Pigeon Number One*. At the start of 1955, the show employed two new writers, Joe Bigelow and Lou Meltzer. As with their predecessors, the two men had worked extensively in radio comedy series in the 1940s, chiefly on *Duffy's Tavern* starring Ed Gardner, but they showed they had little problem adapting to the medium of television in their scripts for Red.

Bigelow and Meltzer came up with several offbeat premises for Red's show, the likes of which were never seen in any other time of its run. Sometimes the concept was better than the finished product, such as their take on Jackie Gleason's hit sketch (and future series) *The Honeymooners* being done in gothic fashion, with the always creepy Peter Lorre playing a ghoulish Ralph Kramden to Red's amazingly accurate spoof of Art Carney's Ed Norton character, complete with hand and arm tics. It was a cute idea, but it ran out of life, pardon the pun, before the sketch ended.

Other efforts fared better. "Helm." in *Daily Variety* reviewed the Jan. 11, 1955, show written by Bigelow and Meltzer involving George Raft in a sketch about the Los Angeles smog problem. "Throwaway lines were as good as some of the big laughs on other shows," said the critic, who added that Red didn't ad lib anything either for once—a testament, perhaps, to the quality of Bigelow and Meltzer's writing.

Yet the ratings did not rise appreciably under the new writers, even with the new time slot (9:30–10 P.M. on Tuesday nights on the East Coast) when they joined the show in January 1955, so they were let go.

But at least they went out with a bang. Billed for some reason as *The New Red Skelton Show*, the June 7, 1955, edition had guest Rose Marie as a dance teacher for Red (playing himself) who thought he was there to teach her a new dance, the "Monkey Mambo," when he entered her studio accidentally bent over with a bad back. This all leads to Red helping Rose Marie's troupe of ballerinas with their recital amid a flighty organizer of the event, wonderfully played by Helen Kleeb, later one of the alcohol-sipping Baldwin sisters on the CBS drama *The Waltons* (1972–1981).

Amid this breezy half hour, viewers got Rose Marie singing up a storm with her interpretation of "Something's Gotta Give" and hamming up the comedy nimbly with Red; great physical comedy by Red "powder puffing" the young girls and being hit constantly by one lass's ponytail in their number, causing him to "yank" her by it off the stage at the end; and plenty of inside jokes. For example, Red made reference to his exiting director and co-producer when talking about getting the girls costumes. "Jack Donohue at the studio can get them for you," Red grinned. "He's leaving anyhow." The episode moves so nicely, and Red does so well not even having to rely on his stock characters, that one almost wishes the show could've been done longer with Bigelow and Meltzer's imaginative contributions to it.

But there was another group of writers being sent in as a last-ditch effort for the show by returning producer Cecil Barker. Leading them was Sherwood Schwartz, the younger brother of comedy writer Al Schwartz who ended up surpassing the latter in fame, thanks to his name being prominently attached to two of television's more frequently rerun, albeit inane, sitcoms—*Gilligan's Island* (originally on CBS from 1964 to 1967) and *The Brady Bunch* (on ABC from 1969 to 1974). Schwartz's tenure on *The Red Skelton Show* fell before those later creations but after Schwartz had an impressive list of writing credits that included *The Bob Hope Show* on radio in the 1940s and the television sitcom *I Married Joan* on NBC from 1952 to 1955.

From looking at Red's show via kinescopes—films of often poor quality of live television shows, usually recorded by shooting at what a monitor camera saw—Schwartz determined two things: Red needed more visual than verbal humor, and Red needed to do just one character per show. Addressing the former, Schwartz told a *Newsweek* reporter in 1959 that nearly two-thirds of Red's scripts consisted of description. "Sometimes, you write five pages of script for Red without a word of dialogue," he said.

The one-character-per-show rule meant no more hodgepodges on each show of shtick with, say, Cauliflower McPugg, then a musical number, then Deadeye or Clem Kadiddlehopper or whoever. The show now would just have Red do the monologue, maybe a short song-and-dance number, and then a main sketch consisting of one of his old characters alternating every week, so, say, you wouldn't see San Fernando Red but once a month at most. These philosophies would basically anchor *The Red Skelton Show* for the rest of its run, proving Schwartz knew what he was talking about.

Wait, amend that last paragraph—Schwartz did add one new person for Red to play in the 1955–56 season. And of all things, it involved a man who probably is better known to younger generations of television audiences today than Red is.

Klinger Joins the Fun

Actor Jamie Farr gained television immortality for his role as Corporal Maxwell Klinger, the cross-dressing soldier, on *M*A*S*H* from 1973–83, but that was nearly two decades away from him as he became a recurring character on *The Red Skelton Show* in the fall of 1955. His appearances on the series grew out of an odd circumstance. Actor Craig Stevens starred in a sitcom pilot called *The Mighty O* in 1955 playing Cookie, a happy-go-lucky sailor, and noticed there was a part for a sailor nicknamed Snorkel because he had a large proboscis. Stevens had played opposite Farr in a Hollywood stage production of the play *Mister Roberts* in 1953 and told the pilot's producer that Farr (then going by his birth name of Jameel Farah) would be perfect for Snorkel.

The pilot didn't sell, but its producer was Cecil Barker, the same producer for *The Red Skelton Show*. When Barker learned Schwartz was thinking about a Navy character for Red to add to his list of characters on the show, given that Red had a lot of Navy jokes, he sold Schwartz on the idea of doing Cookie from *The Mighty O*. An agent backed the idea of having Cookie and Snorkel as a comedy team, so Farr met with Red to see how well they could work together.

"Skelton was one of my all-time heroes," Farr confessed in his autobiography *Just Farr Fun*. He had been a fan since he was a child. "At age 8, I used to listen to him on the radio, in bed, under the covers, so my mother couldn't hear, 'cause [he] came on after my bedtime. And later, when I was old enough to start going to the movies, I never missed a Skelton movie."

Farr met Skelton at the latter's home, where he served up some nose jokes like "Was your mother frightened by an anteater?" Skelton liked him, so Cookie and Snorkel were part of *The Red Skelton Show* cast of rotating characters for two years.

In 1957 Farr learned to his chagrin that he actually was drafted into military service in Korea for two years. Red remained a friend and performed in Korea during Farr's tour of duty, personally requesting that Farr join him. When Farr returned to Hollywood in 1959, he found that he needed to take advantage of Red's offer in Korea to help him get back to work on his return, and Red responded by giving him another year on the show with a few shots of playing Snorkel to his Cookie.

Then Farr decided he had to try to find work elsewhere, so he left Red on an amiable note full of fond memories that remained throughout Farr's lifetime. When the Academy of Television Arts and Sciences, the organization that dispense the Emmys, sponsored "A Salute to Red Skelton" in Los Angeles on Oct. 21, 1998, Farr served as its host.

The character of Cookie crumbled from appearing further on Red's show after Farr's final departure. But on Aug. 21, 1962, another pilot for *The Mighty O* aired on CBS with Craig Stevens again as Cookie, now billed as "Chief Joe Slattery," and no Snorkel listed in the cast. It did not sell—again.

Moving on Up in 1955–56

Red returned for his fifth season on television on Sept. 26, 1955, replacing the summer series *Spotlight Playhouse*, a collection of filmed presentations repeated from various anthology series such as *Schlitz Playhouse of Stars*. *Spotlight Playhouse* would serve as Red's summer replacement series through Sept. 22, 1959.

Red and crew knew they had to prove themselves this season. The show had stayed on the air basically because of his contract with the network and his somewhat surprising alternating sponsorship by Pet's Milk and Johnson Wax that existed by 1955. Executives with that company must have seen something promising about the show that the general public didn't, for the ratings and general recognition of the show were low. A spring 1955 *TV Guide* poll, for example, found that Red's show was not listed in the top 25 cited by viewers as their favorites, although its East Coast lead-in, the sitcom *Meet Millie*, made the cut.

And when the networks unveiled their 1955–56 lineup, *Variety* made no mention about Red's show at all. To that publication, the big news was that Red's previous ABC competition, *The U.S. Steel Hour*, was moving to CBS on Wednesdays 10–11 P.M., thus setting up a new duel at Tuesdays at 9:30 P.M. between the dramatic anthologies *Cavalcade of America* (now retitled *DuPont Cavalcade Theater* in honor of its sponsor) on ABC and *Armstrong Circle Theater*, expanded to an hour starting that season, on NBC.

Yet it was that very competition that probably aided Red that season.

Television watchers were growing weary of the dramatic anthology format by the mid–1950s, with only four of them making the top 20 in 1955–56: *Disneyland* (#4) on ABC, *The Millionaire* (#9) and *G.E. Theater* (#11) on CBS and *Ford Theatre* (#12) on NBC. And with two of them competing at the same time—an infrequent situation even in 1955— it naturally figured that anyone not interested in the format would give Red a try.

Furthermore, NBC's dominance on Tuesdays was waning. *The Milton Berle Show* found itself floundering opposite the sitcom *You'll Never Get Rich* (a/k/a *The Phil Silvers Show*) on CBS 8–8:30 and the western *The Life and Legend of Wyatt Earp* on ABC 8:30–9, and Berle went off the air in 1956, never being able to get another hit on the medium he had so thoroughly dominated a few years earlier that he earned the nickname "Mr. Television." The NBC show following it, *Fireside Theatre*, had been in the top 10 two years earlier but now ended the 1955–56 season at #24, even with film actress Jane Wyman as its new hostess. That still managed to beat out *Meet Millie* on CBS, which ended its run as Red's lead-in on March 6, 1956, after four unexceptional seasons on the air, but the continuing loss of audience meant that Tuesdays were now more up for grabs from NBC than they ever had been.

The biggest beneficiary of NBC's lack of invincibility, however, was the game show that followed Red—*The $64,000 Question*. Debuting on June 7, 1955, it was an immediate sensation, zooming to #1 in the summer and even forcing *I Love Lucy* out of the top position for the 1955–56 season, the first time in three years that *I Love Lucy* was not #1 for a season. Some thought that may have aided Red as well, with the audience sampling his show in preparation for the big new hit, though Red thought otherwise.

Whatever the reasons were for more people trying the show, none would have stayed if Red did not deliver a funny show. The debut failed in that mission, as guest Ed Sullivan proved just as wooden as he had in 1954 when he was a last-minute replacement for Jackie Gleason, who had been forbidden to do the show by his sponsor. But later installments jelled over the season as Red and his new writers, which beside Sherwood Schwartz included Dave O'Brien, Jesse Goldstein and Mort Green, found a comfortable setup for him. In fact, O'Brien, a big, balding guy, acted in bit parts on the show starting with this season. It wasn't hard for him to do so, as he had acted in the movies in the 1930s and 1940s in several cowboy movie serials and the "Pete Smith Specialties" short subjects. (Mort Green was a former performer as well, including being a regular panelist on the short-lived DuMont game show *Where Was I?* in 1953, while Goldstein had been an English teacher who wrote for *The Eddie Cantor Show* on radio in the 1940s.)

It took time—months, in fact—but the show's ratings kept growing in 1955–56. For the week of Feb. 1–7, 1956, the Trendex rating service ranked Red's show at #8 that week, the first time his series had reached that high in nearly five years. Subsequent shows came in close to the top 10 thereafter, and the industry took notice. A musical playlet of "Robin Hood" on April 24, 1956, with Red as the title character, John Carradine as Little John, and Billy Gilbert as Friar Tuck earned the series its first "*TV Guide* Closeup," the magazine's feature of spotlighting shows it felt deserved particular attention from viewers. The following week, the same magazine also profiled him for the first time in nearly three years.

If anyone needed an indication of how Red's luck was turning dramatically for the better in 1956, however, it came from Red turning dramatically on screen outside his series. Red not only was having his best time on television since 1951–52, he also was in his first Emmy race since that same period, thanks to a guest role.

Another Emmy Nomination

As if his rise in ratings weren't enough, Red's performance as Buddy McCoy on "The Big Slide" presentation on the top dramatic series *Playhouse 90* in 1956 went on to earn him his first Emmy nomination since 1952. He had virtually no chance against his impressive competitors—Lloyd Bridges for an *Alcoa Hour* presentation where he was so intense he accidentally used the word "goddamn" in his live performance, and even clergy defended him for the slip; Frederic March starring in "Dodsworth" on *Producers Showcase*, March's third Emmy nomination after being the first actor to be nominated twice in the same Emmy category (for Best Actor—Single Performance in 1954 for "A Christmas Carol" on *Shower of Stars* and "The Royal Family" on *The Best of Broadway*); Sal Mineo starring in "Dino" on *Studio One*, a role he recreated in a movie named *Dino* in 1957; and the winner, Jack Palance as the prizefighter in the Rod Serling–penned classic "Requiem for a Heavyweight" on *Playhouse 90*.

Yet Red could take some small consolation in Palance's victory. You see, Red's mentor of sorts Ed Wynn played a trainer in "Requiem for a Heavyweight," but he worried he could not carry off the dramatic role properly. To give him support, Red made an unbilled appearance with Wynn on camera during the production. The performance won Wynn an Emmy nomination (he lost to Carl Reiner for the latter's work on *Caesar's Hour*) and re-energized Wynn as a performer in demand in the industry. As for "Requiem for a Heavyweight," it won the Emmy for Program of the Year, and *Playhouse 90* won for Best New Program.

A postscript: Red played himself when the whole story about Wynn and his fears of doing the show became a television drama unto itself. "The Man in the Funny Suit" aired on *The Westinghouse Desilu Playhouse* on CBS on April 15, 1960, and also featured Wynn and Rod Serling, author of "Requiem for a Heavyweight," playing themselves. It would be Red's last dramatic role on television.

So, Why the Rise in Ratings?

Near the end of the season, the April 28–May 4, 1956, edition of *TV Guide* contained an article on Red probing him about why and how his series rose in the ratings over the year. He claimed it was not due to any dramatic alterations in its format. "Heck, we haven't changed much. Heck, we haven't changed hardly at all. Heck, we've been in the top 20 all along except nobody ever pays any attention to who's in 11th place."

This last statement was wrong, of course. Red had been struggling long for an audience, and he had to know it. He was more accurate in discounting the notion that because his show aired just before *The $64,000 Question* on the East Coast, that was the reason for its ascension, with people wanting to tune in to be ready for the game show.

"I honestly don't think that's it," he said. "We've had all sorts of surveys made, and our rating is just as strong at the beginning of our half hour as it is at the end. You can't tell me people tune to us a full 30 minutes ahead of time just to be sure they're not going to miss *64*."

Red also spoke some truth in mentioning Sherwood Schwartz's change to the format. "We've tended to run a sort of story line through the sketches rather than a series of blackouts, and we've lately been getting some darned good supporting players, but basically the show is the same thing it's always been."

He was on shakier ground with his contention that the guests helped drive up the audience as well. Does anyone think that viewers looked at their television listings that season and said, "Hey! Keefe Brasselle (or Virginia Grey or Jeanne Cagney, etc.) is going to be on *The Red Skelton Show*! Let's watch it!" Frankly, the guest selection still tended toward the Hollywood "B" list as it had previously, though it would improve over the next few seasons.

And though *The Red Skelton Show* was live in color for the 1955–56 season, hardly any other CBS programs airing at the same time were, and color television sets still were in the minority in homes across the country. (CBS let the show stay in color through the next few seasons, incidentally, one of the few color series on that network in the 1950s.)

Whatever the real reasons were, the bottom line was that Red was back on top. For the next 14 seasons, the series would manage an impressive run of remaining annually in the top 20 listings. Considering that there have been less than 30 nighttime shows to run at least 14 seasons alone, that achievement is even more amazing.

4

1956–1962: "I'm Just Lucky"?

Though he came back into the top 15 in 1956 and would stay there the next five years, it was not until nearing the end of the 1950s that casual television observers suddenly realized Red was about the only comedian to hold his own amid the onslaught of westerns on television during the era. As *Gunsmoke*, *Wagon Train* and *Have Gun Will Travel* retained a lock on the respective 1-2-3 positions in both the 1958–59 and 1959–60 seasonal ratings, Red somehow managed to break through the cowboy action and finish as the top-rated variety show both of these years, at #12 for the first year and all the way to #5 for the second year. (*The Danny Thomas Show* was at #4 behind the oaters that season.) As a result, Red garnered major stories not only in the industry bibles, *TV Guide* and *Variety*, but also in *Time*, *Newsweek* and other publications as they attempted to explain how *The Red Skelton Show* managed to get more viewers than all the other jokesters on the air.

Red himself claimed not to know the answer for his continuing success, and as before, when he attempted to explain it, he stumbled. "Maybe the public felt it had to make a choice between me and the beatniks, and they chose me," he told *Newsweek* in 1959. That comment made no sense. Outside of Bob Denver's portrayal of Maynard G. Krebs on *The Many Loves of Dobie Gillis* (a show that ran from 1959 to 1963), there were hardly any beatniks on television except as guests on news and interview shows.

Red was on more solid ground when he frankly told Dan Jenkins in *TV Guide* in 1960 that "I don't know why I've been able to stay on the air for 10 years. If I knew the secret, I'd phone every comedian in the business and let him in on it. I just don't know. I'm just lucky."

He did gloat to Jenkins about one personal triumph, that of thoroughly whipping his NBC competition *Startime* in the fall of 1959. A big-budget hour show featuring top stars like Jimmy Stewart, Dean Martin, and Ingrid Bergman in presentations ranging from musicals to dramas to variety programs, *Startime* was what NBC, and probably some in the industry, believed would give Red a real run for his money and bring him down. It didn't happen, and as its producer, Hubbell Robinson, used to be the CBS executive in charge of Red's show when it started on that network, Red took glee in its failure.

"Well, the last time I looked at the ratings, his show was down around 100, and I was in the top 10," Red noted. "I consider it a great compliment that his show is opposite mine—and that he now wants to move." Indeed, *Startime* left its slot opposite Red in January 1960 and moved up an hour earlier on Tuesday evenings, but it was no more successful there and ended on May 31, 1960. Even better for Red, Robinson returned to CBS as an executive in 1962 and had to work with Red who was then in a better position to make demands as one of the network's top stars.

But it was not just his competition that Red was outperforming. The comedians who flourished on the early television of the late 1940s and early 1950s found themselves facing cancellation or strongly declining ratings in the late 1950s, often but not primarily due to the westerns opposite them. Some social television historians have blamed this decline on the medium's initial appeal to the more affluent and better-educated viewers in its early years versus its catering to the general public by the end of the 1950s, leading to more programming favoring the lowest common denominator. By such reasoning, many of the television comedians' largely Borscht Belt sense of humor held much less sway with the bulk of America's middle class than did other types of shows.

Whatever the excuse, comics were in severe decline on television by the end of the 1958–59 season. Jackie Gleason and Milton Berle returned after respective one and two-year layoffs from the boob tube only to flop. *You'll Never Get Rich*, *The Ed Wynn Show*, and *The George Burns Show* (without Gracie Allen, who retired in 1958) all went off at the end of the season. NBC moved *The Steve Allen Show* to Monday nights as the competition from *Maverick* on ABC and *The Ed Sullivan Show* on CBS proved too strong. *The George Gobel Show*, which had been the comedy sensation of the 1954–55 season, was canned by NBC and only got back on the air for one more year a half-hour shorter alternating weekly with *The Jack Benny Program*, a show which also found its ratings dropping in 1958–59, when it finished outside the top 30 for its first season ever.

Obviously Red had a lot to be proud about himself, given his series' situation in the late 1950s and early 1960s. As typically happens among stars, this kind of success produced a mixed blessing for Red and his fans, as he exhibited some fine new talents along the way while developing some habits that would later haunt his reputation on television.

Slowing Down His Outside Television Appearances

One of Red's more disappointing activities in this period was to concentrate virtually only on his television series and hardly show up anywhere else, unlike most other television stars. At first, Red continued guesting on other people's shows occasionally in the mid–1950s as his ratings climbed back to the top. In the fall of 1956, he turned up on the debut of *The Herb Shriner Show* (which preceded Red's show for just three months in late 1956), followed by a cameo on *The Jack Benny Program* of Oct. 21, 1956, wherein Red was the surprise winner of a contest between Jack and guest star George Gobel over who would become president of a wealthy boys' club. He returned to *The Jack Benny Program* on Dec. 14, 1958, with another cameo, this time popping out of a piano played by guest Gisele MacKenzie.

The CBS special *Bing Crosby and His Friends* included a turn by Red when it aired on Jan. 12, 1958. Red also made a rare game show appearance on *What's My Line?* on Sept. 25, 1960, when he was the Mystery Guest to promote his live one-man pantomime show from New York City to celebrate the 15th anniversary of the United Nations.

But the most-remembered Skelton guest shot to contemporary audiences had to be when he guested on *The Westinghouse Desilu Playhouse* on Feb. 9, 1959, as part of *The Lucille Ball-Desi Arnaz Show* series of specials. In "Lucy Goes to Alaska," Red played himself as a guest in a hotel in Nome, Alaska, and meets Lucy and Ricky Ricardo and their friends Fred and Ethel Mertz, who find that the land they bought in the state has no value. As complications ensue, Lucy does a "Freddie the Freeloader" performance with Red during their stay and has a wacky plane ride with him as they themselves land it amid a blizzard and nearly hit Ricky, Fred and Ethel.

The specials were hour-long extensions of *I Love Lucy* following the decision to end the show as a weekly series while it was still television's top sitcom in 1957. Though the two stars worked together well, including a pleasant song-and-dance number at the end of the "Freddie the Freeloader" number, the show's producer Bert Granet said Lucy had no patience for Red's ad-libbing and forced him to stick to the script. This difference of approach may explain why Lucy did not return the favor and guest on Red's show. (However, William Frawley, who played Fred Mertz, did guest star on Red's 1958 Thanksgiving show, and Vivian Vance, who was Ethel Mertz, also made several guest shots on Red's series in the early 1960s.)

Because it was filmed and part of the *I Love Lucy* legacy, the show ran as part of a collection of hour-long specials done from 1957 to 1960, then rerun by CBS for five consecutive summers from 1962 to 1967 before going into syndication for rerunning by local stations. The shows regained renewed popularity in the 1990s with their release on home video and constant replays on the Nick at Nite and TV Land cable channels, making this by far the biggest exposure Red had on television in recent years.

There was one other significant fact about "Lucy Goes to Alaska" that ought to be mentioned. The show's writers, Bob Schiller and Bob Weiskopf, would become Red's head writers in 1964, after writing again for Lucille Ball on *The Lucy Show* from 1962 to 1964.

But the greatest potential guest appearance for Red in this period unfortunately did not become a reality. In the April 2, 1959, issue of *Down Beat* magazine, Gene Tuttle reported that Red wanted to do an hour-long jazz special with drummer extraordinaire Lionel Hampton after the two worked at the Riviera hotel in Las Vegas. The two men taped their idea of having Red narrate the history of jazz while Lionel provided backing music.

"How can it fail?" Red asked Tuttle. "Lionel's music is the greatest and with these ideas incorporated into it, it will be a success."

But the project never occurred, probably due to CBS executives' fear about the commercial appeal of jazz. Instead, Hampton did appear in *The Red Skelton Chevy Special* that aired on Oct. 9, 1959, along with several other top guests ranging from James Arness (then starring in *Gunsmoke* on CBS) to Burl Ives. Nearly a year later, on Nov. 30, 1960, *The Red Skelton Timex Special* found Red hosting the likes of Dinah Shore and Frank Sinatra.

But the same year of the last special, Red confided to Dan Jenkins in *TV Guide* that "I don't do very many guest shots. Frankly, nobody asks me. I don't like to do those swap deals where you do your show and I do yours. They're contrived, they're not spontaneous—and I think the audience senses that."

In 1961, talking to another *TV Guide* reporter, Red elaborated on his growing dislike of others in entertainment away from his series. "Actors are strange people. When you tell them a joke, all they do is nod and try to top you. They don't laugh. I stay away from them." The article noted that he belonged to no actors clubs nor did testimonial dinners or benefits so common among other comedians. Instead, he preferred to stay home and watch as much as nine hours of television a day on one of his many television sets.

Despite that activity, Red stopped acting on television in 1960, preferring to make just one or two visits away from his television series, usually on talk and variety shows. He even turned down a request to talk on CBS's top nighttime interview show *Person to Person* ("kinda nosy," he explained to a *Time* reporter). Now that he was back on top, the loner among show business circles felt he had no need to do any other television jobs. It was not an approach that won him fans in the industry, but it made Red happy by all accounts.

Comedy Being Born with Erlenborn

A happier development pleasing everyone, or at least those familiar with the inner workings of Red's series, was the addition of Ray Erlenborn to do sound effects in 1957. He had been doing his profession for at least two decades before he arrived on the show.

"In 1937 I went on staff on KNX radio [in Los Angeles] as a sound effects guy," he recalled in 2002. "There were about 7 or 8 of us, and we would fill in with another guy. Everybody went out and did extra work. When I went on staff, we made $25 a week."

From that modest start, Erlenborn branched into doing network radio shows rather quickly, such as playing a fireman's siren with bells to indicate the opening of *The Texaco Star Theater* in the late 1930s. He created unique noises for all sorts of top radio shows—westerns (*The Gene Autry Show*), sitcoms (*Blondie*), adventures (*Big Town*) and even straight drama (*Dr. Christian*). But he loved comedy the best, and when television came around, he even scored a regular acting role on a syndicated sitcom, playing Mr. Fuddy on *Life with Elizabeth*, starring Betty White as the title character, in 1953.

When he arrived at *The Red Skelton Show*, Erlenborn discovered the star's tendency to wander away from his scripted lines and movements, which, in lesser hands, would make for messy, mistimed gags from the sound effects man. But not in Erlenborn's case.

"Working with Red, I learned to throw away a script and make a cue card for myself," Erlenborn said. Red would vary what he did at each rehearsal, and Erlenborn had to be ready for whatever sound might be appropriate, or maybe perfectly inappropriate, for the comedy Red was concocting. Erlenborn proved he could handle it.

"I came out of vaudeville as a kid, so I knew everything he was doing," Erlenborn said of Red's tricks. "He telegraphed what he was going to do. But a lot of times he tried to throw me off." When he succeeded, invariably Red smiled and maybe giggled to indicate to his audience he'd fooled one of his staff.

Erlenborn's duties on the show varied from everything to making squeaking sounds for doors and windows to imitating a flea. (Try and do that one!) "I did a water sound effect with a water fountain," he remembered. Naturally, he was at his busiest whenever Red did a pantomime.

Erlenborn also provided sound for Red sometimes, including one characteristic people may not have realized. "I did all the snores with Freddie the Freeloader on stage," he said. "[Red] had emphysema and an oxygen tank on stage."

Erlenborn left the show in 1967 to do *The Carol Burnett Show* when it debuted that fall. He was there for a few years and stayed on staff at CBS before retiring in the late 1970s when the idea of providing a doorbell sound to soap operas like *The Young and the Restless* held little appeal for him.

But he remains fond of his association with Red and wishes something as good as that show was on the air now. "Nobody knows how to do comedy anymore," he lamented to me.

Skelton Versus Schwartz

Alas, at the same time Erlenborn worked his magic on Red's show, the industry also noted the obvious dislike between Red and his writers. Though the crew of Sherwood Schwartz, Jesse Goldstein and Dave O'Brien remained with him longer than any of his previous writers, and, in fact, both Goldstein and O'Brien died while still doing the show (Goldstein in 1959, O'Brien in 1969), Red was loathe to pay them too many compliments for helping his show regain its popularity as a top television attraction. Indeed, he often avoided them as much as possible, much less give them any thanks for their efforts.

"Red never talked to his writers," confirmed his pal, entertainment reporter James Bacon. "[Jackie] Gleason was that way too."

This attitude rankled Sherwood Schwartz so much that even though he stayed on the show through 1961 and earned an Emmy from his work on it, he spent much of his later years in interviews criticizing his ex-boss. For example, Schwartz told Geoffrey Mark Fidelman in *The Lucy Book* that "Red Skelton hated writers. Hated writers. He hated to admit that he needed them so much."

What really irked Red's writers was when the comedian made one of his few guest appearances in 1959 on *The Tonight Show* when it was being hosted by Jack Paar (a/k/a *The Jack Paar Show*). The host asked Red how he came up with his funny material for his show, and Red did not mention his writers, but did credit God.

Red recounted the incident this way to a *Newsweek* reporter: "I thanked the producer and the director of my show, and then I thanked God for giving me such wonderful lines. So the writers are objecting because I gave God top billing." Incidentally, the tables would turn on the show that hosted Red that evening, for in 1962, he sued NBC for repeating a later guest shot by him on *The Jack Paar Show* without his permission.

The writers also did not like Red being credited as a writer on the show, as most of the plots and dialogue came from them, with Red adding jokes and ad-libs during the rehearsal and shooting. Nonetheless, Red got Emmy nominations in 1961 and 1962 for writing his show, and, in fact, won with Schwartz and company for the 1961 nomination, to the writers' chagrin. (Oddly, neither Red's show nor his performing received a nomination in 1961, continuing Red's rocky relationship with the Emmy nominating committee. After Red's dramatic acting Emmy nomination in 1956, he had to wait until 1959 for his next one, for Best Comedy Series, followed by the same nomination in 1960 and 1962. Also, Seymour Berns' direction on the show got a nod in 1960.)

Despite those situations, the fact remains that the writing crew was fairly stable in the 1950s and early 1960s. If the scribblers for Red's show felt unappreciated, they certainly did not display any confidence in themselves by leaving the show for other venues, as they certainly could have done with ease, given the hit status of *The Red Skelton Show*. But apart from Schwartz, who left after six years to develop what would become the series *Gilligan's Island*, none of the other writing staff left in this period, and in fact, Martin Ragaway, a writer for Red in 1954–55, came back in 1960 to begin a longer (eight-year) tenure with his ex-boss.

However, there was one notable firing in this time. Al Schwartz, Sherwood's older brother, joined the staff in 1960 to work under his younger sibling. When Sherwood left, so the story goes, Red was so upset that he retaliated and fired his brother Al as well. Thus, in the fall of 1961, there were two new writers to replace the Schwartzes—Arthur Phillips, who had been writing for *The Phil Baker Show* on radio in the 1930s and stayed with Red almost through the rest of the show's run, and Ed Simmons, who assumed the title of script supervisor, meaning he replaced Sherwood as head writer.

Through it all, Red became known as one comic who did not talk with his writers unless absolutely necessary. His pal, columnist James Bacon, offers this reason why: "He was very funny in person. That's probably why he didn't associate with his writers."

But it still doesn't explain the disdain, if not outright contempt, Red constantly showed to his writers. For example, in a 1967 article for *The Saturday Evening Post*, Bill Davidson recorded Red saying, "That sounds like one of my writers' lousy lines" when Red's attorney told the comic he could sue himself for an injury on his own show.

Actually, there could be one good excuse for Red's irritation. A novel co-written by Benedict Freedman, one of Red's writers from the 1951–53 seasons, came out in 1957 and printed a very unflattering portrait of a television comic. It may not have been Red exactly, but what was in it struck so close to home that Red nursed a grudge from it years later.

Lootville

Lootville, written by Benedict Freedman and his wife Nancy, began its saga with cameraman Pete Munger joining *The Zane Cochrane Show*, a live comedy variety series sagging in the ratings thanks to the lousy routines done by its star, who also was its producer. The program was an industry joke, featuring a comedian who preferred old gags rather than newly scripted material, refused to rehearse and laughed constantly after his own jokes. Pete, devoid of other prospects, soldiered on with his job, while various characters, including his girlfriend, grouse about how overpaid and untalented Cochrane is.

Yet Pete had some affection for Zane, who liked his camera work (*The Zane Cochrane Show* is notorious for missed, awkward shots prior to Pete's arrival, partly due to Zane's improvisations) and admitted to him that "I'm wild, nutty, fruity, a low comic, that's what I am." Zane told him about growing up with a mother in vaudeville and other show business stories, all the while loathing network executives who claimed they wanted to improve his show. It also came to light that Zane is a dipsomaniac and throws up prior to doing his show.

Then one night after failing to show for rehearsal, and looking like he will do his worst show ever, Zane suddenly put on a presentation using all of his best old routines. With no one knowing what Zane would do, Pete was assigned to keep him in view at all times. Pete's stellar job in this instance secured the confidence of Zane, who promises to work with him on a television series while inviting him to attend the writers' conferences for his show for input. While there, Pete learned that Zane believes in quantity over quality in his writers, boasting that the higher number of pages his writers have completed means he has more material than any other comic, and that Zane favored simplicity over cleverness in his humor on television.

Zane wound up killing himself amid growing pressure from all quarters, just as Pete intends to kill him after Zane has him fired from his job and planned not to do a television series with Pete as promised. In the aftermath, one character noted that Pete did not hate Zane the human being, who was likable, but Zane the television comic, with all of his money, hangers-on and colleagues, who treated Pete poorly. Zane became an egomaniac, a resident in Lootville.

Oh, and what exactly was "Lootville"? Well, according to Pete, it's where in television the real money is earned, by the "talent" who really aren't that talented. "In fact, I'll give you the latitude and longitude. It's 60 degrees bluff by 40 degrees luck. Here everything works by gimmicks and angles." He presents a truly jaundiced view of the television industry—the writers, actors, singers and so forth really are not talented, but they receive huge amounts of money on the whims of fortune and fake it.

Critical reaction to *Lootville* was mixed. A *Saturday Review* critic claimed that "*Lootville* is too far removed from the facts of life and television to be more than heavy-handed caricature," while a writer for the *Library Journal* noted that "Too rough for small libraries [presumably for its adult situations for the time, such as one character speculating that Zane was gay], it is of value solely as brassy entertainment." Reading *Lootville* nowadays, it's a breezy bit of days gone by, but with the novelty of live television variety gone, it has little impact except for those with a historical background of the period.

Freedman emailed me on Sept. 2, 2002, to explain that the book was not an attack on Red. "As for *Lootville*, it was a work of fiction by Benedict and Nancy Freedman satirizing not just one particular show, but the whole variety format," he wrote. "When it was published, I received phone calls from Red Skelton and Mickey Rooney (whose show I wrote for a year), each accusing us of picking on him." (That show was *The Mickey Rooney Show*, a/k/a *Hey Mulligan*, which ran on NBC Saturdays 8–8:30 P.M. from Sept. 4, 1954, to June 4, 1955, flopping against *The Jackie Gleason Show* on CBS.)

Freedman continued: "I defused the issue by telling Red that Zane was Mickey, and Mickey that Zane was Red. I don't know if it worked with Red, but Mickey was mollified enough to discuss making a Broadway musical out of *Lootville*."

According to Arthur Marx's biography, Red never did accept what Freedman said. Actually, Freedman covered himself against any lawsuit from Red in a tough way—by mentioning Skelton's show in the novel as being even worse than Cochrane's. On page 94, Cochrane and his staff watch the last half of *The Red Skelton Show* and denigrate it thoroughly. "The material was lousy, the acting putrid, the production stank, the whole thing was 'just ghastly.' ...But apparently the intention was to convince Zane, and perhaps themselves, that *The Red Skelton Show* was so bad *The Zane Cochrane Show* must be magnificent if only by comparison."

With such a statement, Red can hardly be blamed for cursing at Freedman for writing it. Actually, Red was doing a lot of cursing at the time, only most television viewers didn't know about it. It happened when he did an off-color rehearsal for his television show, and it became known familiarly by the cast and crew as the "Dirty Hour."

The "Dirty Hour"

Red did not create the idea of a rehearsal where dirty jokes and gags proliferated. It's fairly well known that in the early 1950s, the radio cast of *Gunsmoke* and even the television children's show *Howdy Doody* would use similar tactics as a means of release before doing their live shows. But Red's routine would outlive both shows and gain its own notoriety.

The "Dirty Hour" already was known by *TV Guide* by 1961, where an observer said that "his ribaldry comes over as good clean fun." Former monologue writer Robert Orben concurred with that assessment, telling me that "The so-called 'Dirty Rehearsal' could be shown on *Sesame Street* today."

On the other hand, Red's pal Hollywood columnist James Bacon asserted the rehearsals were not fit for children at all. "They were dirty as hell!" he said. "He got it all out of his system before taping." Bacon said the "blue" rehearsal was an open secret in the industry.

Having acquired a rare videotape of one of those rehearsals, I'd say they'd fall somewhere in the middle between *Sesame Street* and "dirty as hell," maybe under the "14" rating they use on television now. Many sources I've read and interviewed have indicated that only Martha Raye could match Red for these moments, and as fate would have it, the bootlegged rehearsal available on a few videotapes has Red and Martha going over a "Cleopatra" parody in 1962, and it's fairly lively.

Among other events at this rehearsal, where the stars wore their street clothes, Martha mistakenly (?) calls Red's character "King Tit" at one point, and when she takes her hand to feel his muscles, Red grabs his crotch to protect that area from inspection. Martha responds with "All right, throw it over here. Holy Christ!" as she grabs his leg, feigning that she's touching his manhood. "Welcome to Hollywood Knickerbocker—no *ballroom*!" Red cracks. Martha shoots back with "If that wasn't your knee, I'd marry you!" Later comes some other suggestive leers and lines between the two, especially when Martha asks to see his tongue and Red rolls it around his mouth to indicate how it can be used. "A tongue like that, and all he wants to do is hump!" Martha exclaims, breaking Red up.

As ribald as this description sounds, in reality, Red managed to get away with a few good risqué lines on his show by the late 1950s. In a 1959 sketch with Audrey Totter, for example, Red eyes trying to get into her single bed before they go to sleep (double beds were still forbidden on television at the time), following an earlier bit where he and Audrey hid under the bed from criminals and Audrey said, "What are we going to do?" "I don't know, whatcha got in mind?" he ad-libs, making her giggle.

And in another show in 1959 with Nancy Walker, Red played Bolivar Shagnasty as a hair stylist. Asked by one man as he escorted one female client behind a curtain "How long do you think it'll take?" Red eyed the gorgeous woman and ad-libbed "Censored," tickling Walker. Then the woman came out, ecstatic about her new bob, and offered Bolivar to set up his own salon in Hollywood. "I'll even back you," she told him. Red asked her to repeat the line, then rolled his eyes and leered, "Hmm, you will?" then remarked, "We're worse off now than we were with the first one!" (Adding to the slightly adult air of the show at this time, Red had nearly every major bombshell except Marilyn Monroe guest on his show in the late 1950s and early 1960s, including Marie Wilson, Marilyn Maxwell, Jayne Mansfield, Julie London, Mamie Van Doren, Jane Russell, Diana Dors and even Mae West.)

These crackups by guests over jokes that may have been raunchier in the earlier rehearsal sometimes spilled into the actual show too much for many critics' tastes, and some sniped at Red for it. Following a telecast where he and his guest Cesar Romero broke up at nearly every line, *Variety* posted an article headlined "Look Here, Mr. Skelton!" in its Oct. 23, 1957, issue. In it, critic "Rose." griped that Red's spoof of westerns with Romero "was not only in bad taste, with its offensive material, but suggested a sloppiness and carelessness that, in this latter period of television's exactitude and finesse, could hardly be condoned."

Yet nearly a year later, that periodical and many others in the media would be laying critical praises to Red for a different show he did. It marked a turning point in the way many critics and television industry people viewed him. It was a risky effort involving his pantomime talent, which no one had ever taken on the medium, and few have done so since.

The 1958 Thanksgiving Show

On Nov. 25, 1958, Red presented a show where the only talking done except after the main sketch ended came from the voice of his announcer from 1955 to 1971, Art Gilmore, who narrated the tale. The setup had Freddie the Freeloader dealing with a maître d' played by William Frawley who demanded Freddie leave while his restaurant's customers enjoyed a turkey dinner for the seasonal celebration. Freddie thinks he gets a break when he sees a woman lose her money clip and returns it to her expecting a handsome reward, only getting a handshake instead. While Gilmore claims Freddie is saying "Shucks!" and "Darn!" in response, it's obvious and amusing by Red's mouthing that Freddie is saying something more profane.

Next, a man stacks a crate of apples to bring into a store, but as

Freddie grabs for a piece of fruit, a vigilant cop smacks him with his nightstick. The apple delivery man, upon seeing Freddie, gives him an apple in pity, but the cop happens on Freddie again and thinks his apple is stolen, so he takes it away from the hobo. All hope looks lost until Frawley's character offers Freddie a free meal if he'll wash dishes at the busy restaurant. Freddie goes to do the chore, joined by beefy pug-nosed character actor Henry Kulky, but the two make a shambles of the kitchen as Freddie sneezes and drops the dishes and causes other mayhem. He winds up being thrown out by Frawley and looking less likely than ever to get a meal that day.

Act II began with Freddie being so desperate for food he pries into a gumball machine, finally getting a piece from it accidentally, then tries to use the chewed gum to pick up a quarter underneath a grating. He attaches the gum to a man's walking stick without the man knowing, and when the man grabs the stick back, he does a pratfall (to audience applause) as the stick is stuck to the ground by the gum. Finally a customer in the restaurant sees Freddie and insists he eat with him over Frawley's objections. Freddie treats himself like a king, ordering wine and attaching a bag to the glass to make Frawley keep pouring longer than usual, then eats a turkey all the way down to the bone.

But wait! The lady whose wallet Freddie returned earlier now wants to repay him with a turkey dinner at her mansion. Freddie walks back to the restaurant with a full gut, attracting the suspicion of the cop who saw him earlier and resulting in a punch to Freddie's belly. (An incredible innuendo for the time came up as Gilmore said, "What a terrible place to hit Freddie! Right between his white meat and his giblets!") The cop loosens up and tells Freddie that the police have bought all the unfortunates in the area turkey dinners and Freddie has to come eat with him, a thought that makes Freddie green. He passes out at seeing one more bird to eat at the station, forcing him to be hospitalized, where the doctor diagnoses him as having malnutrition and offers him more turkey. Freddie jumps out the window and throws turkeys back at the doctor and nurses until fadeout.

Emerging at the end of the sketch to appreciative whistles, Red noted that singer Roberta Sherwood made the effort to see that night's show as a guest in the audience. (She wasn't shown on camera, alas.) He smiled contentedly during the wrap-up and said, "I hope that answers the thousands and thousands of requests that we've had for me to do a complete pantomime show." It did that, and more.

Red's Thanksgiving show was not the first television show to go without dialogue by any means. Ernie Kovacs, for example, had an NBC special on Jan. 19, 1957, called *The Silent Show* that brought that comedian renewed respect as an expert on using television's visual language to the fullest with his comedy. And by having Gilmore narrate it, arguably it really wasn't a "complete pantomime show" as Red claimed.

But who cares if it wasn't the first silent show or technically not a silent show? It didn't matter, because Red's talents as a clown showed through as never before. He got glowing reviews from many publications on the event, including *Variety* and *TV Guide*, and the world began to realize that maybe, just maybe, this comedian that they had written off a few years earlier as being unable to handle the medium or had come back just due to lucky scheduling had more talent and versatility to offer than they thought. Unlike his usual shows, he didn't resort to old gags or out-of-character moments to get laughs. He stayed true to what was happening and managed to make a show full of both gentle and broad humor, with a small amount of pathos to leaven the laughter.

Of course, Red does not deserve all the credit. Schwartz, O'Brien and Goldstein cranked out a quality scenario, and David Rose added appropriate mood-setting background music. And the cast of supporting actors were solid, including the top-billed guest star Frawley, who, like the other actors, never spoke. (Despite a reputation among *I Love Lucy* historians as being every bit as cranky as his television character Fred Mertz, Ray Erlenborn recalled William Frawley's guest bit on the show with Red as a positive one. "They had a ball working together," he said.)

What made it even more poignant was that many viewers knew that Red had done this virtuoso performance following a horrible period in his life. You see, Red's son Richard died on May 10, 1958, after valiantly struggling against leukemia for a year and a half. He passed away a month before what would have been his 10th birthday.

The Death of Richard

When Red debuted on television in 1951, he often impersonated his son Richard in saying something precocious or adorable in his monologue. That tradition continued until midway through the 1956–57 season, when the diagnosis of Richard's condition made Red stop talking about his son on or off the air, making the writing staff follow suit to remove anything that might be associated with Richard or young boys in general. The show's writers set up a policy whereby no one was to use the word "son" in a script thereafter, and that applied for the rest of the show's run.

But then Richard noticed he wasn't mentioned in his dad's show anymore and wondered why, not knowing about his condition. Red put some jokes back in, but audiences were aware of what Richard was facing and didn't laugh.

Eventually, word filtered to Richard that he had leukemia and faced the possibility of dying. Ever the trouper, Red kept doing his television show, finding it a release from his situation. Meanwhile, fan mail in support of Richard and Red swarmed the show. But even with the prayers and cards, nothing could be done to save Richard.

To handle the show the week Richard passed away, Milton Berle stepped in as a guest host on May 13, 1958, along with a slew of other comedians, singers and actors. They all tried to make light for the show, but at the end, Berle offered his sincere condolences to Red and his family. To thank Milton for doing this, the next season, Red guested on Berle's new series, *Milton Berle Starring in the Kraft Music Hall*, on Nov. 19, 1958, along with the Kingston Trio and Barbara Nichols.

Surprisingly, Red came back to do a few shows to end the 1957–58 season, being as genial as ever. The cast and crew were told not to feel sorry for Red, that he wanted to do his comedy again. But many noted there were several moments when he would stare into the distance, off in another world. Nevertheless, he remained professional on air and kept doing his television show regularly in the 1958–59 season.

"In some respects, Red Skelton's comedy has become more poignant since then," said his producer Cecil Barker to Dora Albert in *TV Radio Mirror* in 1959. "Whenever Red has appeared in a scene with children, it has always had a sympathetic overtone. But now, when he plays such a scene, there is noticeably more heart within him."

Red spoke in detail to Dwight Whitney of *TV Guide* about how he handled the tragedy. "I've tried working just the same. People ask, 'How could you keep on telling jokes?' Sure, I told jokes. And if the little guy were here, I'd tell the same jokes. Others have suffered the same thing." (Red liked Whitney's article containing these and other quotes so much he promoted the *TV Guide* issue with it at the end of one of his shows in 1959.)

One little-known effect of Richard's death was how it resulted in one star being booked for the series. While finishing up a fifth and final series co-starring with a brave dog on *The Adventures of Rin Tin Tin*, child actor Lee Aaker got a guest part because his series had a special resonance for Red. As Aaker told me, "The first show I did with Red Skelton was right when his son died. I was the favorite show his son would watch."

Aaker said he also recalled the loose quality of the show. "When it came time to do the show, you threw the script out and just winged it," he said. Other than that, he told me his memories of doing the show, which aired Feb. 3, 1959, are hazy.

The impact of Richard's death on the show faded over time, and Red went back to making references to his family, including his daughter

Valentina, born one year before Richard in 1947. But many say it was not until he sold his home in Bel Air in 1962 and moved to Palm Springs that Red truly was able to get over Richard's passing.

A New Character—George Appleby

A happier memory for Red fans in the late 1950s concerned a new character he introduced—George Appleby, the most henpecked man in America. Sporting a bowler, bow tie and horn-rimmed glasses, George was a meek soul dominated by his wife Clara, whom George would put down as looking homely as his way of fighting back at her. Nevertheless, each skit usually ended with George telling Clara how much he loved her anyway—sort of like *The Honeymooners*, only if Ed Norton rather than Ralph Kramden had been married to Alice.

George made his first appearance on the show on Nov. 13, 1956. Virginia Grey played Clara. She would reprise the role several times, as would other actresses as varied as Vivian Vance, Pat Carroll and Audrey Meadows (shades of *The Honeymooners* again—she even ended one sketch with him in 1963 saying, "Baby, you're the greatest," the catchphrase that Jackie Gleason as Ralph Kramden usually said at the end of his show to Meadows as Alice Kramden).

George Appleby proved to be an immediate hit, and Red's weaker characters like Willie Lump Lump the drunk and Bolivar Shagnasty the—well, I'm not sure exactly what Bolivar was, although I've been told he was braggart—showed up less often thereafter as George went into major rotation with Freddie the Freeloader, San Fernando Red and Clem Kadiddlehopper as Red's most frequently played characters on television. His fights with his wife were perfect fodder for television comedy of the time, and usually you could count on good jokes about the problems of matrimony from any Appleby skit. He usually spoke in a whiny tone, and it was not uncommon at least one time in every sketch to see George put his fingers to his mouth to indicate how nervous he was.

For helping create this one character alone, Schwartz and his crew of writers merited some sort of public thanks from Red, but never got it, as he preferred to have people think he came up with this sort of thing on his own. He had a lot of fans who believed that, since he had a lot of fans period. Starting with the 1959–60 season in fact, Red would spend all but two of the next 11 seasons as a top 10 attraction on television.

A Popular Favorite, a Critical Question Mark

It would be safe to say that Red's rise as television's top comedy variety star confounded many television critics in the late 1950s and early

1960s. It's not that they did not consider the show unfunny, but rather its reliance on stock characters and old jokes, sometimes of the cornball variety, wore out its appeal with them rather quickly. His occasional cracking up at his own jokes struck them as unprofessional, and the lack of a continuing supporting cast virtually meant that if you didn't like Red, you wouldn't like the show.

(A note regarding the latter charge: The show did have a few new recurring bit players in the late 1950s and early 1960s who sharp-eyed viewers could recall seeing, chief among them Barbara Morrison. She first came on the series in April 1957 and made at least 22 appearances with him over the next eight years as a stout female prop for Red to douse with water, hit with furniture, and so forth. The British native came to Hollywood in 1947, with her biggest credit prior to Red being a small role in the 1953 film *From Here to Eternity*. She died in 1992.)

In contrast, comedians they considered more sophisticated and attuned to broadening the possibilities of the medium, particularly Ernie Kovacs and Sid Caesar, were flopping in several television series at the same time while Red's down-home humor kept people returning. When Federal Communications Commission (FCC) Chairman Newton Minow described network television programming in 1961 as "a vast wasteland," it would not be too much of a surprise to find some discriminating critics thinking Red and his show ought to be part of the rubble.

About the most generous assessment of Red among top television reviewers of the time came from Bob Chandler of *Variety*. Trying to define Red's appeal to the masses, he claimed that "The best attempt to explain it is that Skelton is more clown than comic, his mode of expression is more universal than the others." The Academy of Television Arts and Sciences, which hands out the Emmys, also was somewhat charitable to the show but hedged its bets, giving Schwartz and crew statuettes in 1961 for best comedy writing among a handful of nominations during this period.

Addressing the climate of the time, Red's director Seymour Berns defended his boss and his show to Dora Albert in *TV Radio Mirror* in 1959. "What some professional critics criticize, the public loves," Berns said. "Red sometimes enjoys a joke he is telling so much that he bursts into laughter. Technically, perhaps he shouldn't do this—but who really minds it? The public shares his enjoyment."

Indeed the public did. In fact, more viewers watched *The Red Skelton Show* in the 1957–58 season than the show that followed it, the former #1 show of the 1955–56 season *The $64,000 Question*. (Red's show finished at #15 in 1957–58 versus #19 for *The $64,000 Question*.) *The $64,000 Question* went off in the controversy over the rigging of big money game shows in 1958, and CBS replaced it with *The Garry Moore*

Show, an hour comedy variety series. Despite Moore having been a top draw on daytime television from 1950 to 1958, he had a slow go of it early in his nighttime slot, and few of Red's viewers stuck around to watch Garry's show in the 1958–59 season, when Red finished #12 and Garry didn't even make the top 30. It would not be until the 1961–62 season that *The Garry Moore Show* came close to matching Red's high ratings when it finished #12 for the year. (Red was at #6.) *The Garry Moore Show* went off in 1964.

The only hiccup in Red's ratings in this period came in the 1960–61 season when he finished #19, but this is easily explained. He had surgery in December 1960 to install a plastic diaphragm due to lingering complications from all the pratfalls he had taken over the years. It was the second such surgery he had, and it was a success. But recuperation after such a major operation takes time, so Red did not return to the airwaves with a new show until March 14, 1961, with his old pal Ed Wynn.

Rather than take Red's show off the air or even show all repeats during the three months of his recuperation, CBS made the questionable decision of having guest hosts replace him starting with the Jan. 10, 1961, show. Despite other top CBS talent such as Danny Thomas and Jackie Gleason appearing in the slot, it became obvious that viewers did not like watching *The Red Skelton Show* without Red, and the ratings slid. CBS belatedly realized its mistake, and after five guest host shows, the network ran repeats before Red returned. There was one silver lining in the situation, however: Ed Sullivan's appearance on February 7 as Clem Kadiddlehopper opposite Ed's favorite comedy team, the Canadian duo of Wayne and Shuster, proved how much "the stone face" of Sunday nights had grown as a performer since his stiff turn on the show in 1954. Ed's timing was great, and his hunched-over body in Clem's outfit was worth a few chuckles in itself.

Yet even in a season where Red did not appear in new shows for three months, his show still easily defeated its competition on ABC and NBC, which was respectively the western *Stagecoach West* and the suspense anthology *Thriller*. Both hour shows started a half-hour earlier than Red's, and he had no help from his lead-in, the unimpressive sitcom *The Tom Ewell Show*, which lasted just a year, but he still beat all comers. For the record, the earlier shows seen opposite Red on ABC included the dramatic anthologies *DuPont Cavalcade Theater* (through June 1957) and *Telephone Time* (June 1957–April 1958), the game show *Pantomime Quiz* (April 1958–September 1958), and the cop dramas *Naked City* (September 1958–September 1959) and *Philip Marlowe* (September 1959–March 1960). NBC lost *Armstrong Circle Theater* in 1957 to CBS, so they answered Red at first with the sitcom *The Bob Cummings Show* (a/k/a *Love That Bob*; September 1957–September 1959), the previously discussed *Startime* (September 1959–January 1960), and the musical variety offering *The Arthur Murray Party* (January 1960–September 1960) prior to striking out again with *Thriller*. In fairness to the series mentioned, not all started nor ended their television runs opposite Red; I've just reflected their tenure opposite his show.

As much an audience pleaser as Red had shown himself to be, there was room for him to grow within his empire. And it would become apparent in the 1961–62 season.

Planning to Go to an Hour

For the Oct. 28–Nov. 3, 1961, edition of the "TV Week" insert in *The Chicago Tribune* newspaper, Red wrote an article about "What Trouble Has Taught Me," where he noted at the end the following: "Just think: Television's audience is about 30 million people every night! Even Chicago doesn't have a place big enough for that kind of audience, unless it's Lake Michigan. Maybe that's why I love television."

That medium Red professed to love saw his show move to a different time slot for the first time in six years by the time *The Chicago Tribune* article ran. CBS moved the show up half an hour to start at 9 P.M. on Tuesdays, probably because his show was doing so much better than the rather weak lead-ins it had over the years. *To Tell the Truth* did OK before Red from December 1956 through September 1958 before CBS moved it up to start at 8:30 P.M. on Tuesdays; but after that, Red thrived, in spite of his lousy opening act, in the 9–9:30 P.M. slot, which consisted of *The Arthur Godfrey Show* in 1958–59 and the crime drama *Tightrope* in 1959–60. Both shows failed miserably opposite *The Rifleman* on ABC, and when CBS's next effort *The Tom Ewell Show* bombed in 1960–61, even with no longer having *The Rifleman* competing in the time slot, the network decided they would have a better chance creating a hit in 1961–62 by sandwiching it between the 9–9:30 *Red Skelton Show* and the 10–11 *Garry Moore Show*.

Unfortunately, the show selected to do the job was *Ichabod and Me*, a wan sitcom dealing with the none-too-hilarious happenings at a small-town newspaper between its meddlesome former owner Ichabod Adams, played by George Chandler, and its current operator Robert Major, played by Robert Sterling. Despite having Chandler announce to viewers at the end of all Red's shows in the 1961–62 season to stay tuned to *Ichabod and Me*, few of them did so, and CBS wound up with a ratings loser stuck between two top 15 shows, something they did not want in their effort to build up Tuesdays as a major viewing night for the network.

That situation, plus the fact that the half-hour variety format was dying (the only other show to fit that category on network nighttime television that season was *The Bob Newhart Show*, which lasted just a year), encouraged CBS officials to approach Red and his production staff with the idea of making the show an hour affair in 1962–63. Red's business advisors recommended he accept the idea because CBS was willing to buy Red's Chaplin Studios film production offices, which were a drain on Red's finances, as no one was renting out the ancient facility, in exchange for getting Red to do an hour each week.

Moreover, more air time would give the show more legitimacy and prestige in the industry. The only drawback was naturally that it would require more work of the crew and of Red. It was a slight gamble, but most involved thought it would pay off well in the end, and it did.

Wrapping Up 1956–1962

As *The Red Skelton Show* wound to a close in the summer of 1962, there was a happy freak of nature related to the show's conductor. After years of cutting singles and albums that suffered declining sales since the advent of rock and roll in the mid–1950s, David Rose finally had a hit to equal, and in some eyes surpass, his theme song for Red, "Holiday for Strings." In 1955, while scoring a drama called "Burlesque" for the series *Shower of Stars*, Rose wrote some strip music for one scene. Three years later, having time to kill at a recording session, he dusted off the tune with its wailing brass and drum sections for his orchestra to play, but the material did not get released.

Unbeknownst to Rose, in 1962 someone at the MGM record company went through his recorded material and thought the song, dubbed "The Stripper," would be the appropriate flip side to Rose's newest single "Ebb Tide," back in the days when records came in vinyl form with songs on both sides. But deejays preferred the raucous sounds of "The Stripper," and its short running time (less than two minutes) and lack of vocals made it the perfect tune to use to lead up to newscasts at the top of each hour and other situations where music was needed as filler.

The heavy airplay led to a run in sales, and for the week of July 7, 1962, *Billboard* reported that "The Stripper" was #1 on both its popular and adult contemporary music charts. The same publication later listed the song as one of the top five hits of 1962, and Rose received three Grammy nominations for his efforts on the record. Rose would never have another record even approaching the magnitude of "The Stripper," but its viability in the market at the time brought renewed attention to him and, by extension, his work on *The Red Skelton Show*.

Meanwhile, Red finished off his last CBS half-hour show in fine form on June 26 with Vincent Price as his main guest. As Cauliflower McPugg, Red goes to see a psychiatrist claiming that he's seeing birds. There he meets Price, playing a bird catcher who's seeing imaginary birds as well. McPugg then ventures to Price's "haunted" house for the evening, where he has an amusing routine with an "armchair" whose fingers come to life. After Price does a mock dance to the then-popular Twist craze (which cracks Red up) and similarly fakes a tango with his "invisible daughter," it's revealed that Price is really a psychiatrist too who did the whole charade to cure McPugg of his visions.

Prior to announcer Art Gilmore informing viewers at the end of the show that next week *The Comedy Spot* would begin its summer cycle of showing failed sitcom pilots in the time slot (*Comedy Spot* had run every summer since 1960, replacing the former perennial replacement for Red's show *Spotlight Playhouse*), Red told his audience that this was the last half-hour *Red Skelton Show*. He then wryly remarked, "You know, I was figuring out the other day, and I've found that we've done 336 half hour television shows in the last 11 years. That is a total of 168 full hours. That's exactly the amount of hours in one week. Therefore, I'd like to take this opportunity of thanking all of you for being so kind to a newcomer in television."

That number of shows may not be right—that works out to roughly an average of 30 shows per season, when it was still standard for series to run 39 shows each season. But even if not, it was tweaked for the right reason, of getting a laugh while preparing people for the fall. Red's hope of starring in a big-time variety show finally was a reality, and somewhat surprisingly, it would make him even more popular in the 1960s than he had been before.

5

1962–1967: The Glory Years

With ratings almost always ending in the top 10 for each season (two of them, 1962–63 and 1966–67, at no less than #2) and multiple Emmy nominations, the 1962 to 1967 seasons of what was then called *The Red Skelton Hour* formed the glory years of the series. The expansion of the show to an hour in 1962 gave it new life, making it bigger and bolder than ever without sacrificing Red's charms. Its setup of music, comedy and expanded pantomime bits was unlike anything else on television at the time, and the formula catered well to Red's needs on and off stage.

Because of this, every element of this period of the show is worth examining in depth, including the regular singing and dancing groups, the frequently appearing supporting players, the guest roster, the writing and the production. It's a lot to chew, but getting all the facets of it are needed to understand the appeal—and yes, considerable weaknesses—of *The Red Skelton Hour* in the early to mid–1960s. A good place to begin is what the home viewer saw on it.

Checking Out the Hour Show

Let's pretend it's 1962, and you're watching a typical episode of the new *Red Skelton Hour*. Here's how it would unfold for you:

The show would open "cold"—with no title credits, as was commonly done at the time, and only a few bars of music from the David Rose Orchestra—as the camera focused on Red in some quick setup, known in comedy parlance as a "blackout." Red would start a brief skit taped without the studio audience but with a laugh track, say maybe one set the week after Christmas. Chomping a cigar in an uptown office set, Red does a gangster imitation and speaks the following into a phone:

It's Big Daddy ... I know it's over, but how do I get rid of it? Oh, now wait a minute, that ain't for me, that kind of stuff, that's for the old days, that cement in the river stuff! Beside, it's too big, I couldn't get it in the car! Huh? Yeah! [rolls eyes and grins] Glad you thought of that. Great idea! Nobody could ever put the finger on me, could they? Thanks!

Red hangs up. After muttering "If Elliot Ness is around, I'm dead," he goes into a closet, grabs his old Christmas tree and throws it out the window onto the street below to get rid of the perpetual after-holiday nuisance.

Amid the canned giggles and a smiling Red at the end of the "blackout," an unseen chorus intones "It's *The Red Skelton Hour!*" The sketch shrinks to a pinpoint shot of Red, then is replaced by an opening number featuring the Tom Hansen Dancers, with words and music supervised by Alan Copeland, to introduce the night's major guest star(s) and orchestra leader David Rose, all superimposed over the dancers with the person or persons seen in a five-pointed star outline. This would be modified in following seasons by dropping the opening blackout and cutting to the stars rather than superimposing them in the introductions and involving them in the theme of the number, such as a gift-giving extravaganza on Dec. 8, 1964, wherein guest star Fernando Lamas is pleased to see a woman giving herself to him gift-wrapped in a box.

The number ends with the group introducing Skelton, entering in tuxedo from stage left to deliver his monologue. Generally it would contain jokes, often making reference to Red and his family, like their adventures with getting a horse. Making reference to a cowboy, Red would say that the man was so bowlegged that "when he did the Twist, he looked like an egg beater!" Red would also include a few blue lines in his monologue that never made it into the show. He'd been using to warm up audiences since the 1950s, but of course these were edited out of the final product. Nonetheless, they gave the studio audience something the home viewers would be missing, so they naturally won over the affection of all but the most puritanical types gathered to see him in person.

For home viewers, Red appeared to rush through his monologues briskly, usually punctuated by a shot or two of his mostly middle-aged audience laughing, because he wanted to get to his "pantomine," as he called it, of some activity related to the monologue, such as buying a horse and mounting the wrong way as it ran off. Sometimes he used a hat thrown from offscreen, other times it was just himself conveying the mood. Once the impish comic obviously mouthed, "What the hell is the matter with you?" in a pantomime, and when the audience laughed at what surely would've been bleeped at the time had he spoken it, Red covered himself by innocently asking, "Oh, you speak Japanese?"

Following the pantomime came a musical number, then a main sketch involving Red and his guest star(s) that typically stretched over three acts. Invariably the skit used one of Red's principal characters—Freddie the Freeloader, George Appleby, Clem Kadiddlehopper, or San Fernando Red—with plenty of asides to the audience and private jokes to crack up the cast, often with references about the guest star involved. For example, in a 1966 sketch with Ed Wynn, just a few months before the comic died, Wynn played Freddie's long-lost father, and Red made reference to Wynn's well-known actor son by saying, "I'm glad I'm your little boy, even if it makes Keenan my brother."

After the sketch, Red would do a little routine by himself or with the guest star before introducing another musical number, usually involving a guest vocalist or band. This led into the final portion of the show, the "Silent Spot," wherein Red rarely played one of his characters, just a typical Everyman in some sort of common predicament, such as a forest ranger ineptly patrolling his route, or a private eye out on the prowl in a house looking for a criminal, who turns out to be Red himself, in a clever ending. As befits the title, there was no talking during this segment, just lots of physical comedy done by Red and bit players identified only at the end of the show, not by the guest stars.

The show closed with Red, typically wearing whatever outfit he used in the Silent Spot, addressing the camera with the following benediction: "Thank you, ladies and gentlemen. On behalf of the sponsors and our staff, may we thank you for allowing us to be a part of your evening. So until next week, we say good night for now, and God bless." (It was later modified to end with "On behalf of the sponsors and our staff, we sincerely hope that our entertainment and our products have brought happiness into your homes. So until next week, we say goodbye for now, and may God bless.") A commercial or two ran before the Tom Hansen Dancers did a final number under the closing credits to Red's theme, "Holiday for Strings."

That was the normal show for viewers. Now, here's how Red spent his average work week getting the hour show ready from 1962 through the end of the decade to get the hour show ready. Surprisingly, his routine took just two days.

Red's Routine

Red would arrive at work Monday morning at CBS's Television City studios in Hollywood by 7 A.M. (or at 6:30 A.M. to chew the fat with his production staff; in the first season of the show, rehearsals started on Wednesday mornings for tapings on Thursday nights). He then would

Red was a silly prince to Chanin Hale's dissatisfied princess in this "Silent Spot," date unknown.

read through a script that typically took around five weeks of preparation with the actors for that week's show along with his director, producer and executive producer. The writers would leave Red alone and not contact him directly, only getting notes on what to do from the production assistant or other members of the production staff after the initial reading.

Staging the show with sound effects, camera angles and other crew came next, as the cast worked to remember their lines and staging as well. For learning his monologue, Red would play the tape back from rehearsal in his dressing room to mull over changing jokes in the initial run-through and ask others their opinions of what they heard. As evening approached, there was a preview show with an audience done around 6 P.M. and taped to gauge their reaction. The producer, director and head writers would review that tape and decide what needed to be redone for the next day's actual show. Sometimes this required the writers to work all night to have their changes ready for the cast and crew when rehearsal started again at 8 A.M. Tuesday.

With the new notes, or sometimes completely new scripts, ready to go, the cast and crew would repeat the same process of blocking the show on Tuesday, followed by a run-through and then a dress rehearsal before the actual taping. Interestingly, all the time while rehearsing, Red was known to gnaw, not light, up to 50 cigars in preparation for show time. He also would eat hot peppers to kill his appetite prior to performing.

The show would be taped at 6 P.M. after a dinner break for the crew and cast if they wanted to eat. Doors would close at 5:40 P.M. to allow the audience to get settled and in place, with children under the age of 12 not admitted.

Announcer Art Gilmore would do the audience warm-up routine. According to Ken Shapiro, a page on *The Red Skelton Hour* from 1962 to 1967 who now is a successful Hollywood writer and producer (responsible for the annual Golden Globe Awards, among other honors), for part of the warm-up, the cameramen would surreptitiously take pictures of people in the audience and put them on the monitors, which let them see the show as if they were watching it on television. "They would see themselves and point and laugh, and by the time Red came out they'd be laughing," he said.

The studio audience would never see the opening "blackout" done at the start of the 1962–64 seasons' shows, nor any musical routines for that matter—all of those would be taped later and edited into the final show, meaning that the audience would be present only for the monologue, the main sketch and the Silent Spot. But they would get a few jokes not seen on air, most of them ones Red had been doing throughout his career.

And sometimes even what had been planned for the monologue got changed by Red as much as the main sketch of the show. Shapiro said he wrote a Gertrude and Heathcliff joke and read it to Red one time backstage. "That's good," Red responded, and it was so good that he came out and delivered it as the first joke of his monologue.

"I could hear [director] Bill Hobin say, 'What's he doing? What's he doing?'" laughed Shapiro in recalling the incident. "First joke for television I wrote for Red."

The production schedule had shows taped roughly four weeks in advance of air time, but due to vagaries of vacations and Red's schedule, sometimes the lead time was much less than that. For example, Red's Jan. 19, 1965, show with boxer Archie Moore and obscure British singer Shani Wallis was taped just a week earlier, on Jan. 12, 1965.

After the show ended, usually somewhere around 7–7:15 P.M., Red would spend two minutes changing his clothes, then get into a waiting sedan to drive him to a heliport, where he went up three flights of stairs to board a chopper taking from Los Angeles to the Santa Monica airport. There, Red boarded a two-seater plane as a passenger and flew to the Palm Springs airport, where he drove his Rolls Royce home just in time to watch *The Red Skelton Hour*—usually a tape of last week's show. A technology buff, Red had videotape machines installed in his home decades before the recorders were part of the average American home, thus allowing him to be one of the few people to get to watch his reruns.

Everyone on the staff felt this process worked best for Red, and he agreed. "I'm no good in rehearsal," Red told reporter Noel Busch in 1965. "I only come to life when there are people watching. People talk about stage fright—what scares me most about the stage is not so much going on as coming off." Red added that he believed repetition of material in rehearsal wore down even the best lines and routines.

Red's workweek then basically ended Tuesday night. The rest of the week, though, the staff continued to hone the show, and much of that involved its increased reliance on music numbers. A key figure in that effort was Alan Copeland, though his job evolved over where it started in 1962.

Music, Music, Music

The original job for Alan Copeland in regard to *The Red Skelton Hour* was just to be a member of the Modernaires, a vocal group of four men and one woman, Paula Kelly. The group already had been regulars on a few other nighttime variety series in the 1950s, including *The Lux Show Starring Rosemary Clooney* in 1957–58, the summer series *Perry Presents* in 1959, and *The George Gobel Show* in 1959–60.

"I had joined them in '48 and left them in '56 to do a single," Copeland said of his first Modernaires stint. The result was a regular vocalist job on the last year of the NBC Saturday nighttime television musical show *Your Hit Parade* in 1957–58, followed by many club gigs.

"I went back with the Modernaires in '59, and we had a renaissance of sorts with some new guys," he said. "In '62, Red was going to Seattle at the Town and Country Club, and we opened there. Seymour Berns [Red's producer] came backstage after our show to talk about doing Red's show." Berns had been familiar with the Modernaires when they were regulars on *The Bob Crosby Show* on CBS daytime from 1953 to 1957, as that show was done from Television City in Hollywood next door to *The Red Skelton Show* and, noted Copeland, "We were back in Television City in the same studio we did with *The Bob Crosby Show*," taping *The Red Skelton Hour*.

But a funny thing happened while doing the show. As the Modernaires' arranger, orchestra leader David Rose became impressed by Copeland's musical ability, so he integrated the vocalist into doing special music material for the show. Berns was similarly enthused by Copeland's work, although members of Red's staff seemed less bowled over by what the other Modernaires were doing. As a result, Berns proposed dropping the Modernaires and installing Copeland as musical director of an in-house group that would be known initially as the Skeltones.

Copeland was apprehensive about the idea, given his loyalty to the group, which in 1962, besides him and Paula Kelly, consisted of Hal Dickinson, Chuck Kelly and Vernon Polk. "I was torn, because I had already left the group, and to do it again with the group just left me torn," he said. But he had a family with three children to support, and the idea of a steady income without touring was too alluring for him.

Thus, the Skeltones replaced the Modernaires as the regular music group on *The Red Skelton Show* in January 1963, with Copeland at the helm. Composed of three girls and four guys ("Plus myself, but I didn't work on camera"), the group's membership was somewhat fluid, as these groups tend to be, but included several notable names such as Ginny Mancini, wife of famed composer Henry Mancini. As for where the group's pun-tinged name came from, Copeland laughed, "Probably Red; I don't know."

A year later, the Skeltones officially became the Alan Copeland Singers. Since their musical numbers were shot away from the Tuesday tapings with the audience most of the time (they prerecorded their music with the David Rose Orchestra on Wednesday mornings), Red rarely appeared in them. Copeland saw his nominal boss infrequently, though he knew and respected Red's work. The singer recalled taping the Christmas show in 1967 and "Red was standing there, and he looked at me and said, 'Merry Christmas, Alan,' and I said, 'Merry Christmas, Red.'"

Given that he had vocalized on the show and in the movies, it seems a shame that Red did not involve himself more in singing for the show.

When I asked Copeland about this, he acknowledged, "It never really crossed my mind. Now that I think about it, it would've been nice."

Copeland did realize that his group had appeal beyond just providing music for Red in 1966, when it joined with jazz great Count Basie to record the album *Basie Swingin,' Voices Singin'* and earned a Grammy nomination for Best Performance by a Chorus. They lost to the Ray Conniff Singers for "Somewhere, My Love" ("Lara's Theme from Dr. Zhivago"). Two years later, the Alan Copeland Singers did win a Grammy in the Contemporary Pop Chorus Category for their medley of the Beatles' "Norwegian Wood" along with the theme to the CBS television series *Mission: Impossible*. (Ironically, *The Red Skelton Hour* tied at #11 in the ratings with *Mission: Impossible* in the 1968–69 season.) The group performed "Norwegian Wood" on Red's show on Nov. 19, 1968.

New vocalists were not the only change viewers noticed at home in 1962–63. The show added a peppy group ready to trip the light fantastic as well.

Gotta Dance

"When they changed the show from a half hour to an hour, they changed a lot of the production team," said Tom Hansen. Formerly a top dancer in the 1950s on *Your Hit Parade*, Hansen told me his agent contacted him about the possibility of his becoming the choreographer. All parties agreed, and for the next eight years, the Tom Hansen Dancers were regulars on Red's show.

Hansen's job typically consisted of having to put together a production number at the opening, a routine for each show's musical guest, and specialty material to serve as a buffer (on the final show, that is) between Red's monologue and the two- or three-act main sketch. "If Red's show had a particular theme, like a plumber, we'd do something like a dancing plumber," Hansen said of the specialty dance numbers.

To put it all together, Hansen met Saturday morning with an assistant, a piano player, and later in the run, a drummer and worked on the "billboarding" of guests at the top of the show (the musical numbers at the top announcing "Our guest star..."). In the afternoon, he and the others would rehearse routines with the dancers, which usually were six men and six women.

On Sunday morning, the musical guest's number would be reviewed, followed by rehearsal with the dancers in the afternoon. Sometimes, but not always, the guest would rehearse with the dancers. The guest definitely rehearsed the musical number by Monday and Tuesday, followed by rehearsals of the specialty material and other areas needing practice. All the music would be recorded on those days. During Mondays and Tuesdays, Red would be working on his comedy scenes, so Hansen said he saw the comedian "very little, other than 'Hello' or 'How are you?' He worked the two days, and that was it."

But Hansen said he didn't object to the setup because of the respect he had for Red and vice versa. "He loved dance," Hansen said. "He loved dancers. He trusted me. I will say that in all the years that I was with him, I never heard a criticism from him."

Finally, Wednesday was the day all the numbers were recorded by cameras. "The dancers taped without an audience," Hansen said. Applause was edited in postproduction, as were the numbers in their proper sequences in the show.

On special occasions, viewers got to see more than just Hansen's on-screen handiwork. "I danced on the show maybe once a year with my assistant and my dancers," he said. That assistant was Leona Irwin, by the way.

Yet, as with singing, given that Red danced in MGM musical comedies in the 1940s, it seems a shame that he didn't get involved in the production numbers the way other stars of the time did on their variety shows, such as Garry Moore did in the "That Wonderful Year" tributes on *The Garry Moore Show*. To that end, Hansen reminded me that Red had dealt with a hiatal hernia and had only a limited time he would permit himself to rehearse. Nevertheless, dancing and singing by the star would have made a nice icing on the cake that was *The Red Skelton Hour*.

Red's Other (Sort-of) Regulars— Jan Arvan and Chanin Hale

Keen-eyed observers would note two performers who, more than any others, appeared often in supporting roles during Red's hour-long show. Though never billed as regulars, they were considered family by the show and often relied upon at the last minute should a guest or sketch fall through, as was often the case. Their names were Jan Arvan and Chanin Hale.

Jan Arvan was a mustachioed, irritable sprite who found himself the butt, intended or not, of several jokes or pranks by Red's characters. Born on April 10, 1913, in Wisconsin, he had been doing the show in bit parts at least since 1954. Red's producer/director Bill Hobin noted that "Whenever the book called for a subsidiary performer, it was usually played by Jan.... Jan could do it all."

A director at the Pasadena Playhouse, Arvan worked with several actors to coach them on their roles in addition to appearing often on *The Red Skelton Hour*. Hobin found Arvan a fine, dependable performer to support Red, and not just in the usual sense either.

"Besides being a consummate character actor, he was a sort of 'costumed stage manager,'" Hobin wrote. "If Red missed a cue, Jan would always walk him back into his part, so subtly that viewers would seldom realize that Red had gone up. Although he seldom did, Red came to depend on Jan to help him whenever it happened, and he never let him down."

Arvan's only other regular television role was as Nacho Torres on the ABC western *Zorro* from 1957 to 1959. He died on May 24, 1979. "Jan could have easily become a star," Hobin added. "But he always seemed to be satisfied to be the superb character actor that he was."

Chanin Hale was a pleasant blonde beauty who was cast several times as Red's love interest, even though she clearly was much younger than him. Born and raised in Dayton, Ohio, Chanin (pronounced like "Shannon") had dreams of stardom when she was young. Chanin was not her moniker then.

"My first name really was Marilyn," she said. "But when I started in the 1950s, Marilyn was of course Marilyn Monroe." So why the changing to Chanin, then? "I really, honest to God can't remember why I did that, maybe something with the Chanin Building in New York." (That facility, located on 42nd Street, went up in 1929.)

Her initial story is a familiar one to many aspiring actors and actresses. "As soon as I could get out of school, I went to New York," she recalled. "I did some off-Broadway. I had done a little modeling and dancing in Ohio." After some acting jobs on New York-based television dramas (e.g., *Studio One*) and touring nightclub dates, she finally moved out to Los Angeles in the early 1960s after finding herself one December "up to her ears in snow in Syracuse" while talking to her mother in California who was boasting about how wonderful the weather was.

Chanin auditioned for Jack Albertson for a play called *Burlesque* in Los Angeles when she arrived. "I got the part; it was a wonderful part, but it was only a three-week run," she said. Luckily, a producer with *The Red Skelton Hour* saw her and thought he could use her. She did her first show with Red in "probably '63. I only did the Silent Spot with him. He played a stagehand and I played a star."

After several other Silent Spots, she moved into the main sketches in roles such as secretaries and even Daisy June, Clem Kadiddlehopper's girlfriend. "The first time I did a line, I blew it," she noted. But Red loved her spirit and attitude ("If you are working on Red's show, you had to be prepared to be the brunt of jokes, and I was") and encouraged his staff to use Chanin often.

She learned one rule in working with Red: Don't rely on cue cards. "You never knew what he would use, and if you took your eyes off him, you could be in trouble," she said.

Yet along those lines, Red once convinced her to pretend to read cue cards and make a "blooper" during taping. Going along with his wish, she went out and said, "The war's over! They ended World War Eleven!" (The joke being, of course, that she read "World War II" as "World War Eleven.") To her dismay, a show business insider recounted the incident to *TV Guide* in an article in the 1990s about classic mistakes on series.

Regardless, the series was a plus for her, in her opinion. "Red was the big break for me, because after that, I got to meet other people," she said. She went on to do guest parts on *The Beverly Hillbillies*, *The Dick Van Dyke Show* and other series. She also became beloved enough that for the 1964–65 season, she received an offer to become a permanent part of *The Red Skelton Hour*.

"They called and my agent said, 'They want you to go under contract,' and I had just signed to do *Synanon*," she said, referring to her second movie role. (Her first was a minor part in 1964's *Get Yourself a College Girl*.) Wanting to uphold her film job, she decided against the regular part. "I think I was the only girl they wanted to put under contract," she noted.

Nonetheless, she continued to be a frequent "day player" until Red's series ended. Generally she showed up once every four to five shows. "Sometimes it was six times a year, others only five," she said of her work on the series.

And some of the jobs appeared literally overnight from the show. "Once in a while, I'd get a call about 9 o'clock on Monday evening, and I'd think, 'Uh oh, something didn't work out or somebody got sick or Red didn't like them,' and they'd say, 'Chanin, we need you!'" she recalled.

Even with all those requests, Red's show never gave Chanin the opportunity to show her skills as well as, say, Garry Moore did with Carol Burnett on his series, usually limiting her to just a few lines at best for indistinct characters. Chanin is frank in assessing where she stood on the show: "You always want more, but you go in and do what they give you to do. Sometimes I wanted to do something funny, because I'm a comedian at heart. But I knew it was Red's show, and I was just so glad to be working there."

After Red's show ended in 1971, Chanin acted on a few soap operas, such as *General Hospital* and *Santa Barbara*, before getting married, traveling the world and moving out of Hollywood. She is still open to the idea of acting, but doesn't live for the profession anymore.

"I hoped to be a bigger star, but I had some good times and met some good people, so I can't complain," she said.

The Guest Stars

When it came to picking special guest stars, a few of those seen in the half-hour version managed to make the cut on the more polished hour show. Among these were Jackie Coogan, Audrey Meadows, Janis Paige, Vincent Price, Cesar Romero, Mickey Rooney and a handful of others. "He liked to have the old pros work with him, like Vincent Price and Mickey Rooney," noted his sound effects man Ray Erlenborn. Most of the others who joined Red on the hour shows were newcomers to working with Red, at least in the early to mid–1960s.

Producer/director Bill Hobin described the selection process for guests this way: "The guest star had to be an intelligent person with that illusive capacity to let his hair down and have fun. Virtually any well-known public figure with stage experience and presence was a candidate for the show, if he had that ability."

One guest who did have it with Red was opera singer Patrice Munsel, who got to appear on the show three times, in 1965, 1967 and 1969. "I was thrilled, because he was such a delicious man to work with," she recalled nearly four decades later. "He was so marvelous to the people who worked for him, unlike some people who worked on other comedy shows."

Munsel confirmed what many have said about doing the show with Red, that you had to be prepared for him to go off the script at any moment. "You never knew what was going to happen when you did the show," she said. The show also allowed her to do both comedy, such as playing a saloon gal opposite cowboy Deadeye, as well as sing a few songs, though she did not recall the separation of doing the comedy sketches before a live audience and then taping the songs without one a day later.

One artist who did recall that division was Lana Cantrell, a mellow songstress who did Red's show three times from 1967 to 1969 to promote her records. Now an attorney in New York City, Cantrell is representative of many of the singers who did *The Red Skelton Hour* without taking part in the show's comedy and, as a result, had virtually no contact with the comedian.

"When I did the television Skelton show, I didn't have much communication with him," she said. "I talked to him more when I opened for Red in Las Vegas one month. He painted bears backstage."

Cantrell added that this was a typical production practice for the videotaped variety shows of the 1960s and 1970s. "The only shows that you really interacted with the host was *The Tonight Show* or the talk shows," she said.

One notable trait about Red's guest stars was how many of them came from starring in series that had flopped opposite his show during the 1960s. For example, Connie Stevens popped up on April 7, 1964 (and again on April 20, 1965), the season after her series *Hawaiian Eye* on ABC ended its run opposite the Skelton powerhouse. After *McHale's Navy* went off ABC in 1966, having provided Red with his best competition in the mid–1960s for three years by finishing a strong second, usually in the top 30, its star Tim Conway joined the actor to clown around on Nov. 15, 1966, and Oct. 31, 1967. Red handily beat *The Man from U.N.C.L.E.* in its initial season in 1964–65, but while it ran in a different slot the next year, its star Robert Vaughn guested with Red on Dec. 7, 1965, and Oct. 18, 1966. *Dr. Kildare* spent its last season, 1965–66, in two half-hour slots, one of them opposite Red; the next season, its star, Richard Chamberlain, clowned with the comic on March 21, 1967.

These bookings are more than coincidence for what happened in comparison to other variety shows of the period. Were these bookings suggested by Red as a sly way of saying "I beat you," or was it his way of paying tribute to what he felt were talented people who were his competition? He no doubt could and did watch his competition, having the equipment set up to record television shows at his house in the 1960s on his various sets. Only Red could answer that question, and to my knowledge, no one ever asked him that.

Red's pal, columnist James Bacon, said Red really preferred those in his field of expertise to show up. "He liked other comedians as guests," Bacon said. "He could work with them." Yet as with the half-hour show, most of his guest comedians were not on the same level as Red, being either second bananas (Don Knotts, Bill Dana) or ones he admired personally (Ed Wynn, Milton Berle). The only ones who could be considered his equal were probably George Gobel and Martha Raye. "We loved it when Martha Raye was a guest because she was great fun," recalled Chanin Hale.

In any event, Red's guests certainly were an eclectic lineup in this period. Check the appendix for a full rundown of who showed up.

Rock Comes Red's Way

More time available for music on the hour show meant that guest stars would be needed to help carry the load as they did on other variety series. The first two seasons in the hour format, Red's show used mostly middle-of-the-road pop vocalists, with just a few having rock appeal, such as Bobby Rydell, who did the show several times as a guest star in sketches as well as singing through 1966, and Joannie Sommers. The Beach Boys did pop up twice in the 1963–64 season, the second time to sing their hits "In My Room" and "I Get Around," but *The Red Skelton Hour* remained mostly a haven for "easy listening" performers until a trip to tape a special show in London in the summer of 1964 resulted in a rock onslaught for the show.

The show's production staff received assistance from British television packager Sir Lew Grade, who managed a find for them as "Beatlemania" was in full swing in America. Sir Lew did not get them the Beatles, but he did book an up-and-coming group being compared to them called the Rolling Stones, and even had the group's lead singer act in a sketch with Red. Ever the entrepreneur, Sir Lew offered Red's producer Seymour Berns a package price to tape six English rock groups and use their performances on the series throughout the season. The deal appealed to Berns, so for the next three summers through 1966, Berns and Red's director Bill Hobin came back to Halliford Studios in Twickenham, England, to tape six groups in one day.

"Our entire crew hated rock musicians and their music—our sound man particularly," Hobin recalled. "To him, they all sounded and looked the same—bad." While they loathed it, the show had sort of an exclusive on the acts, and so as a result, *The Red Skelton Hour* was one of the few nighttime variety series outside of Ed Sullivan who could boast of having nearly all the big "English invasion" groups save the Beatles guest on the show. Besides the Rolling Stones, the 1964–65 lineup included the Searchers, the Honeycombs ("Have I the Right?"), the Kinks, and Billy J. Kramer and the Dakotas, followed in 1965–66 by Freddie and the Dreamers, the Animals and the Hollies.

Meanwhile, the show also began featuring American rock acts too, with the Supremes, Dionne Warwick, Johnny Rivers and Jay and the Americans, among others, starting to turn up around 1965. It wasn't a landslide for the music by any means—you were just as likely to have to endure the upbeat white-bread vocalizing of the Doodletown Pipers or even lesser-known "square" music acts—but it did offer the show a contemporary feel, something that other variety shows of the period soon realized they needed to have in order to stay competitive.

Red, a jazz aficionado, apparently was philosophical about booking the rock'n'rollers. "He said, 'you've got to have them, because all the kids like the rock acts,'" said his buddy James Bacon.

One more point: The dealings with Sir Grade also gave Red's show a distinctive look with its summer replacements. In the summers of 1963 and 1965, it hosted revivals of *Arthur Godfrey's Talent Scouts*, without

Arthur Godfrey as host. Instead, Merv Griffin presided over *Talent Scouts* (as it was called) in 1963, while the 1965 version titled *Hollywood Talent Scouts* featured Art Linkletter and did well enough that CBS brought it back in December 1965 as a midseason replacement for *The Steve Lawrence Show*. Alas, the talent show did not make the grade during the regular season and went off on Sept. 5, 1966. Between the various *Talent Scouts* came *High Adventure with Lowell Thomas*, a series of repeats of late-1950s documentaries hosted by the noted news reporter, which aired as Red's replacement from June 16 through Sept. 15, 1964.

These shows paled in comparison with the glossy imports from Britain that Sir Lew Grade provided. *Hippodrome* featured circus acts and other fare typically presided over by American comics and hosts from July 5 to Sept. 6, 1966, while *Spotlight* dropped the circus acts but kept using various American jokesters and singers as hosts during its run that started with mild irony on July 4 (celebrating America's independence from Britain) through Aug. 29, 1967. Sure, it wasn't Skelton, but it wasn't as deadly as summertime fare can often be either.

A New Direction and Writers for the Show, First Wave

As previously mentioned, Bill Hobin was in charge of taping the rock stars in Britain. It was one of his first duties working for *The Red Skelton Hour* when he joined the show in the summer of 1964 to replace Seymour Berns, who was promoted from being the show's director after nearly 10 years to replace Cecil Barker as producer. Hobin's television career to that point had involved mainly series from New York—he received an Emmy nomination in 1957 for his work on *Your Hit Parade*, for example, and had just come off from helming *The Judy Garland Show*, the critically lauded yet ratings-challenged variety series that lasted only the 1963–64 season on CBS opposite *Bonanza*.

The idea of directing Red's show did not strike him as appealing at first when presented to him by his agent. But realizing the show's level of success and guaranteed production schedule, as well as the continuing decline of television work in Manhattan, Hobin bit the bullet and moved to Los Angeles with his family.

Upon meeting Red, Hobin was struck by the comic's intelligence and honesty. He set up a system whereby the crew had to pass suggestions to Red through him, thus cutting down hassles that way for the star. He was not the only new face in a major backstage role by any means in 1962–67, either, particularly in the writing department.

For the hour show, Ed Simmons, head writer since 1961, supervised a staff consisting of three holdovers from the half-hour show—Mort Green, Dave O'Brien and Arthur Phillips—and three new writers, Hugh Wedlock, Rick Mittleman and Bruce Howard.

Of the newcomers, Wedlock had the most extensive resume, having penned numerous movie scripts in the 1940s, including several comedies for Bud Abbott and Lou Costello such as *In Society* and *Abbott and Costello Meet the Killer, Boris Karloff*. He also wrote for *I Married Joan* and *The Jack Benny Program* on television.

The tenure of these new gag writers was remarkably short, given how successful the show was and that all of them earned Emmy nominations in 1963 for their work on *The Red Skelton Show*. Mittleman and Howard left after a year, and Wedlock did so the following year. All three might have left because the show's popularity offered them new jobs, since they continued in the medium with great success through the 1970s at least.

For example, Mittleman received Emmy nominations in 1971 as producer of the short-lived sitcom *Arnie* and in 1977 as writer for the short-lived variety series *Van Dyke and Company*. He also compiled more than 200 writing credits for assorted comedies and dramas over the years, including *I Spy, Bewitched, Get Smart!, The Mary Tyler Moore Show, Remington Steele, MacGyver* and many others. Howard had a more limited slate of credits, including writing for several series supervised by Red's ex-writer Sherwood Schwartz—*My Favorite Martian, Gilligan's Island, It's About Time* and *Dusty's Trail*. As for Wedlock, he was the only one of the trio to claim an Emmy, in 1968 for helping to write *Rowan and Martin's Laugh-In* (he'd earn another Emmy nomination for the show the following year, and yet one more in 1971 for *Jack Benny's 20th TV Anniversary Special*).

When Mittleman and Howard departed, they had just one person replace them. Larry Rhine had extensive writing credits in both movies and radio shows dating back to the 1930s, including in the latter media the sitcom *Duffy's Tavern*, where he met his future wife, actress Hazel Shermet. In the 1950s and early 1960s, he wrote for such television series as *The Colgate Comedy Hour, The Gale Storm Show, Pete and Gladys* and even *Mr. Ed* before joining Red and company.

Though Rhine stayed with the show for five years straight and later returned in 1971, he and the other newcomers to the hour format apparently had little fondness for its star. He recounted to Tom Stempel in *Storytellers to the Nation* how he overheard Red one time quip, "Who needs writers?" In response, when Red requested a new line for a sketch, one scribe shot back, "Let him ad-lib it." And Rhine's predecessor, Rick Mittleman, told Stempel he thought Red wanted to give his fans the impression he came up with all his material and thus ignored his writers.

After Rhine's first year on the job, head writer Ed Simmons left in 1964 for other career opportunities, including a long stint with *The Carol Burnett Show*. This prompted the hiring of a new duo of head writers for the program.

The New Writers, Second Wave

Bob Schiller and Bob Weiskopf first started working together professionally in 1953. Schiller's break as a writer came on the radio comedy *Duffy's Tavern* in the 1940s, where he was hired and fired four times. He did various other radio comedies before going into television to create jokes for Danny Thomas and others on the 1950–53 variety show *Four Star Revue* (later known as *All Star Revue*). Next, he started the second season of *The Red Buttons Show*, which ran on television from 1952–55, until he suffered the fate of almost every writer on that program—he was fired after eight weeks so they could save money. He then partnered with Weiskopf, who wrote three scripts for television's *The Danny Thomas Show* (then known as *Make Room for Daddy*), because he wanted a partner to help him complete the fourth show he had to do under contract.

Prior to his television employment, Weiskopf was a radio writer whose first regular job was with *The Eddie Cantor Show* in 1941. He then partnered with Paul Henning, later the creator of *The Bob Cummings Show* (1955–59) and *The Beverly Hillbillies* (1962–71), among other television hits, and they wrote for *The Rudy Vallee Show* through 1942, when the two split amicably because Weiskopf wanted to work in New York City rather than Hollywood. He then spent nine years writing for radio's *Fred Allen Show* before going back to Hollywood and entering television.

After *The Danny Thomas Show* deal ended, the men struggled for a year to get jobs in television. They wrote scripts for shows that ran less than a year—*That's My Boy*, *Professional Father* and *It's Always Jan*, the latter a 1955–56 sitcom starring Janis Paige done at Lucille Ball's and Desi Arnaz's production company Desilu. *I Love Lucy* producer Jess Oppenheimer overheard them complaining about not getting more of their scripts accepted for *It's Always Jan* and hired them to write for his show, which they did until it ended in 1957 and continued doing so as it aired in monthly specials on *The Westinghouse Desilu Playhouse* through 1960.

The men occupied themselves with other sitcoms in the late 1950s and early 1960s—*The Ann Sothern Show*, which they created, *Guestward*

Ho!, and *Pete and Gladys*—before Ball returned to the weekly grind with her sitcom *The Lucy Show* in 1962. But after two years of working again with her, Schiller and Weiskopf found themselves tired of the star. Her ex-husband Desi Arnaz left as executive producer midway during the first season of *The Lucy Show*, and without him, the two Bobs found Lucy more difficult to handle. Without specifying it was *The Red Skelton Hour*, Schiller told Geoffrey Mark Fidelman in *The Lucy Book* that "we pretty much left Lucy to take a lucrative offer with a variety show." Yet the money they earned from it paled in contrast to how they felt about Red.

Author Jordan R. Young talked to Schiller and Weiskopf for his book *The Laugh Crafters* and got an earful of their distaste for Red. "He viewed his writers as adversaries," Weiskopf claimed. Schiller was more vitriolic. He knew of Red when he was in the Army and hated the comic's routines. "It was awful. Embarrassing. Slapabout, knockabout comic. Very childish, very primitive—embarrassingly primitive. I never cared much for Skelton's stuff." (But he was apparently not so indifferent that he couldn't resist working for a nice salary on Red's television series.)

The reason for such dislike of Red among some of his writers might be understood if one considers how greatly different their scripts could turn out once they aired on television. I managed to be able to compare a script for a show with Merv Griffin with the final product CBS broadcast on March 18, 1969, and the differences were startling, particularly since the script included at least two sets of revisions. A whole routine having Red get stuck in an elevator, which read well in concept, was gone, while Red inserted new insults to the actress playing his date's fat mother, such as calling her "Big Ben" and telling her "Go downstairs and put on your Goodyear sign and come back!"

And the second act was basically shot to hell, as Red, playing a drunk Willie Lump Lump in the audience of what supposedly was Griffin's talk show, improvised jokes left and right involving his audience members' characteristics. He cracked on the huge beehive hairdo of one lass, then spotted a bald man and proclaimed, "That guy's been caught in a hair raid!" It was funny, but could it have been just as good with what the writers gave to him? We'll never know.

There was one other writer added to Red's staff in this period who— and I am not making this up—actually liked working with the comedian. His name was Robert Orben.

The Monologue Writer

The name is a familiar one to many amateur and professional humorists. An author of 47 joke books, Robert Orben has provided gags for everyone from President Gerald R. Ford to, of course, Red Skelton. His six-year tenure writing monologues for the start of the comedian's television shows came after a year stint on his first nighttime television writing gig.

"I had been a writer on *The Jack Paar Show* in New York, and I wasn't too interested in television until doing that show," Orben said. Once that job wound up, Red's then-director Seymour Berns came to New York to interview Orben for the job rather than talk to Orben's agent, who was sick. (I know, it sounds like a comedy routine, but it gets even better.)

"For about 20 minutes, we debated the World's Fair in New York," Orben said with a laugh. For the record, Orben liked it, and Berns hated it. After that, Orben gave him some of his comedy books as samples of his work and "Three or four months later, I had an offer."

Orben's job with Red was fairly limited. "I did the monologue myself. On Monday nights, we had a dress rehearsal, and I helped fix it up," he said. He and the other writers got to watch the dress rehearsal on the monitor to see what worked and what didn't in the first go-round of the show's material. He also had the following week's monologue ready for initial review too.

Regarding the monologue, Orben said, "I pretty much established the subject and wrote it. Red would frequently add jokes to the monologue, sometimes whole chunks, but I really had a lot of freedom."

Orben did not object to Red's additions at all; on the contrary, he welcomed them. "You prayed for the ability, the charisma, the knowhow of a Red Skelton.... Red would give [a joke] a twist it needed."

In fact, Orben's biggest problems on the show came from his fellow writers. The company gave him a big office in which to write at the studio, "But I didn't like it, so I worked at home for all six years. I was really afraid it would create some problems, and I could sense all that." To placate the concerns of his fellow scribes that he was not spending all his time at work, Orben pledged that they could call him anytime at his house, and that if he wasn't there, he'd take them out to eat. He never had to shell out a check for any of them.

Despite his long run with the series, Orben decided not to write for another one when he ended his association with Red. While he knows other writers did not like the man, he does not share the same opinion.

"It has now been 32 years since I left the Skelton show, but I look on that time as one of the happiest of my career," he said.

Highlights (and Some Lowlights) of 1962–1967

The Red Skelton Hour started off strong from its Sept. 25, 1962, season opener, with the impressive special guest star duo of Harpo Marx (not talking, of course) and gospel singer Mahalia Jackson (in an infrequent television guest shot). The main sketch had Red as George Appleby finding out that his guardian angel, played by Marx, could grant him his wishes of escaping from his wife Clara, played by character actress Virginia Grey. One of those powers included making Clara into a young, sexy beauty, played by Dyan Cannon in an early television role. The witty byplay between Skelton and Grey, the solid clowning of Marx and the tricks the crew played on Red, including screwing up a sewing machine he had to use in the sketch, made for an entertaining debut.

From there came a nice assortment of respectable singers and guests throughout the next five years. But one event really holds a special place in this period.

On Feb. 2, 1965, CBS aired a special show billed as "Concert in Pantomime." Hosted by Maurice Chevalier, who only did a brief introduction at the start praising the talents of the participants, this episode of *The Red Skelton Hour* had Red joined by renowned mime Marcel Marceau as they alternated performing at Television City in front of a black-tie studio audience of diplomats from 47 countries. Members of the Tom Hansen Dancers appeared in harlequin outfits to do a few steps and hold up cards announcing the name of each pantomime by Skelton and Marceau.

Marceau, dressed as his familiar character Bip in tight shirt and white pants, performed "The Tug of War," then did "Bip the Dice Player," where Bip gets progressively unnerved by a losing streak, then broke and suicidal until he then cleverly uses his gun to rob other participants. "Bip the Skater" had him move wobbly on an imaginary ice rink at first before getting the hang of it in a beautiful routine, and another winner was "Bip as a Mask Maker," showing Marceau's split-second ability to change extreme facial expressions just by waving his hands. A nice touch to differentiate him and Skelton was that Marceau appeared in light colors on a dark stage during his routines, while the opposite was true of Skelton.

Skelton did a greater variety of scenarios as expected, including "A Girl Dressing in the Morning" (Red mimed a woman hiking her dress up so high her legs buckled, among other complications), "Mixing the Salad" (a chef winds up accidentally sneezing the pepper used, cuts off his fingers and adds them into the mixture), "The Drunken Doctor in Surgery" (the physician unintentionally anesthetized his left hand, among other mishaps) and his sentimental take on "The Old Man Watching the Parade." He joined Marceau for a two-act sketch at the end with Skelton as Gepetto and Marceau as Pinocchio, with all the expected sentimentality leavened by some unexpected humor, including Red sandpapering Marceau's buttocks after getting splinters from spanking

Pinocchio! The two artists' love and respect for each other showed through the sparkling hour.

As for lowlights, there were only a few real missteps creatively. One was the decision to have Red portray his old mischievous character Junior, "the mean widdle kid," starting with the Nov. 20, 1962, show. As Red noted on his television debut in 1951, it was a silly idea to have him play a youngster in a visual medium, and the decision to do it when Red was in his fifties or thereabouts was just pathetic. Junior showed up only sparingly thereafter, but it was not an inspired move to use the character even once on the show, if one cared about treating the audience with respect.

Similarly, not all guests got into the proper spirit of fun. Shirley Temple, in one of her last acting jobs, reportedly projected her "goody-goody" image so well in life that Red did not feel like doing his usual hijinks with her during the "Dirty Hour" rehearsal, and her appearance on the Sept. 24, 1963, fall debut generated some of the worst reviews for Red's show since the 1950s. Otherwise, the show prospered from 1962 to 1967.

As far as CBS was concerned, the great news about *The Red Skelton Hour* was not just that it was a bigger hit than ever, but it was a bigger hit over an hour rather than a half hour, and along with that, a good portion of its audience finally stuck around to watch the show after it. The network put *The Jack Benny Program* from Sunday nights, where it was faltering opposite *Bonanza*, and installed it after Red in 1962–63, prompting it to zoom back toward the top at #12 for the season.

The next year, CBS placed *Petticoat Junction* after Red, and it was an even bigger hit, finishing even ahead of Red at #4. Its ratings fell off thereafter and trailed Red's show the rest of the time it was on the air, but on the four seasons it followed *The Red Skelton Hour*, *Petticoat Junction* managed to finish in the top 25 and help CBS to win Tuesday nights in the ratings.

Finally, Red and crew usually were represented at the Emmys through the mid–1960s, and neither the show nor its representatives ever won. In 1963, it lost the Variety Show Emmy to *The Andy Williams Show*, the Writing Achievement in Comedy to Carl Reiner for *The Dick Van Dyke Show* and the Directorial Achievement in Comedy to John Rich for *The Dick Van Dyke Show*. Blanked out of the awards for some reason in 1964, the show earned a nomination for Skelton as a performer in 1965, followed by a nomination in 1966 for Variety Series, losing again to *The Andy Williams Show*.

Red's Growing Television Clout

With the show now running an hour, Red's starting time moved up a half hour for the second time in as many seasons, beginning at 8:30

on Tuesdays rather than 9 on Sept. 25, 1962. The last time Red had been in that slot, he failed miserably opposite Milton Berle in the 1953–54 season. Now he easily triumphed over his feeble competition: the tired *77 Sunset Strip* knockoff *Hawaiian Eye* on ABC and the modern-day western *Empire* on NBC. *Hawaiian Eye* went off at the end of the season, while NBC curiously decided to redo *Empire* as a half-hour drama titled *Redigo* with a modified cast in the Tuesday at 8:30 slot in the fall of 1963. The latter vanished by the end of 1963 against Skelton, though unlike the previous season, *Redigo* came on midway during Skelton's show.

You see, in the 1963–64 season, CBS moved the starting time of Red's series up a half hour to 8 P.M. on the East and West coasts. Now it began midway through its hour-long drama competition on ABC and NBC, *Combat!* and *Mr. Novak* respectively, with the latter followed by the aforementioned *Redigo* and the former with the military hijinks sitcom *McHale's Navy*, both starting at 8:30. (CBS showed reruns of half-hour *Gunsmoke* shows from the 1950s under the title *Marshal Dillon* to precede Red and run against the first half hour of *Combat!* and *Mr. Novak*.)

Red objected strenuously to the move, having grown into being superstitious about when people watched television. The new time of 8 P.M. was too soon after dinner for people to watch, he believed, and he argued strongly with network programmers to move it back to its previous time slot. Although the show finished at #11 that season, down from #2 in 1962–63, CBS felt it was still strong and wanted to keep it there to use as a building block to entice viewers to watch the rest of the network's Tuesday lineup. But they succumbed to his pressure, and Tuesdays 8:30–9:30 would be Red's time slot from the fall of 1964 until its run on CBS ended in 1970.

(It should be noted that Red's other beliefs on television viewing, such as that few people wanted to watch television on Monday nights and 9 P.M. being too late a starting time, simply do not hold water, especially given how Red had prospered in the "late" starting time of 9:30 P.M. from 1955 to 1961. As for his belief about Mondays, look at how *The Lucy Show* and *The Andy Griffith Show*, among other 1960s series airing that night, remained top 10 fixtures throughout that time. Red simply was showing his irrational behavior with these ludicrous television "theories.")

And after much clamoring to do so by Red, the hour series finally went to color in the fall of 1965. He had done his half-hour shows since the 1955–56 season in color, feeling correctly that it would be the wave of the future; but the cost of doing an hour show in color in the early 1960s was prohibitive, given that the majority of television sets sold then were black and white. Now, with more color sets being sold and more of television being done in color thanks to pressure by NBC, which had an almost-all color lineup by 1965, CBS acceded to Red's wishes and stopped taping the hour show in black and white. (NBC's competition against Red in the 1964–65 season, *The Man from U.N.C.L.E.*, was filmed in black and white that year, as was ABC's competing *McHale's Navy* and *The Tycoon*, the latter a one-year sitcom starring Walter Brennan. ABC kept *McHale's Navy* in 1965–66 while replacing *The Tycoon* with the sitcom *F Troop*, while NBC moved *The Man from U.N.C.L.E.* and replaced it with a half-hour version of *Dr. Kildare* followed by movies.)

His ratings definitely were getting him more power in the industry, though curiously he didn't use much of it outside of his series during the 1962–67 period. He did only a few guest shots and had no big spinoffs from his series by his production company, unlike, say, Danny Thomas, whose production company gave CBS the huge hits *The Andy Griffith Show* and *The Dick Van Dyke Show*, or Lucille Ball, whose Desilu production facilities created such hits as *Mission: Impossible* and *Star Trek* before she sold the operation to Paramount.

One of the few exceptions to this situation was Red's Nov. 9, 1966, special on CBS called *Clown Alley*, which included many frequent guests on his show—Amanda Blake, Jackie Coogan, Audrey Meadows, Robert Merrill, Vincent Price, Martha Raye, Cesar Romero, and Bobby Rydell—covered in greasepaint while having the comic preside over their routines in a setting he loved naturally. It was well received, but curiously prompted no further specials from Red thereafter until his series ended.

There was one little-heralded instance of Red gaining ground in the industry, and of all things, it involved a science fiction series. Well, some people argue it barely merited being called that, but there's no doubt that the show was a hit—and an unlikely product tied to Red's name.

The "Lost in Space" Connection

Nicknamed "The Space Family Robinson" in its original treatment and within the television industry itself, *Lost in Space* told the story of a husband and wife and their two daughters and sons trying to return to Earth following their spaceship being sabotaged in that then-faraway year of 1997. Doing the damage was shifty, hammy Dr. Zachary Smith, played by Jonathan Harris, a character intended to be a supporting one in the series, who ended up overshadowing the other characters, and the show itself, by his comically theatrical reactions to the alien terrors that constantly bedeviled the group. As the show progressed during its three-year run, the nemeses and Dr. Smith became more outlandish to appeal to children, to the dismay of hardcore science fiction fans.

What does all this have to do with Red Skelton? Well, his Van Bernard production company was one of the backers of the show, and thus got a piece of the profits. (It originally ran for 83 episodes on CBS from Sept. 15, 1965, through Sept. 11, 1968, followed by countless reruns over the next 30-plus years.) One of the show's stars claims that CBS involved Red's company in it as a way to keep him signed to the network.

"It was offered as a carrot to get him to re-sign in '64 and '65," insisted June Lockhart, who played the mother of the *Lost in Space* clan. "They gave him participation in the show to keep him there."

A year prior to *Lost in Space*, Lockhart had been the mother on *Lassie* from 1958 to 1964, being forced to leave once it was determined her television son, played by Jon Provost, was too old for playing a kid in charge of a remarkably clever collie. *Lassie* continued to air on CBS Sundays 7–7:30 P.M., as it had since Sept. 12, 1954, while *Lost in Space* ran on the same network Wednesdays from 7:30 to 8:30 P.M.

Lockhart's involvement with Skelton stretched back two decades before *Lost in Space*. "I had been a fan since he started on radio," she said. "My father, Gene Lockhart, was a great fancier of Red's, and I knew him on the MGM lot around 1944 to 1946."

She said Red had nothing to do with the show beyond his company's monetary support. When I suggested it would've been a great idea to have Red guest on one show opposite Jonathan Harris's Dr. Smith for an amusing competition to see who would've mugged it up more, Lockhart disagreed, citing her late co-star's ego. "I think that Jonathan Harris would've objected severely to that," she said. "Totally impossible."

As for Lockhart, she does hold the distinction of being the only cast member of *Lost in Space* to guest star on Red's show, in 1967 and 1969. The 1967 show was a spoof titled "Loused in Space," with Skelton playing San Fernando Red. Lockhart got onto the show in an odd fashion.

"I was over at CBS having my hair done for some sort of show I was doing," she said. "The hairdresser said, 'The next Red Skelton show, they're doing a takeoff on *Lost in Space*.'" Intrigued, she contacted the show's executive producer Guy della Cioppa about being a guest on it. "You would want to?" he asked incredulously. When convinced she did, della Cioppa installed her on the show.

"We had grand fun, and he was wonderful to work with," Lockhart said of doing Red's show. She also acknowledged that she could keep up with Red in the "Dirty Hour" rehearsal by catching him off guard by giving him an unexpected phallic symbol.

"I had some sort of a long wand that I was supposed to tap him with, and I put this thing between his legs and brought it up," laughed

Lockhart. "We were all just convulsed. People didn't expect us to be down and dirty."

One final note about that appearance: When Lockhart's episode ran on April 25, 1967, somewhat incredibly, *The Red Skelton Hour* was the top-rated show on television.

We're (Almost) #1

By the end of the 1966–67 season, many pundits were caught off guard to learn that the top-rated series each week was *The Red Skelton Hour*, now in its 16th season. How in the world could such an old program be pulling in the biggest audience? It was an unprecedented feat, then and now.

Some possible explanations can be easily dismissed. It certainly was not the guest list. Were viewers really excited about seeing Ozzie and Harriet Nelson after their ABC sitcom ended a 14-year run in 1966, or likewise Richard Chamberlain after his *Dr. Kildare* drama ended five years on NBC? Not likely. Oh, there were some big name movie stars popping up to appeal, for sure, such as Janet Leigh and Cliff Robertson, but by and large it remained the same sort of guests seen on other variety series, such as Frank Gorshin, Jack Jones, Edie Adams, Polly Bergen, and so forth—fine talent, but hardly reasons to attract a larger audience than before.

No, *The Red Skelton Hour*'s rise to the top was not just based on the show's merits, but on the television scene around it as well. Basically, the series stood firm while the other shows around it lost ground.

A tremendous help for *The Red Skelton Hour* in 1966–67 was the relative lack of new hits that season. Of the 22 series introduced by ABC, CBS and NBC in the fall of 1966, only nine received ratings high enough to be renewed for the 1967–68 season: *The Iron Horse*, *The Rat Patrol*, *Felony Squad* and *That Girl* on ABC; *Family Affair* and *Mission: Impossible* on CBS; and *The Monkees*, *Star Trek* and *Tarzan* on NBC. Though many of these titles are familiar to television viewers today thanks to their reruns, most of these were not big ratings hits this season and usually finished second at best in their time slots. The biggest ratings winner was *Family Affair* at #15 for the season, and that was thanks in large part because it aired after *The Andy Griffith Show* (#3 that season). The next highest-rated show was, surprise, surprise, the less-remembered *The Rat Patrol* at #24, which would flop the following season when *Rowan and Martin's Laugh-In* defeated it handily.

The Rat Patrol did do well enough to take away more than a million viewers from its opposition, *The Lucy Show*, which had been #3 in

1965–66, while Red's show finished at #4. So that obviously aided Red there. Then there was one other CBS program in 1965–66 that Red had to overcome.

Gomer Pyle, U.S.M.C. was a smash on Fridays in 1965–66 for CBS at #2 for the season. The network probably assumed that it would fare even better following *Green Acres* on Wednesdays in 1966–67, as that was another rural-based comedy, than it had been with *Hogan's Heroes* as its lead-in on Friday nights in 1965–66. But that move deprived children who could stay up late on Fridays to see the show, and the loss of those viewers dropped it to a still-respectable #10 for the year. Nevertheless, CBS moved it back to Fridays for the 1967–68 season.

In contrast to all this, Red managed easily to whip his 1966–67 competitors on ABC and NBC. ABC offered two weak sitcoms, *The Rounders* and *The Pruitts of Southampton*. Both performed so poorly that ABC cancelled *The Rounders* on Jan. 3, 1967, and moved *The Pruitts of Southampton*, retitled *The Phyllis Diller Show* in honor of its star, to Fridays from 9:30 to 10, where it stayed until it ran out of gas on Sept. 1, 1967. Replacing them on Jan. 10, 1967, was *The Invaders*, a science fiction twist on *The Fugitive* by the same executive producer that had Roy Thinnes star as a man running away from aliens. The premise had even less appeal than the sitcoms did for Red's mature audience, but nonetheless ABC renewed it for the 1967–68 season.

Meanwhile, NBC put up its own loser sitcom, *Occasional Wife*, a contrived affair about a single man who had to pretend to be married at home to please his boss, for the first half hour against Red. Following it at 9 was *Tuesday Night at the Movies*, a series of motion pictures first released in theaters from 1949 to 1963 that were making their television debuts. This was back nearly a decade before it became commonplace for Hollywood to sell its titles to cable channels prior to network airing. By the 1990s, releasing theatrical movies for home sale took precedent before the cable showings, and under that schedule, fewer and fewer theatrical movies aired on the networks, as the ancillary markets for most of those films already had been exhausted before that kind of exposure.

But back to 1967. While one may think that movies would be solid opposition to a comedy variety series, the fact of the matter was that *Tuesday Night at the Movies* was the weakest of five movie nights from the networks that year. NBC's *Saturday Night at the Movies* offered *Rear Window, Roman Holiday, Sabrina, The Man Who Knew Too Much, White Christmas, The Joker Is Wild, Donovan's Reef, Stalag 17* and *Lonely Are the Brave* in its stellar lineup in 1966–67. ABC's Sunday slate that season scored big ratings at the start with *Bridge on the River Kwai*, followed by *Bus Stop, Can Can, High Society* and *King Solomon's Mines*, among other titles. CBS had Thursdays and Fridays sewn up with the just-as-impressive collection of *Psycho, Lilies of the Field, Breakfast at Tiffany's, Advise and Consent, A Raisin in the Sun, The Music Man* and *Bye Bye Birdie*.

Compared to all that, the 1966–67 *Tuesday Night at the Movies* was the television equivalent of a store's video bargain bin. Few of its movies had as much commercial and/or critical prestige as the other network motion picture showcases that year, with such blah offerings as 1962's *My Six Loves* and 1956's *Omar Khayyam* being typical fare. Most tellingly, its debut presentation, Elvis Presley's *Blue Hawaii* from 1961, was repeated not once but twice in a seven-month period, a good sign of how barren the lineup was. Not surprisingly, NBC's Tuesday movie series was the lowest-rated of its genre in 1966–67, and the only one not to finish in the top 30 that year.

With CBS hits from the previous year faltering a little, Red's own competition sputtering, and no new real hits emerging in 1966–67, Red's only problem from reaching the top spot was *Bonanza*, the NBC western that had been at #1 in 1964–65 and 1965–66. But even though it stayed at #1 for a third consecutive season in 1966–67, it did have considerable erosion in its audience thanks to the arrival in January 1967 of *The Smothers Brothers Comedy Hour* on CBS, a variety show running opposite *Bonanza* that ate into the latter's audience and wound up a very strong #16 for the season. With less than a ratings point separating *Bonanza* from #2 *The Red Skelton Hour* for the season, it is entirely believable that had *The Smothers Brothers Comedy Hour* started airing a few weeks earlier than it did, *The Red Skelton Hour* would've been #1 outright for 1966–67.

Yet amid the joy about this triumph, the series took an unexpected hit to its reputation. And it was delivered by none other than Red himself.

"We've Never Been Fired Before This"

The Red Skelton Hour was ranked #1 the week before Skelton did the unthinkable: He dismissed his head writers Bob Schiller and Bob Weiskopf. The two Bobs had written the #1 sitcom of the 1950s (*I Love Lucy*) before becoming the lead scribes for television's #1 variety series of the 1960s. Now, after three years of keeping the show no lower than #6 per seasonal ratings, they were out of a job, and with no reason given whatsoever. And there remained one more show to tape before the season ended.

Hal Humphrey, a television columnist for *The Los Angeles Times*, got wind of the axing and went to Schiller and Weiskopf to get the story. His column of their comments ran on April 20, 1967, and did not present a pretty portrait of Red as an employer.

Noting the show's rating, Schiller told Humphrey: "We've never been fired for excellence until now. In fact, we've never been fired before this—not as a team anyway."

Both men said they tried to talk to Red about it but could not reach him, and, in fact, neither had dealt with him directly at any time during their tenure. Schiller said, "I guess I saw Red less than a half-dozen times, and Weiskopf saw him less than that. It's very difficult to talk to him." He did mention that Red did send them a thank you note at the end of their first season.

Humphrey said at least two people tried unsuccessfully to talk Red out of the dismissals. He did not get a quote from the comic, but an unnamed "Skelton lackey" told him that "Red has been considering shaking up the writing staff for a long time." Why he had done so remains a mystery, although Schiller offered this caustic assessment to Humphrey: "Working for Red apparently is the same as going to junior high school. After three years you're out. Red's last two writers lasted only three years too."

The latter statement was false, if Schiller presumably meant head writers. (Other writers had come and gone on other schedules, as has been noted.) Their predecessor Ed Simmons did leave after three years of being head writer in 1964, but before him, Sherwood Schwartz departed in 1961 after six years of service. And both Simmons and Schwartz left on their own volition.

Schiller's comments seemed especially odd and disappointing considering the praise he lavished on Skelton to Bill Davidson in a cover story on Red in the June 17, 1967, issue of *The Saturday Evening Post*. Davidson had talked to Schiller before Red fired him and included favorable comments by the writer in his article without noting that Red dismissed him a few weeks later.

"This man's the greatest pantomimist in the world," Schiller told Davidson. "I know it's not chic among the intellectuals to like Skelton, but the intellectuals' darling, Chaplin, couldn't do this day in and day out, not in a million years." Schiller even compared Red's comedy improvisations to what a jazz artist comes up with in his music.

For his part, Weiskopf made the following backhanded compliment to his ex-employer to Humphreys: "Red does add to the scripts usually, as any comedian would and should, reaching into old routines for an appropriate or sometimes inappropriate line of business here and there."

Red read the column and was steamed about it while taping his final show of the year. Schiller recounted the aftermath to Jordan R. Young in *The Laugh Crafters*. "Skelton said, 'I'll show those sons of bitches. I'll read it the way they wrote it.' It went much better than the stuff he would bring in. It was the first time we ever had an example of our work on the air.... But that was his way of showing us we didn't know what the hell we were talking about." The show's taping ran seven minutes longer than usual due to more laughter.

When I asked Robert Orben if he understood why Red let go of his head writers, who were also Orben's bosses, he told me, "God only knows. They were absolutely stunned and made the practical error of taking out their woes to a television columnist, and they nailed the coffin shut for their coming back."

So, the firing held firm. Schiller and Weiskopf recommended another veteran comedy writer, Charles Isaacs, to assume their role, and he took the job, while Red went back to ad-libbing. But the publicity of the situation in the industry left a negative impression among industry insiders. To fire a hit-making team without any reason was a terrible error in judgment by Skelton, and hereafter those in the know largely gave up on him and his show, perceiving Red to be a power-hungry comedian unappreciative of those who took him to the top.

This was reflected in the 1967 Emmys. There was not enough sympathy apparently to nominate the two Bobs to spite Red, possibly because he would've received a nomination as well since he was still credited as a writer on the show. But *The Red Skelton Hour* got no other nominations in any other category either, although tellingly its director Bill Hobin did get a nod for his job helming *The Sid Caesar, Imogene Coca, Carl Reiner, Howard Morris Special* on CBS. The producers and writers of that special won Emmys in their category; Hobin lost to Fielder Cook for a production of the musical *Brigadoon*.

To not score at the Emmys is one thing and made little difference to the show, which had done well even without nominations, and would continue to do so into the future. In fact, it would have just one more Emmy nomination thereafter, in 1970 for an "Unidentified Flying Objects" dance number by Tom Hansen on the Nov. 25, 1969, show with Walter Brennan that competed for Best Choreography, with Hansen losing to Norman Maen for an episode of *This Is Tom Jones*. (Hansen might have had more nominations had the producers encouraged him to put his material up for consideration for an Emmy. "That was the only time I was approached to submit anything," he told me.)

But there were other factors clouding Red's success after 1966–67, all stemming from a changing television industry that he and his staff apparently failed to grasp until it was too late. The result would affect Red and the way he viewed his series and even television for the rest of his life.

6

1967–1970: "We Had No Concept of That Show Being Cancelled"

During the late 1960s, Red's ratings remained the envy of almost any other comedian on television. He finished no lower than #11 in the seasonal ratings, admittedly not as close to #1 as he had been in 1966–67, but still strong, especially for a show that had been on the air for so long. Yet that was a poor way to gauge Red's true standing in the television industry.

If Red and his staff had been a little more observant, they would have noticed there were changes afoot threatning their hit status. There is a tendency of not making waves on top series that sometimes results in stagnation in creativity, as the same old show becomes far too same and old for many viewers. And so it happened with Red's program.

The waning press coverage should have been one of those indicators. Red would not be the subject of a *TV Guide* article for more than four years after a profile in August 1966. His last general interest magazine cover of the 1960s came with *The Saturday Evening Post* in the summer of 1967. As Red never much liked being interviewed, he didn't seem to mind that state of affairs, but others on his staff should have sensed that when you are not being talked about, a lack of popularity in the media can easily translate into a lack of interest among network executives.

There were other factors that Red and company should have heeded in this period if they really wanted to ensure a good standing beyond their audience to the industry at large and prevent the events that led to the program's cancellation by 1970.

1) *There was a new marketing tool advertisers favored, that of demographics. And Red's results were none too encouraging.*

The idea of looking at the viewership of television series by different characteristics rather than just raw numbers was one long promoted by

ABC executives in the 1950s and 1960s, who realized that with their fewer number of affiliates than CBS and NBC, they would need a different method of enticing advertisers to buy commercials on their programs. By showing affiliates they could target their sales to shows appealing more strongly to specific groups, such as young women with prime buying power, ABC managed to win over a goodly amount of revenue it otherwise might have missed just based on ratings alone, where the network almost always ran third each season.

By the late 1960s, the use of demographics among television advertisers was becoming commonplace, what with businesses having less money to allot for commercials as the economy went into recession. The more finicky sponsors wanted to attract sophisticated audiences—viewers that were younger, more urban, richer and smarter than the average television audience. With those qualifications as a measuring scale, *The Red Skelton Hour* was in serious trouble to tempt those companies to spend their dollars on the show. Simply put, the show was virtual demographic poison.

A June 1968 survey by *TV Guide* of series on the air from Oct. 23 through Dec. 3, 1967, indicated Red's dubious appeal. He finished at #4 among series in three categories, as being favored by those with incomes of less than $5,000, by blue-collar employees and by those with a grade school education. In contrast, he was out of the top 10 among series liked by those with incomes of $10,000 or more, by white-collar employees and by those with more than one year of college. He also ranked #6 among viewers in the South while not even in the top 10 programs of the Northeast. About the only surprise was that his show was not in the top 10 among viewers over the age of 50, but it had to have ranked in the top 20 if not at #11 itself.

Other surveys in later seasons by trade papers such as *Variety* confirmed Red's continuing poor standing among young, college-educated, affluent and non-rural types. So, how did a show that just a few years earlier had seemed to be appealing to everyone now find itself ignored by hip, upscale audiences?

A chief culprit was that Red kept largely the same crew of men his age working on his show as he had through all the 1960s, with little change in their approach. Not helping matters were those few additions. The 1968–69 season debuted with "The Olio," routines based largely on old vaudeville jokes that all but drove away audiences younger than Red's generation. Red also brought out on Nov. 21, 1967, his one new character during this period, Charlie the Swinger, who tried to be cool in the "happening" world around him. One can hardly imagine a more ironic and less-effective characterization out of touch with the times.

There were some more obvious conservative elements creeping into the series that may have put off younger, more liberal viewers. Details about them will come later in this chapter in "The Shows 1967–70" section.

Yet some of the problem had to be linked with the booking of guests as well. Red's visiting stars were falling into somewhat of a rut in later years, especially in the 1969–70 season. The show booked Walter Brennan for its second episode and brought him back eight weeks later. Almost the same situation existed for Vincent Price, who popped up on Jan. 6 and reemerged on March 10. Those who missed Audrey Meadows in November had no worries because she returned again in February. George Gobel followed his Nov. 18 stint with another shot on March 31.

To book these stars twice in a season gave off the air that Red's show was either insular in its booking or could not or would not book new talent. As most of the names involved were middle-aged performers seen almost annually with Red in earlier seasons, it only added to an impression that the show was wearing out the same talent. Obviously, this did nothing to attract new viewers.

The series did try for new names in its musical acts in 1969–70: Paul Revere and the Raiders, Three Dog Night, and most unbelievably on the season premiere, the proto–heavy metal band Iron Butterfly (doing their bone-crunching hit "In-a-Gadda-Da-Vida") all turned up for a show. In his memoirs, Bill Hobin claimed CBS executives pressured him to hire more rock acts that season and wanted Red not just to introduce their taped segments but also talk with them. "I suppose to somehow show that Red, himself, was 'with it,'" Bill wrote. The theory, so it appeared, was that the 18–35 age group would watch *The Red Skelton Hour* because of the rock music, and after seeing that Red was 'rock friendly,' they would stay for the rest of the show and come back, week after week."

That strategy did not work, of course, with its forced nature on air apparent to everyone. The setup died during the season when it was clear it did not get many more young adults to watch, and, in fact, the one musical act to show up twice that season was the mainstream vocal trio the Lettermen, doing their middle-of-the-road hits "Hurt So Bad" and "Traces." Actually, the show would've been better off booking younger, hipper guest stars for the comedy sketches to attract the "in crowd," but apparently no one on the staff thought much about it, preferring to go with what already had been working.

Linked along with all this is our second factor:

2) *Newer variety series made Red's show look more unfashionable and outdated every season.*

The show that helped Red nearly claim the #1 television show title by hurting *Bonanza* in 1966–67, *The Smothers Brothers Show*, was, in a certain sense, the anti–*Red Skelton Hour*. Unlike Red, Tom and Dick Smothers preferred a heavy dose of political humor in their act, often against right-wing targets, including Vietnam War proponents. And when they had rock acts as guests, they did not do some sterile introduction taped without an audience and at a different time from the actual performance. Tom and Dick instead met the performers, shook their hands and joked with them too, seeming to appreciate them more. Not surprisingly, Red hated their show. So did CBS, who eventually cancelled them even though they were in the top 30 in 1969 because the network found more of its material objectionable. (They weren't alone; the network reported that *The Red Skelton Hour* drew only a tenth of the complaints by mail that *The Smothers Brothers Show* did.)

Another irreverent variety show in its own way was *Rowan and Martin's Laugh-In*. Debuting on January 1968, it became the television sensation of the late 1960s on Monday nights, claiming the #1 spot in the 1968–69 and 1969–70 seasons and revolutionizing the pace of television. With its fast edits of videotape (some bits ran less than a second) and mocking sendups of typical variety show production numbers by a spirited cast of young newcomers, including Goldie Hawn, it made Red's show look like a lumbering dinosaur.

But the one that might have hurt Red most in CBS's eye was *The Carol Burnett Show*. Debuting in the fall of 1967, Carol's series would run 11 years to great acclaim from the critics and the audience, even though its highest number of viewers never equaled Red's. (It never finished in the top 10 for a season, for example.) Like Red, Burnett was a light-hearted redhead comic who did skits at Television City in Hollywood. But unlike Red, Carol connected to her audiences more strongly by having more involvement on air. She began each show not with a monologue but by taking questions from her audience. Her sketches were broad like Red's and often contained some ad-libbing from her or her regulars or guests; but unlike Red's, those comments usually were new jokes, not old ones, and often seemed germane to the sketch at hand, not out-of-character asides to the audience that interrupted the flow of the show.

Moreover, Carol's ego was not as large as Red's. She had no problem sharing the spotlight with her regulars Harvey Korman, Vicki Lawrence, Lyle Waggoner and Tim Conway, and even let some skits go on without her in them. Yet at the same time, Carol also indulged in singing and dancing in big production numbers with her regulars and guests, something Red rarely did. It made her look more of the trouper than the comedian did on most of his shows. In a sense, *The Carol Burnett Show* was what *The Red Skelton Hour* could have been if Red had put only more effort and discipline into it. Which leads us to point #3...

3) *Red seemed less ambitious than ever, and people in the industry noticed it.*

One of the rarer things to find on television in the late 1960s was Red Skelton making a guest shot outside his series. Apart from when he popped up twice on *The Ed Sullivan Show*, Red was virtually AWOL from visiting other television venues.

A notable exception was the debut of *The Jonathan Winters Show* on CBS on Dec. 12, 1967. Red mimed with Winters, who idolized Red, in a sketch where the two played lusty lumberjacks between other segments with guests Barbara Eden from *I Dream of Jeannie*, Ivan Dixon of *Hogan's Heroes* and, believe it or not, the rock group the Doors playing their hit "Light My Fire." But Red's Van Bernard Productions company financed the series, so it's not too surprising their star showed up on this part as well. It didn't help; the show went off in less than two years.

In fact, Van Bernard Productions had only one production on television when *Lost in Space* went off in 1968—*The Red Skelton Hour*, of course. The company tried selling just one more pilot while *Lost in Space* was on the air. *Shoestring Safari*, a sitcom starring Andy Davis and Kelly Jean Peters as a father-daughter team who tried to con visitors to Africa into thinking they're seeing a scary tour of the jungle using prerecorded noises and props, found no takers at CBS and did not make the network's 1966 lineup. Otherwise, the production company had no other activity.

Additionally, Red clearly was not understood by network executives. Perry Lafferty, vice president of programming at CBS at the time, described Red to me this way: "He was kind of a hermit. Nobody really saw him." Apart from Red's habit of having a huge amount of cash on hand and the "Dirty Hour," Lafferty said he has few memories of the star.

If you're a star who works only two days a week, acts odd, and barely does any other guest shots nor proposes new material for the network, how do you think the brass would feel about you and your dedication to helping them? That thought no doubt crept into the minds of several CBS executives as the years went by, especially in light of this point:

4) *ABC and NBC offered Red stronger competition than ever.*

In the middle of the 1967–68 season, ABC moved *The Invaders* to the Tuesdays at 10 P.M. slot and replaced it on Jan. 9, 1968, with the upscale crime drama *It Takes a Thief*, starring Robert Wagner. It was not a huge audience grabber, but it did have more urban appeal than Red or its predecessor, for that matter, and ABC had enough faith in it to keep it in its slot for a year and a half before moving it to Thursdays for the 1969–70 season, where it ended.

A bigger threat came that same season when ABC inaugurated its *Movie of the Week* series against Red. It was the first series consisting solely of television movies—films made especially for television. The novelty was strong enough that the series generated ABC's best ratings in the slot in years, finishing at #22 in the 1969–70 season.

But topping ABC's moves was NBC, which moved the so-so comedy variety series *The Jerry Lewis Show* up 30 minutes after the 1967–68 season (it would be cancelled at the end of the 1969–70 season) to allow for a much more imposing competitor for the start of *The Red Skelton Hour*. *Julia* starred Diahann Carroll in the first sitcom with a black female lead since *Beulah* in the early 1950s. But while the latter had a stereotypical maid as its central character, *Julia* played a more relevant middle-class nurse. *Julia* actually beat *The Red Skelton Hour* in the 1968–69 season, placing #7 while Red tied for #11, and still remained a contender the following year, even though it wound up at #28.

At the same time, NBC whipped up a better slate of films for its movie showcase than it had in 1966–67 to run against the second half hour of *The Red Skelton Hour*. Like *Julia* it made the top 30 in the late 1960s, and while it didn't surpass Red in the ratings, it had enough appeal with the "right audience" to make it attractive to upscale advertisers.

Herb Schlosser, head of West Coast programming at NBC from 1966 through 1972, said the network went against *The Red Skelton Hour* with urban, sophisticated programming like *Julia* and movies in the late 1960s due, to a certain extent, on demographics.

"Red skewed old and rural. The demo situation, though an important counterprogramming situation, was not as large as then as today," Schlosser confirmed to me. "The emphasis on demos was not as laser-like as today."

But the demos that were there were better for ABC's and NBC's shows than Red's, and with their ratings not too far behind his, NBC and ABC could handle being a not-too-distant second or even third in this kind of competition. In fact, sophisticates had already written off his show to the point where writer Robert L. Mott, who we'll meet shortly, found that when he moved to Beverly Hills in 1969, some of his neighbors thought the show already was cancelled. It wasn't, but to almost everyone's surprise except CBS officials, it would be a year later—even though it still was in the top 10.

The New Personnel

Some things that were not affected by outside influences remained the same within Red's world. One was that his new head writer, installed in the fall of 1967 to replace Bob Schiller and Bob Weiskopf, maintained a tradition by hating his boss.

Charlie Isaacs told Jordan R. Young in *The Laugh Crafters* that "Skelton was mean-spirited. Insulting. Autocratic." Asked to elaborate, Isaacs said, "Skelton just thought you were nothing. He hated to have to talk to you, even. Skelton was really the one who felt he should get all the writing credit." Considering that Isaacs wrote for nearly every major comic of the 20th century, from Edgar Bergen to Bob Hope to Dean Martin and Jerry Lewis to Johnny Carson, that's a pretty strong statement to make.

A steady presence in writing comedy for radio and later television since the late 1930s, Isaacs' longest-running television job before *The Red Skelton Hour* was writing for Jimmy Durante for *All Star Revue* in the early 1950s. Though primarily a writer, Isaacs also wrote and produced three sitcoms that ran just a year: *The Duke* (1954), *Hey Jeannie* (1956–57) and *The Tycoon* (1964–65). Bob Orben called him "A sweet, sweet guy."

Others joining the writing team in 1967–68 were partners Fred Fox and Seaman Jacobs. Their television credits included many sitcoms of the 1950s and 1960s, including *How to Marry a Millionaire*, *The Andy Griffith Show* and *Mona McCluskey*. Like Isaacs, they lasted with the show for three years. The next few years, other writers were added, chiefly under the instigation of Bill Hobin, who in the fall of 1968 went from being the series' director to its producer.

Hobin claimed in his autobiography that Seymour Berns, who had been the show's producer since 1964 after 10 years of being its director, seemed unlikely to return to the job for the 1968–69 season. "He had been spending a great deal of time on outside projects, devoting too little time to the writers and the show in general," Hobin claimed. "He had also had a few unpleasant confrontations with important people on the show."

Given the situation, Hobin announced he would not return to direct the show if Berns stayed as producer. Others made similar requests of having no confidence in Berns as producer anymore, so Berns was canned and Hobin took over his job.

As the new producer, Hobin met with the writers to determine if they could work with his vision of doing the main sketches for the show. He determined that Larry Rhine and Martin Ragaway could not, so he fired them. In their place, he hired Tony Webster, an Emmy winner for three years in a row (1955 to 1957) for writing *You'll Never Get Rich*, followed by writing nominations in 1962 for *Car 54, Where Are You?* and in 1964 for *That Was the Week That Was*. Webster had a reputation of hitting the sauce, which had hampered his career and made Hobin wary of hiring him until he had Webster checked out and approved. Webster worked out fine and stayed with the show through its run on CBS.

The following season, in the fall of 1969, there was a death in the writing staff. Dave O'Brien, who had written for the show since Sherwood Schwartz rejuvenated it in 1955, passed away. To replace him, Hobin brought aboard Robert L. "Bob" Mott, a pal of his from back in the 1950s when the two worked together on *The Andy Williams Show*.

Mott was a sound effects man for the daily morning CBS children's show *Captain Kangaroo* when Hobin offered him the chance to write Red's pantomimes in the monologue. Despite a chilly initial reception from Mort Green, who thought Mott joined the staff to usurp him if he asked for too big a salary increase, Mott displayed such inventive talent devising pantomimes based on Bob Orben's monologue themes that Mott said Green appropriated them to use in his "Silent Spot" segments, forcing Mott to find another concept.

Mott learned the basics of Red's pantomimes, including Red using only a chair and a fedora to create his situations and the use of such terms as "jaws" to indicate when Red would pretend to be screaming in anger at something or someone. Mott also indicated when and where in the pantomime to add sound effects and music. As for his job's drawback of being basically forbidden to meet with Red, he was philosophical. "I've often thought that whatever communication he withheld from his writers, he gave his audiences in full," Mott wrote in his autobiography *Radio Live! Television Live!*

Another addition in 1969 was George Balzer. A longtime writer with Jack Benny on radio and television, his time on *The Red Skelton Hour* came near the end of his career, as he did his last regular television writing gig on the ill-fated 1970–71 comedy variety series *The Don Knotts Show* on NBC.

"It was the last year [of Skelton on CBS], and I don't know if I made him go off the air," Balzer joked when talking to me. He demurred in speaking about his time on the show, saying that he didn't want his brief tenure there to be exaggerated by a book on the series.

"There's nothing I could tell you that you wouldn't have anyway," Balzer added. "I did a good job. Thanks for asking."

But Robert Orben remembered Balzer vividly on the staff. "I think George had spent 25 years with Jack Benny, and whenever we discussed a joke during writing, George would say, 'Well, Jack would do it this way,'" laughed Orben.

In with Quinn, Plus Stanley Green

While Hobin became producer and shuffled the writers, Howard Quinn moved up to assume the director's chair from 1968 to 1970. Quinn had been associate producer on the show since at least the 1961–62 season. Replacing Quinn in his old role was Stanley Green.

"I did a lot of preparation work," Green said in recalling his role more than 30 years later. For example, he would consult with the art department about graphics to be used on the show, among other duties. But most of them centered on editing and timing the shows.

For the show's musical production numbers, Green would ready the shots during rehearsal. He worked closely with Quinn on that aspect of the production, plus pickup shots—scenes that were missed or omitted during the main taping that could be edited into the show during postproduction.

Editing was a considerable part of Green's function, as he devoted Thursdays and Fridays to the task. He would review with the director the shot selections for about an hour and then do editing. Green said meshing the different elements of the show could be difficult in those pre-computer days: "It was physical editing of 2½-inch tape, with a lag between audio and video," he said. "You'd try to cover it with applause or other sounds."

Green also let loose a secret about how he timed the show: He made Red's opening jokes the variable element that he would lengthen or subtract from the final show as needed. Basically, he said that he used the monologue as "filler" for timing the show in editing.

There was one last element in place for Green to do each week. After he edited the whole show, he would "sweeten" it to comparable audio levels throughout the show. In other words, he and the director would add a laugh track, applause or whatever other sounds were needed to finish the show.

Green liked his producer, recalling that Bill Hobin was one of the nicest people he worked with. But he admits that working with director Howard Quinn was intimidating at first.

"I'd just seen him around and he sounded like an ogre," Green laughed. "He had been a Marine Corps general." But with time, Green's assessment of Quinn was the same as of Hobin: "Howie turned out to be one of the nicest guys to work with."

As for Red himself, Green did not see much of him. "I didn't deal directly with him. He was always pretty nice to Howie Quinn and Bill Hobin. He could be awfully hard with Guy della Cioppa." Like many others, Green stayed with the show until its sudden cancellation by CBS in 1970.

The Shows 1967–1970

The only noticeable change on air on *The Red Skelton Hour* with regulars involved replacing Alan Copeland with Jimmy Joyce as musical

Red and Chanin Hale as bumblebees, date unknown.

director in the fall of 1969. Copeland said his ouster stemmed from when he joined the syndicated talk show *The Donald O'Connor Show* in 1968 as musical director. Copeland had done work outside Red's show before, so he did not think there would be any difficulty with his new job.

"I got the bandleader gig, so I was doing both Red and Donald

O'Connor," Copeland said. "I don't know who it didn't sit well with, but they brought on Jimmy."

The Jimmy Joyce Singers had been regulars on *The Smothers Brothers Comedy Hour* in 1967–69 as well as two summer series, *The John Gary Show* in 1966 and *The Summers Smothers Brothers Show* with Glen Campbell in 1968. They had no hits to speak of, and unlike Copeland, they never even had a Grammy nomination, but they maintained the Alan Copeland Singers' standard of pleasant middle-of-the-road music for Red's viewers during the last season on CBS.

Content-wise, the show did have a few memorable highlights. Red did a one-man show on Jan. 16, 1968, reprising all of his classic routines. On April 29, 1969, the show went to Massachusetts to have Red clown around with Arthur Fiedler and the Boston Pops. (The orchestra played a few tunes written by Skelton on the show.) Mac Davis made his network television debut on March 17, 1970, singing two hits he wrote for Elvis Presley, "In the Ghetto" and "Memories."

And John Wayne made a rare variety show guest appearance on Oct. 28, 1969, a year before his more celebrated shot on *Rowan and Martin's Laugh-In*. Naturally, it included a western spoof with Red playing Deadeye, plus Chanin Hale played a saloon girl who got in this crack on Wayne and his famous stride: "Hey, where'd you get that walk?"

The most prestigious of Red's outings came on Feb. 27, 1968. Vice President Hubert Humphrey introduced Red doing yet one more pantomime show, this time before the United Nations, called "Laughter, the Universal Language," joined by actor David Sharpe and Chanin Hale. "I did the Silent Spot," Hale said. "We played chickens. And we were in the most wonderful costumes you've ever seen!" Other than that memory, Hale recalled only the party held after the affair.

In contrast, the weakest entries of the period had to be Red's two Christmas shows. Once rife with strong comedy to cut through the sentiment, the holiday presentations now sunk into schmaltz far outweighing the laughs. To compound their sluggishness, these shows also were taped without a live audience, and the lack of any sounds of giggling made them deadly to watch and endure.

It's not surprising to report that Red had a hand in writing these clunkers. Credited as writing the original story for both, they have such a distinct heavy feel from the other shows done without him that it brings credence to the claim that Red did not always know what was right for himself. Aiming for the heart, these heavy-handed concoctions missed their mark entirely.

The first to air was "A Christmas Urchin," originally seen on Dec. 19, 1967, and repeated on Dec. 23, 1969. In it, Freddie the Freeloader finds an orphan, played by Linda Sue Risk, who is so desperate to eat she tries to abscond with his dog food. Following a fantasy sequence wherein a ballerina named Jillana dances in a snow setting, the orphan finally tells Freddie details about herself. Freddie's cop friend, played by Howard Keel, helps reunite the girl with her mother, played by Joan Freeman.

Wouldn't it be nice to get that girl a father and her mother a husband, Freddie thinks? And wouldn't Keel's cop be the perfect match? And isn't this so obvious, and yet the story must drag with slow exposition, new Christmas carols (one written by Red) and an overwhelming air of pathos that it makes you want to scream at the set? Of course, the answer is yes to all three.

Between the Yuletide showings of "A Christmas Urchin" came "A Christmas Story—1777," airing on Dec. 24, 1968. Ballerina Jillana shows up again, but in a far different scenario. Here the main action centers on soldiers fighting the Revolutionary War at Valley Forge in late December. In this treacly drama, Red plays a sentry who actually engages in the following preachy dialogue with an escort soldier and another sentry:

SKELTON: Do they know we starve here?

ESCORT SOLDIER: Yes, but we are far away and the war is not popular with everybody.

SKELTON: ("incredulously," as indicated by the script): Fighting for freedom is not popular?

ESCORT SOLDIER: There are young men on the streets who make speeches of protest.

SENTRY: ("angry," again according to the script): If those fighters for liberty put self before country, ask them to come up here on the battle line—both sides can take shots at them.

Get the message, you unwashed hippies protesting against America's involvement in the Vietnam War? Only the dullest of viewers could have missed the "America—Love It or Leave It" undertone of this dialogue. This show had all the trappings of what would be later known derisively as "a very special episode" of a comedy, wherein melodrama overwhelms the usual humor in a show to make a Big Statement about important issues of the day. To comment on war protest in such a manner was didactic and unbecoming for a comedy show like Red's. It only reinforced the feeling that he was a hawk out of touch with why so many people objected to the war.

What really politicizes the show is the fact that it is narrated by Republican Senator Everett McKinley Dirksen of Illinois. Red loved this politician and featured him often on his show in later years, including writing a song called "The Everett McKinley Dirksen March," which he introduced on his show on Jan. 16, 1968, followed a mere three weeks later by the Tom Hansen Dancers doing a routine to that same number.

Fortunately, these instances were the most overt and somewhat awkward cases of Red showing his conservatism. He did have another instance that some may consider right-wing pandering, while others may view it as patriotic. As far as Red and his hardcore fans were concerned, however, it's one of his greatest moments on television.

"The Pledge of Allegiance"

In late 1968, Bob Orben found himself with an unusual request by Red. He didn't want the standard monologue to kick off the show, just some words reminiscing about school days. Red would use that setup to introduce a bit he created himself.

Red wrote a narrative on "The Pledge of Allegiance," describing how his teacher Mr. Lasswell broke down the words in the statement and explained what they meant because he felt that his students were reciting it with monotony. It began this way: "*I*—me, an individual, a committee of one; *pledge*—dedicate all of my worldly goods to give without self-pity; *allegiance*—my love and my devotion..." and so on.

He ended by noting this: "Since I was a small boy, two states have been added to our country, and two words have been added to the Pledge of Allegiance: 'under God.' Wouldn't it be a pity if someone said that is a prayer, and that would be eliminated from schools, too?" (The latter part was indeed introduced by law by President Dwight D. Eisenhower in 1954 to the pledge; Red's reference was to the ruling against school prayer by the U.S. Supreme Court in 1962.)

Red's rendition appeared on the show first aired on Jan. 14, 1969, and caused a sensation with his viewers. Following a year filled with assassinations, public protests gone violent and the endless unproductive military campaign in Vietnam, Red's "Pledge of Allegiance" struck a chord with them about patriotism and what's right with America despite what had gone on previously. The fact that he put it out in the midst of the inauguration of the country's first Republican president in nearly a decade was not lost on several observers either.

In the wake of the broadcast, CBS received around 200,000 requests to get a copy of "The Pledge of Allegiance." It caught them off guard, as Red had little success on records outside of his soundtracks to the MGM musicals on which he sang in the 1950s. For example, in 1955, he recorded two songs, "Little Babe" and "The Foggy, Foggy Dew," backed by the David Rose Orchestra, of course, and both flopped.

Likewise, two 1966 albums of instrumental music composed and conducted by Red, *Conducts Music from the Heart* (with a period piece gauzy color photo of a young couple nuzzling their heads on the front, and a picture of Red and his wife and daughter on the back with liner notes) and *Red Skelton Conducts* (which had a picture of Freddie the Freeloader on the front) generated few sales, even with Red promoting *Red Skelton Conducts* on his Dec. 13, 1966, show by giving it to guest Robert Goulet as a gift.

Nonetheless, within a month, the network's record label put the audio recording of "The Pledge of Allegiance" onto a single to satisfy the sudden demand for the work. In the March 8, 1969, issue of *Billboard*, an unsigned blurb noted that "Columbia issued orders for a mass pressing in all of its plants so that the record would be shipped to radio stations and retailers across the country last week." The magazine also reviewed the single as part of its "Special Merit Spotlight" section ("Spotlighting new singles deserving special attention of programmers and dealers") and said it "could easily prove a left field sales giant. Brilliant performance."

Red's record fared better than some of the other 19 reviewed, including some by groups who never made *Billboard*'s Hot 100 singles chart (e.g., the Bards, C and the Shells, Downtown Collection, Alice Clark, B. B. and the Oscars). It began to enter the charts and move up steadily the next few weeks. It held the curious distinction of being the only record listed on the Hot 100 at that time without a writer or producer credit.

But *Billboard* and other music industry charts measure a records' performance by a combination of both sales and radio airplay, and it was with the latter that "The Pledge of Allegiance" lagged. As of the March 29 issue, only one station out of 14 surveyed by *Billboard* named the record as an add-on to their playlist. The lack of airtime hurt the sales beyond the core buyers who wanted in the first place, and as a result "The Pledge of Allegiance" peaked at #44 on April 12, 1969.

What prevented stations from playing a record by the top-rated television comic in the country? Was it his lack of hits previously? Possibly, but that has never stopped thousands of "one-hit wonders" from making the singles charts either. Was it because it was a spoken word record, and those rarely have become hits in a music-dominated singles market? Again, possibly, yet some spoken word singles made the top 10 after Red's record went off the market, including "Desiderata" by former television talk show host Les Crane in 1971.

What about its message? Was it a diatribe that turned off the left-leaning entertainment industry? That's another possibility; but if it had sold more copies, the stations no doubt would've been forced to play it. Two years previously, another spoken word record, "An Open Letter to

My Teenage Son" by Victor Lundberg, ended with the narrator telling his "son" that if he burned his draft card, he would no longer be his father. That managed to get enough sales and airplay in many markets to become a top 10 hit, even though many younger listeners probably objected to it.

The real reason probably lay in its running time of four minutes and 13 seconds. Of the 279 records to make the top 40 in *Billboard* in 1969, only 22—less than 10 percent—ran more than four minutes. Airtime is a precious commodity among broadcasters, and was especially so during that period, with most record producers realizing they had to have cuts that ran around no more than three and a half minutes to be considered for the playlist. The few records that did violate this time limit were virtually restricted to the biggest hitmakers of the day (e.g., Elvis Presley's "Suspicious Minds," Frank Sinatra's "My Way," and the song that was at #1 when "The Pledge of Allegiance" peaked, the Fifth Dimension's "Aquarius/Let the Sunshine In"). To give up nearly a minute more than usual to a middle-aged comic's recitation did not appeal to many programmers, and so with little airplay, once those wanting copies bought them, there was little other exposure for "The Pledge of Allegiance."

The recitation later became a standard part of Red's touring act, and sometimes he would sell copies of the record at his shows. It also became a "flexidisc" (a thin plastic square single you could put on your turntable) distributed by the Burger King restaurant chain later in 1969, and judging from the eBay website, more people apparently have copies of this version of "The Pledge of Allegiance" lying around than they do of the original single sold in stores. It had the familiar Rene Bouche caricature of Red in the upper left corner on the front, along with the Burger King logo, and the words of Red's speech were printed on the back. Red also delivered "The Pledge of Allegiance" in a July 4, 1970, celebration at Washington, D.C., which was recorded and released by Landmark Records on album titled *Proudly They Came*, along with other performances by Bob Hope, Dinah Shore and many more.

"The Pledge of Allegiance" also received much publicity from Red's camp about how it garnered 42 awards. I've never been able to find an exact list of what they were, but it's probably safe to say they came from various patriotic civic groups across America. One award that it did not receive was a Grammy Award for music excellence in the spoken word category. Red's "Pledge of Allegiance" was not even nominated in a field of five contenders that included "The Great White Hope" by James Earl Jones, "Home to the Sea" by Jesse Pearson, "Man on the Moon" by Walter Cronkite and the *Robert F. Kennedy: A Memorial* album. The winner was Art Linkletter, whose "We Love You, Call Collect" featured a dramatic dialogue on the phone between the longtime television personality and his real-life daughter Diane, playing a runaway girl confused about her life, including the drug scene around her, after which her father, played by Art, beseeches her to call him. Sadly, Diane later fell to her death from a window after taking drugs in 1969.

After his death, Red's "The Pledge of Allegiance" was pretty much forgotten by collectors until a ruling in June 26, 2002, by California's 9th U.S. Circuit Court found in favor of an lawsuit by Michael Newdow, an atheist, that the phrase "under God" in the pledge violated the policy of separation of church and state and needed to be omitted. Negative public outcry was immediate, and within a day, the court put a hold on its ruling. But in the wake of the controversy, many people remembered what Red said at the end of his recitation about whether "under God" would be removed from the pledge. As a result, prices for the copies of the record, even those of the flexidisc, went into double figures over the next few weeks, even though most collectors' guides valued them as worth less than that, and the website for Red's estate offers recorded copies of it for sale as well.

Meeting the President

Red performed "The Pledge of Allegiance" to perhaps his most important audience a year after he did so first on television. On Jan. 29, 1970, Red was the featured performer at the first "Evening at the White House," a planned series for famous entertainers to perform for newly inaugurated President Richard M. Nixon every four to six weeks. He did 50 minutes of jokes and routines and earned a standing ovation at the end.

In introducing the comic, President Nixon quipped, "He's been on television for 19 years, and the Vice President [Spiro Agnew] has never had an unkind word to say about him. Agnew says he's going to ask for equal time." Nixon's press secretary Connie Stuart said the idea for the evening series and for Red to be the opener came from the President.

Red had a surprise visitor there—his recurring player Chanin Hale. "Red turned around to me and said, 'Are you every place?!'" Hale laughed when recounting the ceremony.

The event made the front page of *The New York Times*, although it may have stunned Red if he read it when it jumped to page 31 and ended next to a large ad promoting an X-rated pornographic film called *Female Animal*. Reporter Mel Gussow got one very telling quote from Red after his performance: "You know, if I gave up television and worked on the things I do best—as Marcel [Marceau] told me to do—I'd be remembered."

He had no idea that with an announcement made two weeks later in the same paper, Red would get the chance to put that concept into practice.

The Bombshell Cancellation

In the Feb. 19, 1970, edition of *The New York Times*, television columnist Jack Gould wrote that CBS Chairman William Paley and President Bob Wood had removed Red's series from the 1970–71 lineup as part of an effort to update the network's image in the face of advertisers crying that television needed to be "modernized." The article came after the announcement that CBS was dropping *The Jackie Gleason Show* as well.

The odd thing about the item was that its headline was wrong—"CBS is Dropping Red Skelton After 16 Years as a TV Regular," when, in fact, he had been on CBS 17 years and 19 on television altogether—plus it called the network president Bob Woods rather than Wood. These are not typical errors for "The Paper of Record," and yet no corrections about them appeared in the next day's paper.

What did show up was an article saying that "Red Skelton is Moving to NBC" in an unsigned item. In making the announcement, NBC said Skelton's sustained appeal did meet that network's demographic needs for viewers in the 18–49 age range.

A series in the top 10 seasonal ratings cancelled—it was incredible, unheard of, unthinkable. But it happened to Red, for the first time ever in television history. Oh, there can be two technical arguments where it happened before, with *Gangbusters* in the middle of the 1952–53 season and *The Buick Circus Hour* in the 1952–53 season. But both shows were alternating weekly with two other top series—*Dragnet* and *The Milton Berle Show* respectively—and were designed to not run long per the whims of their advertisers.

In contrast, the cancellation of *The Red Skelton Hour* was a decision by CBS executives, and it was to a series that had run almost as long as coast-to-coast network television had been in existence. This cancellation was unprecedented and huge within the television industry.

Such an unusual circumstance prompted many questions, the most pressing of which I will attempt to answer fully now:

1) *Who was responsible for thinking up the notion?*

In his memoirs, Bill Hobin assigned the blame of the show's demise to CBS executive Fred Silverman, but that seems unlikely. Silverman had only become the assistant to CBS programming chief Mike Dann on Feb. 4, 1970, just two weeks before the cancellation was announced. Silverman did rise up to take Dann's position shortly thereafter, as Dann was upset with CBS for canceling its top shows and left to take a position with the Children's Television Workshop, the organization behind public television's hit children's series *Sesame Street*.

Most accounts have Bob Wood, who died in 1986, pushing the strategy to remove Red along with Gleason and *Petticoat Junction*, a rural-based sitcom that aired directly after Red's show from 1963 to 1967, in the initialize phase of "reverse aging" CBS. However, in his autobiography *As It Happened*, CBS Chairman William Paley claimed that he wrote a memo in 1965 to Wood's predecessor, Frank Stanton, about the problem CBS had with attracting too many old and rural-based audiences with its hit comedies, because the longer they ran, the older their viewers became. But he gave credit to Wood for laying out a strategy of how to handle the situation, namely by abandoning those series for new ones that appealed to younger, more urban audiences.

Others say Paley had to be convinced that Wood was right, especially on the idea of giving up on longtime stars Skelton and Gleason. According to Lewis J. Paper in *Empire: William S. Paley and the Making of CBS*, Broadcast Group President Richard A. "Dick" Jencks and President of the CBS Network Jack Schneider both backed Wood, who told Paley that "CBS is falling behind the times, and we have to get back in step."

Paper added that Skelton's audience had some of the worst demographics to attract advertisers in 1970. "Almost half the people who watched *The Red Skelton Show*, for example, were over the age of 50, and much of the remainder was probably under 12," Paper wrote.

When the discussion about the plan took place among all CBS executives, Paley said it did not go down easily, and that one researcher cried about the decision. Mike Dann also objected vociferously to the plan at the meeting, but Paley overruled him. Yet Paper claimed that even after Paley gave his seal of approval to the operation, he nonetheless called Wood once more to make sure the latter knew what he was doing.

2) *Why target a top 10 program like Red's? Weren't there other CBS series with similar demographics that had worse ratings?*

There certainly were, such as *Green Acres*, but they didn't have another component that loomed especially large on Skelton and Gleason: their salaries. Paper said both comedians asked to have their television contracts renewed for three years with raises, but they were doing so while the network figured Skelton generated only a $25,000 profit for CBS, while Gleason actually lost the network $300,000 with his costs.

Robert Orben insisted to me that canceling the show was more about prospective salary increases than demographics. "The excuse given with canceling Skelton's show was that it didn't have the right demographics. But we were all, individually, our contracts were up, including Red. When I joined the show in 1964, I had a six-year contract."

Associate producer Stanley Green concurred with Orben's take. "The show was doing well, but the show got more expensive. Everyone's contract being up and wanting more money affected it, but Red's particularly."

3) *Finally, was this a personal vendetta CBS Chairman William Paley had against Skelton?*

The true answer to that one may never be known. Sally Bedell Smith wrote in her biography of Paley, *In All His Glory*, that he "was known to consider Skelton uncouth," although she did not say specifically who told her that. To back this statement, she reported the fact that "Red Skelton wouldn't even take a phone call from Paley," without realizing that Red had a well-known aversion to talking to everyone on the phone, so perhaps her opinion should be taken with a grain of salt.

For his part, Paley wrote only three lines about Red in his autobiography, concluding that Red was "unique and a master" at doing skits. Such terse wording, and the fact that Paley had more glowing things to say about Bob Wood's strategy of dumping the down-home comedies ("In my mind, a good programmer always tries to stay ahead of his audience's tastes, rather than follow them blindly"), lend credence to the concept that Paley really did not agonize over dropping Skelton, and may have even enjoyed bidding him good riddance.

However, once that decision had been made, it was not Paley but Bob Wood who informed Red's executive producer Guy della Cioppa that the show was going off the air. Della Cioppa then had to relay that information to his staff while they prepared to tape what would be the final two shows on CBS.

The Staff Learns of the Cancellation

The first one della Cioppa told was producer Bill Hobin. He was shocked. "There had been no talk—not even rumors—concerning possible cancellation," Hobin recalled. He also learned that Red had not been told, so the two men met with him in his dressing room after taping his second-to-last show on a Tuesday night.

Hobin and della Cioppa instructed everyone but Red to leave his dressing room, then locked the door. This action was as unprecedented as the cancellation itself. Hobin delivered the news. He said Red didn't believe him, then made a joke before leaving. "He was probably still in a state of semi-shock when he went home," Hobin concluded.

"I think everybody knew how furious he was that he had been cancelled," June Lockhart said in recalling the show business buzz about Red at the time. She herself had been a victim of the demographic purge at CBS that year when the network canned *Petticoat Junction*, having replaced Bea Benaderet as the show's female lead in 1968, following the latter actress's death from cancer.

Yet unlike Red, Lockhart had been through cancellation before, when *Lost in Space* went off in 1968, and even from being dismissed from a hit show, when the producers revamped *Lassie* in 1964. As a result, she was more philosophical about her show's cancellation in 1970. "I like to look at the long range of a career," she said. "It being cancelled didn't affect me one way or another."

But on Red's show, few crew members handled it as smoothly as Lockhart did. The morning after he had told Red, Hobin addressed all the writers to deliver the news. Robert Orben quoted Hobin as saying, "Bob, what I'm about to tell you, I'm not kidding. We're cancelled." Orben thought it was a joke, as did his fellow scribes.

"It came as such a shock to us. We had no concept of that show being cancelled," he said. "We all thought we were fat and happy doing that show."

As Orben and the rest of the writers absorbed the information, Hobin summoned the rest of the production company together to drop the word. It hit the staff hard and off guard, and it did the same among Red's friends and industry observers, of which columnist James Bacon was both.

"I think a lot of people thought it was crazy, because kids were watching too," Bacon insisted. "I know my kids were, when they were teenagers."

Given the show's high ratings, there naturally was second-guessing among the show's staff as to what was the unstated cause for its cancellation. Hadn't they done everything the network wanted? When CBS suggested they hire as a guest Tiny Tim, a novelty act best known for his screechy freak hit record "Tiptoe Through the Tulips," didn't they do so willingly? And what about all the rock acts they put on too? It couldn't have been that they'd gone over budget, since Hobin had $93,000 left over to throw a farewell party, right? Whatever could it have been?

These questions slowly faded away a week later when the whole crew involved with the show had a farewell bash. In a transcript available on the website www.idoodit.com, Red came out to 45 seconds of applause on stage to the cast and crew, then quipped somewhat darkly "This is like having your own eulogy without a box!"

Red then recalled his years there at CBS and on television and thanked his personnel. Oddly, given all accounts of how he had reacted, Red told those assembled not to be angry with the network executives who canned the show, and to continue working for CBS if the network employed them. "These are all fine gentlemen, and they are still my friends, and to keep your jobs going, they find it necessary to change, and I hope for the best," he said in a calm voice.

After a few more words summarizing how much he loved the television industry, Red thanked those assembled again at the end of a six-minute speech, and the staff indicated their love for him with another 45-second round of clapping.

And then it was over. But only on CBS.

Moving Over to NBC

Ahead of the going-away party, executive producer Guy della Cioppa had taken matters into his own hands and met with NBC executives about transferring Red back to his former network. He was able to do so, but it might not have been the wisest thing to do at the time, in some people's opinions.

Red's frequent co-star Chanin Hale, for one, faulted the producer for being too quick in forcing the change, rather than holding out for the best deal for Red. "It was a case of moving too fast and miscommunication and bad decisions by a few people," she said. "NBC was not prepared to give him an hour and support him."

Where exactly did NBC stand at this time? Well, when recounting whether his fellow NBC executives were as taken off guard by CBS canning Red as Red's staff, West Coast head of programming Herb Schlosser told me, "I think we must've been." A top 10 show, even with the audience Red had, was not something one easily dismissed out of hand by the network, especially with a known name like Red.

"Skelton had a track record, so we took him," Schlosser said. "It was the wrong demo[graphic], but we felt it was worth trying."

Schlosser also acknowledged that doubts about the abilities of some new series on the planned 1970 fall schedule versus a known property like Red played on the minds of NBC programming heads. "It was true then and true today: No matter how well you do at development, you always say, 'Dammit, we're missing something,'" he said. Skelton fit the bill for NBC's need.

With all that in mind, NBC negotiated with della Cioppa, and the best thing the two parties could hammer out was a last-minute change in the 1970 fall schedule so that come September, Red would air on Mondays from 7:30 to 8 P.M., leading into TV's biggest hit at the time, *Rowan and Martin's Laugh-In*—the same show that made Red's brand of TV comedy look ancient. Such slotting struck some observers as odd, given the contrast in the two shows' appeal, but Schlosser said since both were comedy variety shows, it was felt that the younger, more upscale audience for *Rowan and Martin's Laugh-In* might give Red a chance and sample him before their show started at 8.

As for the show's reduced length, it's naturally easier to clear a half hour of TV time than a full one. And given Red's situation, he and della Cioppa pretty much had to accept what was offered if they wanted to be back on the air at the start of the next season, although in retrospect, he might have been better off holding out for a midseason replacement deal for a full hour show for Red instead, or even just staying with CBS or any of the other networks doing a series of specials. But that's all hindsight.

The final *Red Skelton Hour* aired on June 23, 1970. CBS replaced it and the hour western that preceded it, *Lancer*, with a two-hour slot of movies. (Earlier summer replacements had been *Showtime*, a London-based variety show from June 11 to Sept. 17, 1968, and *The Liberace Show*, also a London-based variety show hosted by the flamboyant pianist who guested on Red's show in 1964 and 1968, which ran from July 15 to Sept. 16, 1969. The deal Red's production company had with Sir Lew Grade about sharing entertainment since the mid–1960s resulted in the airing of these British-based variety shows, just as had happened with *Hippodrome* in 1966 and *Spotlight* in 1967.) Less than a month after his last airing on CBS, Red went into production on his half-hour series for NBC.

So Red Skelton, who had started TV on NBC with a half-hour show 19 years earlier, returned to the same network in the same length of time. One could say his television career was going full circle. The only problem was that it turned out the circle would be broken after just one more season.

7

1970–1971: "It Would Be Presumptuous to Change, Modernize or Innovate Skelton"

Going into its 20th season, people involved in *The Red Skelton Show* gave the impression to the outer world that the important fact was that Red still was on the air, and not the way CBS had dismissed him from their schedule a few months earlier. But anyone familiar with the television industry realized that *The Red Skelton Show* (not *The Red Skelton Hour* anymore, nor just *Red*, as David Inman's *The TV Encyclopedia* referred to it in 1991) would have some formidable obstacles to overcome when it debuted in the fall of 1970. Among them were the following:

1) *A change in networks:* Red had switched from NBC to CBS in 1953 in a period where it was rather common for shows to change networks, since often in the 1950s, the sponsor had more control over when and where a show would run rather than a network. But the big money game show scandals of the late 1950s resulted in more controls by the networks of the series in response to how advertisers meddled in the outcomes of such programs as *Twenty-One* and *The $64,000 Question.*

As a result, hopping from one network to another in the 1960s was infrequent, especially among nighttime shows. There were only 11 series that changed networks during continuous nighttime runs in the 1960s, and of those, eight lasted only one year after their transfer. (They were *The Detectives, Get Smart!, The Ghost and Mrs. Muir, Hazel, The Jack Benny Program, The Joey Bishop Show, Peter Gunn* and *The Price Is Right.*)

For the other three, *Wagon Train* came to ABC in 1962 after spending its fifth season on NBC as the #1 show on television. NBC retaliated by programming an even more elaborate western, the 90-minute *The Virginian*, opposite it, which knocked *Wagon Train* down to #25 in the

1962–63 season, only a few notches ahead of *The Virginian*. *Wagon Train* struggled thereafter before ending on ABC in 1965 after three years on the network. That same year, *Alfred Hitchcock Presents* (also known as *The Alfred Hitchcock Hour*) ended a 10-year run that included hopscotching from CBS to NBC in 1960, back to CBS in 1962, and then finally to NBC for the last (1964–65) season. The remaining show in this setup also had a milestone in 1965, when *My Three Sons* left ABC for CBS under a seven-year contract that turned out well for the latter network in the ratings.

So there you have it—only three shows in the decade prior to Red's move flourished more than a year by the switch in channels, obviously not a pleasant precedent.

2) *A reduction in running time:* Going from 60 to 30 minutes cuts down on the perception of a show's prestige. However, like switching networks, it was a common practice in the 1950s, with around 40 nighttime series shortening their time periods, which became rare in the 1960s. And in this case, all the news was bad. The first to do so was *Fair Exchange*, an hour-long situation comedy that produced low viewership for CBS on Friday nights from September through December 1962. Irate fans protested enough that the network gave it a half-hour incarnation on Thursdays; but it didn't work either, and the show was gone by 1963.

The series that replaced part of the hour-long *Fair Exchange* was *The Twilight Zone*, which stumbled in the time slot as a revamped hour series starting in January 1963. When it came back in the fall of 1963 as a half-hour show, it lasted just one more year. The same happened with *Wagon Train* in the fall of 1963, when ABC decided to emulate *The Virginian* and make it a 90-minute oater. Unfortunately, ABC put it on against the CBS hits *The Lucy Show*, *The Danny Thomas Show* and *The Andy Griffith Show*, and *Wagon Train* went down in flames. It shrunk back to 60 minutes in its final season of 1964–65, withering opposite *My Favorite Martian* and *The Ed Sullivan Show* on CBS and *Walt Disney* on NBC.

Several series in the fall of 1965 went from 60 to 30 minutes and vanished a year later (a few sooner than that). The teen rock shows *Hullabaloo* on NBC and *Shindig* on ABC went this route, although *Shindig* aired two half-hour shows, on Thursdays and Saturdays. One other variety show, *The King Family Show*, slimmed down as well following a run as an hour show since January 1965; a year later, the show was off ABC's Saturday lineup. And NBC's *Dr. Kildare* took a page from the success of *Peyton Place* on ABC and attempted to revive the show's sagging appeal by making it a continuing 30-minute drama on Mondays and Tuesdays. It didn't work; the show ended in August of 1966.

This track record was horrible. If there was any solace in considering it, it was that another show on the 1970–71 schedule was undergoing the same predicament. ABC subtracted half of *Love, American Style* from its lineup to move it up before the variety series *This Is Tom Jones*, but that show's audience fell off enough that ABC pumped the former show back to an hour into the latter's time slot in January 1971. As for Red's show ... well, keep reading.

3) *The series it replaced*: *The Red Skelton Show* took over the time slot of *My World ... and Welcome to It*, a distinctive sitcom adored by the critics. Based on the humor of cartoonist James Thurber, it incorporated animation in telling the whimsical pressures befalling artist John Monroe at home and at work. The series won the Emmy for Outstanding Comedy Series in 1970 despite having already being cancelled, making it the only sitcom to run just a year to win the honor. (The competition for the award reflected how barren the sitcom field was in 1969–70, which included *The Bill Cosby Show*, which ran just two years with the comedian playing a teacher, and should not be confused with the later hit *The Cosby Show*; *The Courtship of Eddie's Father*; *Love, American Style*; and *Room 222*.) The show's star, William Windom, won an Emmy for Outstanding Continuing Performance by Actor in a Leading Role in a Comedy.

To think that such a series was to end in favor of a comedian who'd spent 19 years on the air with less lofty artistic goals galled the critics and no doubt predisposed them to hate Red's show, no matter how much improved it might have been. Indeed, Goodman Ace, one-time writer for *The Milton Berle Show*, noted with scorn in his television column in the March 14, 1970, issue of *Saturday Review* that in an upcoming season where the networks were emphasizing "relevance and social awareness," his beloved *My World ...* was being replaced by the aging *Red Skelton Show*. The truth was that NBC already cancelled the sitcom, with its lackluster ratings, before adding Skelton in its place.

Despite all these concerns, Red's team planned to keep the show on NBC mostly the way it had been on CBS, only on a reduced scale. They thought, "Why mess with success?" and assumed large Red's audience would follow him wherever he would go.

Oh, how wrong they were.

Welcome Back to NBC, Red!

At first, things augured well with Red's arrival to NBC behind the scenes. Herb Schlosser recalled the star making a hit with the executives by amusing them during the following incident: "When we had done the deal and scheduled the show, [NBC Vice President] Tom Sarnoff, threw a luncheon for him. There were about 10 or 12 of us executives, and Tom asked each of one of us to get up and speak 30 seconds. It was all very nice.

"When Skelton got up, he then mimicked the manner all of us got up to speak. Some slouched; some shot up quickly. He did it to a 'T.' I know he did it perfectly with me."

So much for Red's talents. But the show's somewhat fossilized format did have the executives concerned, and Schlosser thinks they had discussed the possibility of changing it before relying on the production crew to make whatever changeovers they thought Red could handle. "It was not like when we took Jack Paar, which was a different formatted show on nighttime [1962–1965] than what it was when he was on late night [on *The Tonight Show*, 1957–1962]," Schlosser said.

In the end, the format of *The Red Skelton Show* was left the same with a revamped staff for new ideas. And an interesting one it was.

Meet the New Crew

When Red's executive producer Guy della Cioppa sold the star to NBC, he halved the budget of the CBS hour show, forcing a reduction in the writing staff. Also, most of the other personnel who worked on the CBS show were employees of the network and not Red, so they did not make the transfer either. In effect, the show was starting from scratch, apart from head writer Mort Green, who continued to do the "Silent Spot."

The new writing team consisted of Jeffrey Barron, Lionel Burt and Pat McCormick. Of these three, McCormick is probably the most familiar name, as he later would go on to be head writer for *The Tonight Show Starring Johnny Carson* for most of the 1970s and act occasionally in the show's skits, usually with some outrageous outfit affixed to his tall, bulky frame. He also attracted general notice playing shifty Big Enos Burdette in three *Smokey and the Bandit* movie comedies with Burt Reynolds from 1977 to 1983.

When he joined Red's show, McCormick already had won an Emmy (for Outstanding Writing Achievement in Variety in 1966 for *The Danny Kaye Show*, where he served as a staff writer in 1965–1967) and both wrote and served as on-air sidekick on *The Don Rickles Show* in 1968–69. After his brief tenure with *The Red Skelton Show* came much performing and writing for television series and specials, including regular roles on *The New Bill Cosby Show* in 1972–73 and *Gun Shy* in 1983.

Sad to say, I attempted to contact McCormick in the fall of 2002, but his former personal manager Larry Spellman told me the writer/performer is now too ill to do interviews. As for Lionel Burt, he seems to have fallen through the cracks of television history, while Jeffrey Barron rebounded to win an Emmy for Outstanding Writing for a Variety or Music Program in 1982 for *SCTV Network*, followed by three nominations in the same category for the same series in 1983. He also wrote for *Wonder Woman* in the 1970s.

Supervising them all were writers-turned-producers Dee Caruso and Gerald Gardner. They came to prominence in the early 1960s, with Gardner credited as author of a few humorous political books while Caruso served as co-editor of *Sick* magazine (a lackluster imitation of the satirical *Mad* magazine that went out of business in 1980). The two men then earned Emmy nominations for writing for the satirical New York-based comedy *That Was the Week That Was* in 1963–64 before going to Hollywood to do scripts for *Get Smart!*, *The Ghost and Mrs. Muir* and *The Monkees*. For the latter, they wrote nearly half the sitcom's episodes and also served as script and story editors.

Upon getting this new job, Gardner told Dwight Whitney of *TV Guide* that "It would be presumptuous to change, modernize or innovate Skelton.... What we're trying to do is create a show faithful to a character people love."

But while trying to do that, Gardner and Caruso learned they had to create a show Red loved too, which was not as easy to do as they thought. They would end up leaving before the end of the season, as would writers Barron and Burt, who were replaced by Red's old writers Arthur Phillips (who had been with the CBS show from 1961 until the network canned it) and Larry Rhine (who worked with Red from 1963 to 1968). It turned out to be too little too late, however; but let's not get ahead of our story yet.

Don't Forget Our New Director

Also coming on board was Terry Kyne to replace Howard Quinn as the series' director. Kyne came to prominence in Canada by producing and directing a late-night series called *Nightcap* from 1963 through 1967 written by Chris Bearde, who then went south to America to score fame and fortune on *Rowan and Martin's Laugh-In*, among other series.

"I came down in 1969," Kyne told me. "I worked on *The Steve Allen Show* [a syndicated talk show hosted by the comedian from 1968 to 1972] for a season. There may have been one in between on CBS, and then I got a call from someone at NBC."

That someone was Herb Schlosser, who wanted a director with a comedy background to do the show, Kyne noted. Kyne met with della Cioppa and then Red, who told Kyne about his concerns regarding the direction on his most recent CBS shows. Specifically, della Cioppa felt the director wasn't getting any close-ups or reactions of Red. A look at any of the 1970–71 shows can attest to the fact that Kyne fulfilled Red's request, as the comedian always was seen closely and clearly as needed for each sketch.

Kyne had no problems on first meeting Red. The star was friendly and gently chided his British accent. The director had been familiar with his work despite not being in America long, noting that he had watched Red's movies while he was a boy growing up in England.

But Kyne had one obstacle going against him—with the show going to just a half hour this year, it was decided Red needed only one day to rehearse and then tape his material, rather than the Monday rehearsal and Tuesday taping as had been done for years on CBS. Kyne found out he had rather busy Mondays to deal with his star.

"We used to meet Monday mornings at 7:30," Kyne recalled. "They would give him scripts a week ahead, and he would give his opinions and be nice about it, but he often told the writers, 'I don't know if this will work too well,' meaning he wanted them to change some material."

Next came dress rehearsal on stage with Red. Red would walk through the sketches, then let a stand-in walk through his part while he would be in the bleachers. Red would watch, usually without saying much, according to Kyne, as the stand-in would also rehearse with the guest stars. Kyne would give the guest stars directions while Red watched.

Meanwhile, as before, Red mulled over jokes to insert into the proceedings, and Kyne found during taping that he had to watch his star carefully for unplanned ad-libs or activity. As before, Red did a lot of ad-libbing, so it was a little difficult for Kyne to follow him all the time.

But at least Red listened to Kyne's critique of each rehearsal, as the director would give him notes about what he thought was not working by saying, "It's not funny to me, Red," or some similar statement. Red's respect for Kyne's comments over those of Caruso and Gardner soon became apparent, much to the producers' dismay. "He never would listen to producers, only directors," Kyne said.

Actually, Gardner's and Caruso's problems with Red started as soon as they did the initial show for NBC. It was clear they had not earned the comedian's trust the way their predecessor, Bill Hobin, did as producer, and their tenure on the show did not run past the end of 1970.

The Taping of the First Show

Red started working on his first NBC show on July 13, 1970—his 57th birthday. He told Dwight Whitney in *TV Guide* he still didn't quite understand why CBS had canned his series. "I don't know what this 'demographics' bit is all about," he said. "They say they want a group I don't reach. I'm a comedian who does one thing. No way I could reach out and get fans I haven't got already. All you do is kill what's already there."

In that spirit, della Cioppa, Gardner and Caruso had set up the show to be done much the same way the CBS hour shows had been, only in a condensed format. Red would do a monologue and brief pantomime, followed by a sketch involving one of his characters, his "Silent Spot" routine, and if time permitted, a song by a guest or two. There was a basic assumption that people already knew the characters involved, even though the show aired earlier and on another network that season, so there was very little to accommodate or attract a new audience on purpose, a decision that is quite questionable in retrospect.

Nevertheless, the show proceeded with Mike Connors, then starring in the hit CBS detective series *Mannix*, as Red's guest star and a tune from a never-was chanteuse named Robin Wilson. Connors did a sketch where Red's Clem Kadiddlehopper pretended to protect the former in a hotel room from being attacked before testifying about a crime. It was the sort of silly thing done previously for years by Red, although he had to juice up the proceedings more than usual due to weak jokes ("I'm a private eye," Clem said to the hotel maid, played by busty blonde Carol Wayne, later the Tea Time Lady on the Art Fern sketches on *The Tonight Show with Johnny Carson*. Wayne responded with "Well, your other eye doesn't look too private").

The one real item of note about the sketch was an ad-lib that elicited a good amount of audience laughs and applause for those familiar with his just-ended reign at CBS. Eyeing Wayne's physique, Red said, "I frisk her and we won't last 17 years here, I tell you that!"

Otherwise, the taping did not go altogether smoothly. The first sketch involving him playing a gangster who was really a mayor confused him, and he also received coldly a "Silent Spot" involving him as a dentist. After the taping ran later than usual, Red met with his producers backstage to complain about what he had been given to do.

"You picked the two worst subjects—crime and dentistry," he told them testily as Whitney quoted Red. "I can quit right now, and there's not a damn thing NBC can do about it." Someone in the room responded that those bits had some nice moments, to which Red shot back, "I want funny moments. I don't want nice moments."

Apparently the "nice moments" didn't appeal to NBC either. It wound up as the fourth show on the air rather than the first. Soon thereafter, Gardner and Caruso left the show. Director Terry Kyne thinks they were eased out, even though they were nice, because they didn't seem to have too many ideas as producers that appealed to Red and della Cioppa.

Kyne pointed out one example of the problems with Gardner and Caruso as producers. For music, they wanted to have as regulars a contemporary group like Harpers Bizarre (a male quartet who hit with the easy-listening recording "Feelin' Groovy" in 1967 and appeared on Red's show as guests that same year). But they couldn't get Harpers Bizarre, so they settled on the Burgundy Street Singers, a group of about a dozen or so young males and females who were regulars on the 1969 CBS summer series *The Jimmie Rodgers Show* but otherwise had nothing much of note in terms of professional success. Kyne said the men looked for the photogenic quality of the group members rather than singing ability to determine who would get the most time on air, and as part of that decision-making process, they didn't pick the lead singer, because of the way he looked.

But before Gardner and Caruso left, they stayed on to produce what turned out to be the debut show of the season. Judging its reviews, though, they might have been better off leading with the Connors show.

Guest Starring—Jerry Lewis and Spiro Agnew?

Of all the people a star might have wanted to introduce their series for its debut in 1970, Vice President Spiro T. Agnew probably was way, WAY down the list. One of the more controversial individuals to hold that post, Agnew's blasts against liberals, including those in the media and Hollywood, made him a divisive and hardly endearing figure. But Red had entertained for him and President Nixon at the White House in January and apparently thought that having someone in his position would give the show credence.

As if Agnew's introduction wasn't odd enough, the show also offered Jerry Lewis as its first NBC guest star. Lewis already had bombed twice as host of his own television variety shows on ABC in 1963 and NBC from 1967 to 1969 and was on the wane in popularity—hardly the person you'd want to use to attract viewers. Yet here he was, and in a rare situation for a "Silent Spot," which usually used no guest stars, he was doing physical shtick as the helper to Red's magician. He was booked for the show because he had starred in a World War II movie comedy Gardner and Caruso wrote, *Which Way to the Front?*, which opened and closed in most theaters in the summer of 1970 within a week.

Agnew and Lewis in no way aided Skelton when it came to reviewers assessing the show when it hit the air on Sept. 14, 1970, although most commented on Lewis solely and unfavorably. And it wasn't just Lewis that came off badly either. "Mr. Skelton appeared ill at ease in his foreshortened format," wrote Jack Gould in *The New York Times* in a terse review, one of his last before stepping down as the paper's television critic in 1971.

A *Variety* reviewer complained that "Even at half its previous length, which is a decided improvement, the Skelton brand of comedy isn't for the young swingers or even the middle-aged now people.... It does seem bound to an old—accent old—formula, the new production and creative staff notwithstanding."

Underlining that opinion was television scribe and critic Harlan Ellison of the *Los Angeles Free Press*. After acknowledging he was no fan of Red's, he summed up the show as "Old, old, incredibly old. Pratfalls, the perennial seagull jokes, that moronic Silent Spot, his unfailing phony laughter at his own jokes, and in case no stone of low comedy was left unturned, the abominable Jerry Lewis (fresh from new horrors on his telethon) added a maudlin show biz note of cheap sentimental homage a la Danny Thomas."

The latter comment did have some credibility. Yes, Lewis had just been seen the previous weekend as host of the annual Muscular Dystrophy Association's Labor Day telethon, and he did pay tribute to Red on the air at the end of the magician play. Stopping the music and motioning for the microphone to come down, he said the following (I've kept his garbled syntax and grammar intact for the sake of accuracy):

"I would just like to step out of character for a moment, due to a coronary arrest [audience laughs]. I feel that I would be remiss if I allowed this to be any normal television guest appearance sketch, where a guest comes on a show and they perform and they exit and they're thanked by the host. This is an exceptionally unique and exceptional performance in that I have been referred to by many as a clown, and I guess this is the first time in my life that one of my dreams have come true, and that was to work with the clown mastery of the master. I know that he's embarrassed, but that's what he is [audience starts applauding], so I leave the stage to him."

And he did so, to a surprised, delighted Red. The sentiments wear thin, however, when you realize that the two worked together as guests on *The Steve Allen Show* in 1958. And if Lewis really had wanted to perform with Red before, why had it taken two decades to find a time and place for them do so?

Putting that issue aside, in truth, the Lewis skit was not as bad as reviewers said. (*Variety* termed it "a belabored sketch that was as slovenly for the mashed eggs and prop debris as it was funless.") "The Magic Act" did suffer from poor editing and, like most of the sketches on Red's show this season, ran too long, but it does have a modest amount of charm to it. The two do a cute *pas de deux* routine between doing tricks; Red sticks a saber into a box that comes out the other side in a different angle in a clever visual gimmick; and Lewis manages to crack up his host as he fights against being put into another box to be sawed in half.

No, the most upsetting thing about the sketch is how old Red looks in it. His hair is unkempt and scraggly within a minute of the start of the routine, and his face has beads of sweat popping up on his lined face. He looks every bit his 57 years here. And unfortunately, as the season progressed, the series revealed its age as well, as routines became more hoary, trite and unfunny. Somehow, when it went to half its length, *The Red Skelton Show* lost even more than that amount of enjoyment that season.

All these critiques mean nothing in television compared to the ratings, as any regular viewers knows. So here was the final judgment on the debut; the show's competition on CBS, *Gunsmoke*, which appealed to a lot of the same viewers as Red had, finished at #9 that week; Red came in at #40. He did better than the series running opposite him on ABC, the leaden drama *The Young Lawyers*, starring Lee J. Cobb as head of a legal firm in Boston with two hip attorneys ready to defend the poor and downtrodden (in essence, a courtroom knockoff of the hit detective drama *Mod Squad* that some derided as "The Lawed Squad"). But it was clear Red no longer was a huge television presence, both then and in succeeding weeks.

Promotions and Cast Additions

Despite the lackluster start, indications are NBC did want Red's show to be a hit. They spent the next three shows having their top stars under contract introducing the show—Dean Martin, Jack Benny and Johnny Carson—and also had leads from their other big series guest as well, including Raymond Burr from *Ironside*, Michael Landon and Dan Blocker from *Bonanza* and James Drury from *The Virginian* (retitled *The Men from Shiloh* that season).

The Drury shot was a favorite booking of Red's, according to Kyne. "He told him, 'My wife and I watch you every week, and we want to give you a special gift,'" Kyne said. And with that, Red gave some authentic western guns from his collection to the man who played television's Virginian.

Red also guest-starred on the first *Dean Martin Show* of the season, and made himself available to the network in two high-priority specials, *Jack Benny's Twentieth Anniversary Special* on Nov. 16, 1970, and John Wayne's patriotic *Swing Out, Sweet Land* on April 8, 1971. He also popped up on *The Tonight Show Starring Johnny Carson* on Feb. 7, 1971, along with an incredible assortment of other name guest stars—Jack Benny, John Wayne, Peter Falk, Ben Gazzara, John Cassavetes and Ann-Margret.

(Interestingly, all this activity didn't seem to make everyone realize Red had moved to NBC, even the editors of the fan magazine *Modern Screen*. A gossipy article titled "Money Can't Buy a Daughter's Happiness," about Red's concern over his child Valentina's marriage in the September 1970 issue, concluded with a note to "See *The Red Skelton Show* on CBS.")

Moving on, two performers this season showed up often enough to be considered the closest thing to regulars on the show along with Red, the Burgundy Street Singers and David Rose's orchestra, although other sources have listed other people who, in truth, barely turned up in even half the shows. Chanin Hale and Jan Arvan popped up most frequently, although that originally was not the plan. Asked if she thought she'd be able to do the series when it changed to NBC, Hale told me, "I didn't expect to, because they wanted a new crew, new writers and so on. But he [Red] wasn't happy, so he brought me and Jan back. It wasn't a couple of weeks before they brought me in again."

Authors Tim Brooks and Earle Marsh, in their *Complete Directory to Prime Time Network TV Shows*, liken Arvan and Hale and a few others who weren't really regulars as part of a "repertory company" for the show. It actually was more of the same series as before, with one player—Red—hogging all the good lines and most of the camera time while the others barely had anything to say or do. Often their characters did not speak, even outside of a "Silent Spot," and stayed within the background in skits. They were not identified at the show's start either. Any chance that Hale, Arvan or any others would become a star here, such as what happened to Carol Burnett as a supporting regular on *The Garry Moore Show* in 1958–64, was squelched from Day One of the new season.

"The Best (?) of Red Skelton"

All the efforts to promote the show and change its cast were in vain, because the production and writing simply were not up to what the show had received on CBS in the 1960s. Taking a look at the four videotapes compiled by the Skelton estate as "The Best of Red Skelton" in 1998 reveals the show's warts all too obviously.

The pacing is sluggish. The jokes are unexceptional. As a result of both, Red is ad-libbing constantly, often straining to create excitement. Red had not done this sort of desperate measure since the mid–1950s, and it looked just awkward. The few young guest stars who appeared with him came across as unamused by his cracks, such as "Mama" Cass Elliott and Chad Everett in a leaden bit where San Fernando Red attempted to get Cass married to Chad without the latter knowing about it amid lame fat jokes about Cass.

"The Best of Red Skelton" does not present whole shows from 1970–71 except for another dreary Christmas show written by Red and done without an audience, with Freddie the Freeloader befriending some needy children with the help of a cop played by Leslie Nielsen (during his stolid serious acting days, unfortunately for us). The other bits presented as Red's "best" make you worry about how awful even the "average" ones were. Among many problems, special sound effects are timed improperly, and Red's characters are placed in tiresome circumstances, such as Clem Kadiddlehopper questioning Gene Barry for the 1970 census while Barry is hiding his lover from his wife.

Worst of all had to be when Red reprised Junior, the "mean widdle kid," in one show where Audrey Meadows played Junior's mom. The sight of middle-aged Meadows and Skelton pretending to be much younger than their years—without any special makeup—was insulting to them and the audience, and the plotline of having Junior trying to wake up his mother early was just irritating and humorless. It's as if the writers were at their wits' ends trying to come up with new material for these characters.

Even a new character Red introduced—Ludwig von Humperdoo, an eccentric scientific inventor with a Teutonic accent and a vest tightly covering what looked like a distended stomach—was as uninspired in action as he sounds in description. He showed up only twice during the run, first on the Nov. 23, 1970, show, and probably is not remembered even by the most devoted Skelton fan. (Red had used the surname in love letters to his wife before the character debuted.)

Also, Red's age did not seem to be taken into account, particularly by Mort Green in his "Silent Spot" material. Twice on the tapes, Red plays men lusting after younger women (one of them being the ever-youthful-looking Chanin Hale), a none-too-appealing setup given his obvious aging in close-ups. And if there was any doubt as to the conservatism of Red's comedy, just listen to his unfunny, very dated monologue about feminism. The monologues this season had a few taped bits interspersed between them, and in this one, an actress playing opposite a similarly unbilled Jack Riley (later to be the ultra-neurotic Mr. Carlin on *The Bob Newhart Show*) informs Riley that even though she's the American president, she can't meet with him at one time because she has a beauty appointment at the same hour. Har de har har.

Chanin Hale also pointed out to me the following weakness that came across when she viewed the collection: "By that time, [Red] had a very definite style, a rhythm. I will have to admit he did fall back on his old tricks, and it shows in watching the sketches back to back, which it did not when we did it weekly."

There are a few bright spots on the tapes. David Rose and his orchestra transferred with Red from CBS and provided background music that is smoothly performed and relaxing, doing a great job of setting the mood in the skits all the time. Thank God no one decided to get rid of Rose during the transfer to NBC.

The new opening to the show is also appealing. The word "RED" appears in stylized letters as the camera zooms out, then at what would be to the right of "D," Red as his character Deadeye ambles and smiles at the camera. Then there's a cut to two clean-cut blondes in vintage 1970s white go-go outfits (both members of the Burgundy Street Singers) bringing up a swing that has "The Red Skelton Show" title superimposed on it. Another cut puts Deadeye going back and forth on the swing and flashes the name of the night's guest star, followed in similar fashion by George Appleby, Clem Kadiddlehopper and so on. Visually, it's what people in the industry would call a "grabber."

Beyond those points, there's precious little else about the tapes to enjoy. If nothing else, the tapes confirm that there were two sets of producers that season, a situation barely recalled by the second one, Perry Cross. I tried to interview Gerald Gardner and Dee Caruso, but I could not find Gardner, and Caruso cut me off when I talked to him on Sept. 19, 2002, by curtly noting he was under the gun to get a script done and didn't have time to talk. After saying "Thank you for considering me," he hung up. I didn't call him back.

Enter Perry Cross

Perry Cross had spent nearly 15 years in network television production prior to his association with Skelton. "I started producing in 1956," he said. "My first show was Ernie Kovacs. We replaced *Caesar's Hour* for the summer."

From there, he worked on other shows, most notably *The Tonight Show* with Jack Paar and the early years of Johnny Carson in the 1960s, as well as the disastrous *The Jerry Lewis Show* in 1963. His experience with such strong comic types made him an obvious choice to be considered as producer of Red's show.

Cross said NBC contacted him about doing *The Red Skelton Show*, and he met muster with Skelton and executive producer Guy della Cioppa to do the job, so he was hired. He carried on largely the same mission that Gardner and Caruso had received.

Cross said his duty on the show was to create a similar show as Red had on CBS, in the hope of capturing the audience he had at the time. He considered updating the show to appeal to a younger, more sophisticated audience before nixing the notion.

"There was some thought given to that, but it was difficult to do that with Red, because he was so used doing his characters his way," he said. "It's very hard to change someone who's used to doing something one way their entire life."

Terry Kyne, who remained as the show's director under Cross, concurred with that assessment. He recalled how writers would present new ideas to him and add, "Red, it's funny," but Red would insist, "You may think it's funny, but I'm me. I can't change."

So even as the show floundered, Skelton stuck by his process of doing his same routine with his old characters taped within a day's time. Cross said the process was the same with him and Kyne doing the show as it had been under Caruso and Gardner—they blocked it, did a run-through without Red using a stand-in, and then taped it with him.

Still, there was one disaster that showed Red could be as cantankerous as in his CBS days if a sketch displeased him during a rehearsal. Kyne said during one Silent Spot where there were problems showing the passage of time in the skit, Red was so infuriated with it that he left the studio for the parking lot.

"He's gone. He won't be back," David Rose told the stunned crew, as Rose was used to the occasional irrational outburst by Red. Cross didn't believe him and chased Red, then came back stunned and announced, "Did you know Red got in his Rolls Royce and nearly hit me?" "We had to cancel the shoot," Kyne concluded.

Cross said another obstacle was the show's half-hour time limit to do routines and a song. It made it really constricting to get guests, according to Cross. That shows up particularly in the lineup. Many of the last guests were repeats from prior seasons—the aforementioned Martha Raye, Audrey Meadows, Vincent Price, Mickey Rooney, George Gobel, and Walter Brennan. They were the same old guests, getting older.

With stale guests, a star obstinate enough to make changes despite a staff eager to try new approaches, and a fair amount of backstage turnover, *The Red Skelton Show* clearly was on its last legs creatively. The ratings reflected a downturn too, but there was more than just a reduced audience that hurt Red this season.

The Changing Face of Network Television

If it had just been the ratings alone being used to measure whether to renew *The Red Skelton Show* in 1971, the series actually might have stood a decent chance. It was no blockbuster, but it consistently finished around the top 35 to 40 programs each week—a borderline case, but still acceptable for renewal under normal circumstances.

Unfortunately, there were several complicating factors at the time. Red's audience remained as old as it was on CBS, and therefore not too appealing with advertisers wanting younger buyers. In fact, if anything the demographics argument grew louder in 1971 than when CBS kicked off Red in 1970, and all the networks went after anything deemed as having too many rural or old viewers. *Mayberry R.F.D.* and *Hee Haw* went off CBS even though they finished an impressive #15 and #16 in the ratings (*Hee Haw*, by the way, inherited Red's CBS time slot on Tuesdays), and not far behind them, NBC got rid of *The Men from Shiloh* (formerly *The Virginian*) at #18.

Another problem for Red was that the FCC succeeded in passing a ruling that the networks had to limit their nighttime programming a half hour less each night to allow for more local and syndicated (sold individually to stations or groups of stations) programs. The networks decided to release the 7:30–8 P.M. periods back to stations, and as a result, shows already in those slots that were not faring well were prime candidates for extinction.

Herb Schlosser said these factors, especially demographics, probably played a part in NBC deciding to cancel the show, although he emphasized he was speculating about the reasons for an event that happened more than 30 years ago. He thought that deciding what shows would most appeal to advertisers played a key role in Red going off NBC.

"We were probably trying to think of something with a longer life, and it may have taken longer to sell his show at that time," he said. "The demos were beginning to become more important."

And whereas Skelton was gangbusters in rural areas, particularly the South and the Midwest, he lacked considerable appeal in the major markets, according to Schlosser. "He would not be able to deliver to New York, Los Angeles and Chicago," he said.

Whatever the real reason, in the Feb. 3, 1971, issue of *Variety*, reporter Bill Greeley broke the news that *The Red Skelton Show* "is doubtful to return" on NBC the next season. The paper made the announcement official in its March 10 issue, at the same time noting the show was finishing a respectable #35 in the last week's rating period.

Red wasn't the only one hurt by the business factors either in 1971. That spring had the biggest wave of former top hits being canceled in one season ever. Beside the ones listed earlier, and Red of course, CBS took off *Lassie, Hogan's Heroes, The Ed Sullivan Show, Green Acres, The Beverly Hillbillies,* and *Family Affair*. NBC brushed aside *Wild Kingdom, The Kraft Music Hall, Julia, The Name of the Game* and *The Andy*

Williams Show. ABC dropped *The Johnny Cash Show, The Lawrence Welk Show* and the nighttime versions of *The Newlywed Game* and *Let's Make a Deal.* (The latter ran on ABC starting in January 1971 opposite Red's show to replace the moribund *Young Lawyers.*)

Some of these familiar names reappeared in the fall of 1971 as syndicated shows in new productions—*Hee Haw, Lassie, Wild Kingdom, The Newlywed Game, Let's Make a Deal* and *The Lawrence Welk Show.* Red wasn't among them, though.

Finishing Off Red's Run

The latter situation brings up an interesting question: Since his ratings were just as good, if not better than Welk's, with somewhat similar demographics, was there any talk about keeping Red's show alive in syndication? "Not that it came to my attention," according to Perry Cross. "I don't think [the idea] ever came up," concurred Hollywood columnist and longtime Skelton pal James Bacon.

Chances are that Red probably was tired of the grind, and the thought of having to make another change of allegiances for the second time in as many years (from CBS to NBC to syndication) following two public dismissals by these networks probably did not thrill him. "He was peeved at the cancellations," Bacon noted.

And so Red's show ended its Monday night run on March 15, 1971, with its 24th and last original installment, the first of several ironies during his last season. Here, it featured a spoof of *Ironside* (whose stars had appeared on Red's second show that year) with Sebastian Cabot, whose sitcom *Family Affair* likewise bit the dust that season on CBS after a five-year run. Cabot was back in the slot the following week narrating the cartoon *Winnie the Pooh and the Blustery Day,* which had pre-empted Red's show earlier in the season on Nov. 30, 1970, then the British sitcom *From a Bird's Eye View* ran in the slot from March 29 through Aug. 16, 1971, before stations got control of the time period.

Red returned in the summer in reruns—the first time ever that had happened for him, so that NBC could defray the costs of the shows. In a somewhat complicated maneuver, Red replaced *The Bill Cosby Show,* which, in turn, took over the time slot of the departing *Julia*—the same sitcom that ran opposite *The Red Skelton Hour* from 1968 to 1970. Red returned on Sundays 8:30–9 P.M. on June 6—coincidentally the last time for *The Ed Sullivan Show,* running opposite Red on CBS. The latter network ran a few movies opposite Red that summer, then buried him toward the end with the five-week run of a new comedy variety series called *The Sonny and Cher Comedy Hour.* Sonny and Cher so outrated

Red up through his final show on Aug. 29, 1971, that CBS brought them back as a midseason replacement on Dec. 27, 1971. They broke up personally and professionally in 1974, finishing the season at #7—the same rating Red had when CBS canned him in 1970.

Though the last year for Red on television was lackluster, at least one participant didn't come out bitter from the experience. "I enjoyed it," said Perry Cross. "It was very difficult to know him, because we didn't have a history. And I'd heard he'd had problems with others. But not with me. He tried everything he could do."

Gig Young embraces Chanin Hale as Red as Freddie the Freeloader offers them a huge apple in a bit from the 1966–67 season opener.

Likewise, Terry Kyne enjoyed his time with the show. "I thought it could've worked, if it had been put together without too many people interfering with it," he said. As with Cross, Kyne said he concentrated on the show rather than worry about its ratings per se. Kyne stressed again his love and respect for Red—"A great guy, he was."

Saying Goodbye to The Red Skelton Show

Much of the media had little to say in detail about ending *The Red Skelton Show* after two decades. Part of it had to do with CBS canceling it a year earlier, which attracted more headlines because the show was a top 10 hit then. Now, half its size and audience, there was less appeal to discuss the show's demise. Moreover, Red was just one of a wave of longtime former television hits now vanishing in the wave of the new season, as mentioned earlier, and as such few felt the need to single him out amid the rubble.

To top it off, the upcoming season was littered with former movie stars coming to the small screen in series due to fewer motion pictures being made in an uncertain economic time. With the arrival of Glenn Ford (*Cade's County*), George Kennedy (*Sarge*), Gene Kelly (*The Funny Side*), Shirley MacLaine (*Shirley's World*), Anthony Quinn (*The Man and the City*), Rock Hudson (*McMillan and Wife*), and Tony Curtis (*The Persuaders*), who cared about a worn-out comic like Red? It was too early a period for television nostalgia; most people wanted to see the medium move forward, and not be stuck in its old ways.

The only major outlet to offer an in-depth tribute to the show was, not too surprisingly, the conservative *Saturday Review* magazine. In a piece titled "So Long Clown" in the July 21, 1971, issue, writer Martin Williams wrote movingly about missing Red without deifying him. He allowed at the top that "Although he is one of our most frustratingly erratic and uneven performers, Red Skelton is also one of the most individually gifted comics we have." He termed the show's cancellation "a sizable loss" for the medium and noted how Red's casual style influenced other television hosts such as Dean Martin.

Williams acknowledged he was not a fan of the NBC version of the show, calling it "a temporary, uncomfortable refuge." He concluded with "As I say, the loss is ours. And one can hope that Red will be back, and soon."

Well, he was back, but not soon. And not too often either. Over the next few years, Red was able to show he could do without television; but he forgot that television could do just as easily without him—and that would be a much greater problem for him and his legacy than it would be for the television industry.

8
1971–Present: "It Should Be 'Red Skelton, Red Skelton, Red Skelton'"

There would be more than a 25-year span from when Red Skelton's last show of his series aired in 1971 until his death on Sept. 17, 1997. During that same period, his national television appearances averaged less than once a year, even though by most accounts, he remained a vital performer on stage up through a few years before his death. But the medium where he had his most success, television, he strangely shunned and even denounced during his later years.

It's a depressing commentary on Red and the image he projected for fans and would-be fans. While his contemporaries such as Jack Benny, George Burns, Bob Hope, and Milton Berle, to name only a few, worked either into their nineties or almost to their deaths doing major and frequent television work, Red seemed content to be "semi-retired" in the medium, and you really had to look to find him in his infrequent guest shots.

Indeed, Red spent much of his time in the 1970s through 1990s staying at his home in Palm Springs, Calif., and doing his paintings by his pool, along with occasional in-person appearances in tours across the world. Television became an afterthought to him.

It's hard to think of another performer of Red's background and stature virtually avoiding television, especially with the opportunities available after his show ended on NBC. For example, why didn't Red star in specials on the network, like his contemporaries Bob Hope and Jack Benny (until he died in 1974)? After all, he had a track record similar to theirs of entertaining the masses on radio during the 1940s and on television in the 1950s and 1960s in drawing top audiences.

"I don't know. I don't know. I don't know," said Herb Schlosser, with an air that indicated in our phone conversation he was shaking his head while saying it deliberately each time.

Schlosser could only guess that since Red's audience had remained predominately older and he seemed unwilling to change what he did, advertisers were not interested. In contrast, he said, Bob Hope always looked younger than his years, and "He would get the latest entertainers and football players on his shows."

So Red wasn't considered a hot starring property for specials by advertisers anymore. Well, how about guest-starring on the innumerable variety shows that littered television in the 1970s? He would've been great bouncing off jokes on *The Carol Burnett Show*, *The Sonny and Cher Comedy Hour*, *Tony Orlando and Dawn* or *Donny and Marie*, to name just a few. These shows would have given him the latitude to do his shtick and ad-libs and not taken much time to tape. But apparently Red did not want to be seen as a guest star on someone else's series, as he had shown in his declining outside work during the 1960s, so he did not do them.

Red also would have been a perfect candidate to do quips on *The Hollywood Squares* like his former guests Milton Berle, Vincent Price, Mickey Rooney and many more, but once again, his ego seemed to prevent him from wanting to be one of nine stars on that top-rated game show, or any other celebrity-laden game show of the 1970s, of which there were many at the time.

And since Red had given up acting for several years, he decided not to pursue doing two shows of the 1970s that would have been perfect for him—*The Waltons* (1972–1981) and *Little House on the Prairie* (1974–1983). Both series were homespun dramas set in times past that had room for lighter moments. Red would have been wonderfully at home as a friendly old-timer or sly con man character on an episode, and maybe even earn an Emmy nomination if he did it right. But as noted before, it never happened, for reasons Red never explained; and for a Skelton enthusiast, it's frustrating.

So, Why the Disappearance from Television?

In Red's defense, when considering his attitude toward the television industry, one must take into account the turmoil going on in his personal life around the time of his CBS and NBC cancellations. In 1969 Red became acquainted with Lothian Toland, the daughter of famed cinematographer Gregg Toland, the man who created the deep-focus technique with Orson Welles for the latter's classic film *Citizen Kane*, before he died in 1948. Lothian was some two decades younger than Red. Their friendship proved to be more than that as the months passed, and by 1971, it was known publicly that she shared a suite with Red as he entertained in Las Vegas. Not surprisingly, Red separated from his wife Georgia after 26 years of marriage in August 1971. He married Lothian on Oct. 9, 1973.

Yet no one I talked to mentioned Red's personal life as a possible motive for not doing television in his later years. Instead, when I asked friends and former colleagues about his attitude, most thought Red remained angry about his series being canned and as a result decided to have little to do with television.

"I think the failure of the NBC show disillusioned him," his longtime choreographer Tom Hansen said, noting that Red also was well off thanks to his years of doing Las Vegas and other clubs during the summer hiatus for his television series.

"He was peeved at the cancellation," friend James Bacon said. "He'd go on a talk show with Johnny Carson or whatever, but I think he was really pissed off about being cancelled. He was very bitter."

"I think he was hurt, frankly," opined Chanin Hale. "There was this fiasco with CBS, and then he had only one year on NBC."

"He got upset with the whole thing," concurred his former sound effects man Ray Erlenborn. "NBC, they didn't get him what he wanted. I think he lost his spunk. He didn't want to try again."

His last series director, Terry Kyne, gave a different tack. "I think that time passed him by." In Kyne's view, Red became set in his ways and rather than accomadate the medium with television's more sophisticated comedies like *All in the Family* and *The Mary Tyler Moore Show* he simply ignored it as much as possible.

"I think maybe Red made his own mind up," Kyne added. "I don't think he was trying to get anything going."

Red gave credence to Kyne's opinion in one of the few interviews he gave in his later years to *The National Enquirer* tabloid in its Dec. 10, 1974, issue. "I was thrown off television because I didn't think rape and abortion and murder were funny," he claimed.

He followed that up with Hal Glatzer for *People* magazine in 1980 by saying he hated current commercial television programming for being too violent. "It isn't entertainment anymore," he said. "It's propaganda to spread fear."

It's quite possible Red was making reference to the shows that replaced him on CBS Tuesday nights by 1972—the sitcom *Maude*, starring Beatrice Arthur, later one of *The Golden Girls* from 1985 to 1992, as a liberated, four-times married lady, which did have an episode dealing with abortion; and *Hawaii Five-O*, a crime drama starring Jack Lord, which started in 1968 and did deal with rape and murder. Both shows were intended for adults and bore little of the kind of frivolity Red had employed on his television series.

They were also huge hits for CBS, ranking in the top 10 for three seasons in a row, 1972–75, while on Tuesdays in Red's old slot. In fact, *Hawaii Five-O* finished #3 and *Maude* #4 in their first season together on Tuesdays, 1972–73. They were the kinds of shows attracting young, more urban, more educated audiences that CBS wanted but were not getting from Red a few years earlier. It proved to network executives they were right in their judgment of canning him rather than retaining him for a few more years, so they had no incentive to want Red back on the air. And, by extension, neither did NBC nor ABC.

So by the early 1970s, Red hated television because television hated Red, in his opinion. The truce eventually would be broken by Red, but he paid a serious price for his decision. He would never star in a series or even a special on network television again.

Easing Back into Television

Actually, there was good reason to believe that Red never would do television again shortly after his show went off. In his first major public appearance after the event, an engagement at January 1972 at the Las Vegas Hilton International prior to a return visit by its top draw, Elvis Presley, Red ended his final performance by announcing not only his retirement from entertaining but also his unhappiness at the way network television executives had treated him, saying, "My heart has been broken." His words were recorded in *Variety* and as such gave little incentive for the networks to want to deal with a man who bad-mouthed them in front of everyone, even if there was some truth in what Red said.

For a time, Red held fast to his word, not showing up anywhere on television. But there was a sadder aspect to this as well. On Sept. 10, 1972, the 90-minute special *A Salute to Television's 25th Anniversary* aired on ABC. It was the first big nostalgia special dealing with television's history, and as such it included clips from some 400 shows and guest appearances by 25 stars, including Lucille Ball, Milton Berle, James Arness, Bob Hope and Ed Sullivan. Prominent among the missing was Red Skelton, and not just as a participant on the show. Reportedly, Red refused to let any portion of his television series, which he owned, be used on the special.

If this decision was his way of getting back at network officials, it was a horrible one for Red's fans and even Red himself. By excluding highlights of his series from such retrospectives, which would proliferate over the next few decades, Red unintentionally made his contributions to the medium forgotten among many of his contemporaries and little known to later generations. It was a petty decision that has helped cause Red to be marginalized in entertainment histories since the 1970s.

Anyhow, Red remained little on view on television or anywhere else through the mid-1970s, when he decided that retirement in southern California was not as satisfying as he thought it would be. (Interestingly, two of his contemporaries who announced their retirements from show business in the 1970s, Frank Sinatra and Mickey Rooney, also reversed their decision within a couple of years.) Red's first major television appearance in nearly four years came as a guest on the July 11, 1975, edition of *The Tonight Show with Johnny Carson*. According to a program description from Carson's official website, www.johnnycarson.com, Skelton discussed hiring Carson as a writer 22 years earlier after Red guested on his local television show, shared a few more memories, did a mime of an astronaut in space, portrayed his crazed scientist Dr. Ludwig von Humperdoo, whom he created in the 1970-71 season, and even conducted the band playing one of his own compositions. He followed it up with another talk show visit on the syndicated *The Merv Griffin Show* in a program aired first in top markets on Oct. 30, 1975.

If the talk show appearances were an attempt by Red to get attraction from television producers for another show or special, it fizzled. He would not get another big television appearance until he popped up on the "America on Parade" celebration on *The Wonderful World of Disney* on April 3, 1976. Then a month later, tragedy struck. On May 11, 1976, Red's second wife Georgia committed suicide by gunshot. Many noted the significance of the date—18 years to the day of their son Richard's death. Red's activities regarding television and other ventures were put on low priority as he mourned Georgia's death for several months.

Then Red did his first real acting work on television at the end of the year by providing a voice for *Rudolph's Shiny New Year*, an animated special on ABC that aired on Dec. 10, 1976. Arthur Rankin, Jr., and Jules Bass produced and directed the special as a sequel to their annual Christmas classic *Rudolph the Red-Nosed Reindeer*. Red served as narrator and voiced the character of Father Time in this special which, while nice enough, was not as popular or as repeated each season as the original. Being only a vocal part, it did not require much of Red and thus was easy for him to do, but at the same time, it was hardly the type of role to catapult him back into prominence.

So let's recap what Red had done in the first five years after his television series ended. A talk show. A children's show. A cartoon. What kind of resume is that for a man who had been a fixture of television two decades prior to that time?

They are the kind of jobs you get when you retire from television for some four years, that's what they are. That small period of time is an eternity in network television, a full regime or two worth of network presidents and vice presidents who come and go. The new ones had only fuzzy ideas about Red, most stemming from the association of bad demographics surrounding his earlier cancellation and the fact that he was getting older. The old network presidents remembered him only fuzzily as well, and not wanting to be accused of being out of step with the times, they likewise ignored Red in favor of newer talent.

With such a situation, Red got television bookings only through the goodwill of friends and fans in the industry. Luckily for him, that list grew in the late 1970s, when it looked like Red might be coming back to his old buddy television. But alas, that flirtation proved to be false.

Late 1970s: A Flurry of Activity, but Nothing Too Substantial

Red had a solid launch back onto television at the start of 1977. He could be seen on New Year's Day in the annual Tournament of Roses Parade from Pasadena, Calif., waving from a float as Freddie the Freeloader. The crowds in the street and at home loved him.

A few months later, Red secured the one guest shot that got him the largest audience by far in a while—the 1977 Oscars. Presenting the Sound Award, Red did a few routines and joked about the cover put over the orchestra pit. "It's the first time I ever worked with a net," he cracked.

One viewer of that appearance was Red's former director Terry Kyne. "He was the funniest thing I saw on that show," Kyne said. Many other critics concurred in reviewing the evening.

Also in 1977, Red appeared on *The Mike Douglas Show* as a guest co-host for a week. In his autobiography *I'll Be Right Back*, Douglas mentioned how Red would spend time with the show's crew and audience before the show and during its commercial breaks. The "common man's comedian," as Douglas called him, also consented to doing a skit with Mike as a fellow hobo along with Red's Freddie the Freeloader, despite Mike's initial worries about asking Red if he wanted to do so.

"He gave me tips on how to walk and how to flick the ashes from the cigar butt," Douglas wrote. "I was touched, and worked hard to make it perfect. Afterward, he gave me a big, heartfelt hug and made me an 'honorary Freddie.' Some comics can be difficult in real life. Red Skelton was a saint."

The spot was well received, yet Red appeared reluctant to do many talk shows thereafter. About his only other visit to a national one came on Dec. 6, 1983, when he sat down with Johnny Carson again on *The Tonight Show*. Red discussed touring with his act on college campuses, portrayed several of his old characters, and talked about his HBO specials. I recall seeing the show and hearing Carson ask Red why he wasn't on television regularly anymore, and Red deflected the question by making reference to the HBO specials. Carson could sense it was an area Red didn't seem to want to get into, so he switched topics. (By the way, neither of Red's appearances on *The Tonight Show* is available for sale, at least not as of this writing.)

Red spent more time in 1978 through 1980 appearing on several oversized variety specials to do his routines briefly. Indicative of his declining stature in the industry, Red would co-host just one of these affairs. And most would be nostalgic celebrations, which only reinforced the belief that Red was an act whose time had come and gone.

Perhaps Red's best outing came as one of six hosts of *TV—The Fabulous Fifties*, a loving remembrance of the days when video grew from a novelty to part of everyday life. Videotaped without a studio audience, Red spoke affectionately of the medium along with Lucille Ball, David Janssen, Michael Landon, Mary Martin and Dinah Shore. The tasteful affair ran an hour and a half on NBC March 3, 1978.

Later that same month, Red turned up as a guest on the same night on two opposing specials. On March 26, 1978, NBC gave *A Tribute to "Mr. Television": Milton Berle*, and Skelton showed up to salute his old colleague.

That same night launched *CBS On the Air: A Celebration of 50 Years*, the network's celebration of its half-century in broadcasting with a weeklong string of specials themed to celebrate series and specials on what nights they aired, starting with Sundays. For example, that night spotlighted highlights from former Sunday favorites *The Ed Sullivan Show* and *Lassie*. Anyhow, as part of the first night's festivities, Red and nearly 100 other CBS stars past and present stood on a set that marked off each night they represented for the network and Red, naturally, was front and center on the Tuesday night label.

The odd thing is that when the hour-long Tuesday night special rolled around two days later, Red was nowhere to be found, either as host or in clips of his series. "I kept waiting to see him," recalled Chanin Hale when she watched the special.

Instead, that night's hosts were Phil Silvers, whose *You'll Never Get Rich* sitcom ran less than three years on CBS Tuesdays, and Alan Alda, whose *M*A*S*H* series ran about three years on Tuesdays too, but by the time of the special was running on Monday nights! Incredibly, Skelton and his show, cornerstones of the CBS Tuesday lineup for most of the 1950s and 1960s, were nowhere to be found on the special, undoubtedly adding to the effect of erasing Red's standing in television history. It was a low point that showed what a deep grudge Red still had against CBS, much less all network officials, in not letting himself or his material be part of this high-rated affair.

Moving on, Red showed up as one of what seemed like half of Hollywood to wish *Happy Birthday, Bob: A Salute to Bob Hope's 75th Birthday*, which monopolized three hours of the evening on NBC on May 29, 1978. Ann-Margret, Pearl Bailey, Lucille Ball, Johnny Carson, Sammy Davis, Jr., Fred MacMurray, Elizabeth Taylor, Danny Thomas and John Wayne, along with Red, comprised the 40 different acts that performed on the tribute.

On Sept. 29, 1978, he popped up on the two-hour special *The General Electric All-Star Anniversary* on CBS. John Wayne hosted the affair with an A-list cast (Lucille Ball, Henry Fonda, Bob Hope, Jimmy Stewart, and Elizabeth Taylor) mixed with top television talent of the time (e.g., Cheryl Ladd of *Charlie's Angels* and Suzanne Somers of *Three's Company*).

Red's last big special guest shot was on *Sinatra: The First 40 Years*, a celebration of singer Frank Sinatra's four decades in show business. Apart from working at MGM and in Las Vegas with him, Red had little in common with "the Chairman of the Board," yet he showed up anyway to offer a tribute to him on this two-hour extravaganza that aired on NBC Jan. 30, 1980. (Four days later, Red would be seen in an old clip for the special *Bob Hope's Overseas Christmas Tours* on NBC.)

All these appearances did very little for Red other than show fans and the industry that he was still alive and in top shape to perform. (Red also could be seen in commercials in 1979 for House of Windsor cigars, even though he did not smoke the stogies.) Network executive and television producers cared little about him by now, and Red never did much more beyond these scattered shots on network television until his death in 1997. The irony was that as his television work slowed to barely a trickle, people who had worked on his series were prospering quite nicely.

The Triumphs of the Ex-Skeltons

For the writers who worked on Red's show in the 1960s and disliked him, the 1970s would prove to be especially sweet revenge for them, as their stock on television grew stronger while his grew weaker. The "two Bobs" he fired so notoriously in 1967, Schiller and Weiskopf, wound up getting an Emmy Award for writing an *All in the Family* episode dealing with lesbianism in 1978, the same year they had another nomination in the same category for writing another *All in the Family* episode about a rape attempt. These topics were light years away from Red and his brand of comedy, yet they were among the top-rated shows of the season.

Schiller and Weiskopf served as script consultants on *All in the Family* from 1976 to 1978. During the same period, another 1960s ex–*Red Skel-*

ton Hour writer, Larry Rhine, served as a story editor on the same show. He was nominated against Schiller and Weiskopf in 1978 also for his work on *All in the Family*.

Red's most vocal critic, Sherwood Schwartz, had his own triumph with his sitcom creation *The Brady Bunch* on ABC from 1969 to 1974. Though not a huge hit in its initial run, its popularity in repeats in syndication led it to become the only series to reappear as a cartoon (*The Brady Kids*, 1972–74), a variety show (*The Brady Bunch Hour*, 1977), a sitcom sequel (*The Brady Brides*, 1981), a television movie (*A Very Brady Christmas*, 1988) and a dramatic sequel (*The Bradys*, 1990).

Even one writer who liked Red, monologue writer Robert Orben, secured a prestigious job after his years with Red by serving as a speech consultant to Vice President Gerald Ford in 1974, following the latter's appointment to his post to replace Spiro Agnew. His title became speechwriter for President Ford in August 1974 after Richard Nixon resigned, then it changed to Special Assistant to President Ford and Director of the White House Speechwriting Department in January 1976. Through it all, he was tapped to provide humor at a time when the freshly appointed president—and the country, for that matter—needed a laugh from the White House where the joke was not on the public. Ford's defeat to Jimmy Carter in the 1976 presidential election led Orben to leave political speechwriting and get back to doing humor-oriented books.

Others associated with the show prospered as well. For example, choreographer Tom Hansen received an Emmy nomination in 1972 for his work on the special *The Fabulous Fordies* starring Tennessee Ernie Ford. He also was the choreographer for two series, *The Tim Conway Comedy Hour* in 1970 and the 1974 summer revival of *Your Hit Parade*, the 1950s show on which he was a dancer.

"I'd done everything from Vegas to Disney until musical television died," Hansen said. He last worked on television in 1978. "After that, it became Vegas and nightclub acts. I did five nightclub acts for Jim Nabors. He was next to Skelton at Television City." (*The Jim Nabors Hour* aired on CBS from 1969 to 1971.)

So obviously, the end of *The Red Skelton Show* was not the end of many people's careers as it seemed with Red after 1971. You would get the impression that the latter was the truth just by taking a look at the books coming out in the same period.

Forgetting Red

In the introduction, I cited some books from over the years that contain incorrect information about Red's show. A few others from the 1970s should be examined, just to give a full impression of how thoroughly ignored Skelton had become as the decade progressed.

Max Wilk's *The Golden Age of Television* came out in 1976 and glossed over Skelton's contribution to television, with few words about the show and no interviews with any participants, even though it concentrated on 1950s television, a decade where Red's show was in the top 10 for two seasons. A year later, Jeff Greenfield released *Television: The First 50 Years*, which had just one picture and one paragraph on Skelton, stating that the comedian had spent nearly 20 years on CBS, with no mention of his NBC years.

The NBC dates did appear in 1977's *TV Book*, edited by Judy Fireman. But while there were nine photos of Red from over the years in the book's timeline at the bottom of each page, there was next to nothing about him in the top section of main text. There was, however, room for a full-page appreciation of *The Gene Autry Show*, Red's one-time failed competition and lead-in.

Most ridiculously, 1980's *TV Guide Almanac*, edited by Craig T. and Peter G. Norback, gave the listing of all the top-rated television shows by season since 1950–51. When it mentioned *The Red Skelton Show* finishing #4 on NBC in 1951–52, it nevertheless claimed that the series actually started on CBS in 1953. How did that get by them and their proofreaders?

They all managed to get away with these misstatements simply because most of Red's fans were aging, ill or dead, and as noted before, Red was doing little television currently and refused to have his series in repeats. Besides, the really damaging printed material came in 1979—an unauthorized biography of Red himself.

The Biography

Arthur Marx, son of comedy great Groucho Marx, wrote *Red Skelton* as one of several books he created over the years examining the lives of famous comedians, covering everyone from his father to Bob Hope. With *Red Skelton*, Marx presented a portrait of a man who had "lived the Pagliacci myth," as the book flap put it, contrasting the comedian's happy-go-lucky image with his often unhappy personal life and occasionally stormy professional life. The biggest shock for his mostly conservative fans had to have been the portrait of Red as a person who enjoyed profanity and dirty jokes privately all the while denouncing those who performed them publicly.

As far as it covered Red's television series, a lot of the dates regarding people's tenures on the show were off by a year or two, and a great deal about the show was omitted or based more on opinion than fact. But Marx did a very good job in capturing the series in its relation to Red, especially given how research into television history was still in its relative infancy in 1979. With Red's show not in syndication, and hardly any videotape copies of them available even as bootlegs at the time, Marx had very little to go on to verify claims of his interviewees against any actual shows, and did well in this challenge.

Still, it was the personal strife in Red's life that gave the book its selling point to most potential readers. In fact, excerpts from the book arrived in the Aug. 7, 1979, issue of the weekly tabloid *The National Enquirer*, the same publication that interviewed Red about his feelings concerning television in 1974, with a front-page photo of Red and the headline "Tragedy and Torment."

A considerable amount of the material that Marx used came from several previously printed sources, including James Bacon's 1976 book *Hollywood is a Four-Letter Town* (which contained racy anecdotes about Red's personal life and off-color comments he made in private). But Bacon did not care to see Marx's book in return. "Never read it," he told me.

Truth be known, the book may not have done particularly well, given the decreasing interest in Red in general at the time. I did not uncover a single interview with Red where he was asked about Marx's book. Then again, Red never did that many interviews, particularly in his later years, so that's not really a surprise.

What Red's friends and former co-workers did recall better from this period was his final attempt to sever any and all ties with television. If the powers that be had consigned him to the hell of being an ex-television star without a show, he was returning that situation in full to them by bringing his own creations to burn in that same hell with him.

A Series Up in Smoke

Besides overtaking Red as CBS's most successful variety show star in the 1970s, Carol Burnett also did the unprecedented in 1977: She managed to sell reruns of her series, albeit edited from an hour to a half hour, usually with the musical numbers subtracted, to local television stations under the title *Carol Burnett and Friends*. The package, consisting of programs that ran originally from 1971 to 1977, was a huge hit and proved that contrary to earlier wisdom, a comedy variety show could be seen in reruns. Naturally, people began to think other shows could do it too, including Red's. But he had different ideas.

In an interview with Hal Glatzer for *People* magazine in 1980, Red announced to the world that upon his death, the original kinescopes and videotapes of his television series were to be burned. "I worked hard to make them, and they're not going on the market for someone else to use," he said. Red did allow that he would reconsider his plan with "the right offer" to sell them on videocassettes.

Predictably, Red's writers were incensed when they got wind of this. Thirteen of them filed a civil lawsuit to stop what they claimed was Skelton's vow to destroy his programs or have his executor do so after his death, claiming they would be robbed of residuals they would have received had the shows been syndicated or offered for home sale. The writers' attorneys, Ben F. Goldman, Jr., and Kenneth G. Petrulis, claimed Skelton had an obligation under the series' original contracts with the writers to make an effort to sell the reruns and earn them money in the process.

Myrna Oliver of *The Los Angeles Times* reported that one former writer, Jack Ritchard, submitted a sworn statement that he had heard Skelton say, "I have in my will that when I die, all my tapes will be burned within a half hour of my death. I figure if I wasn't important enough during my lifetime for the networks to do something with the reruns, there's no reason to leave these things for anyone else to profit from."

In response to the claims, Skelton's attorney Stephen J. Koundakjian denied that any plan stated by Ritchard existed and that any statements made by Skelton about destroying his show were made in jest. The attorney said that Skelton did not oppose syndicating his reruns but wanted them done in the "proper context" so that people understood what made the show funny.

To avoid a protracted trial, Skelton agreed on Sept. 4, 1980, to preserve about 250 of his television shows. He would later try to make a major syndication deal for them that fell through (see the upcoming section "The Plan to Rerun Red"), but never did secure a home sale deal for them during his lifetime.

Interestingly, the only time that any of my interviews for this book went flat occured with Red's ex-writer Robert Orben when I mentioned the lawsuit. I asked if he was one of the parties involved in suing Red, and Orben said, "I signed into that." Then I asked if he thought Red was serious about setting fire to his shows, and Orben said, "No way of telling." With such short, unexpressive answers, I moved on to other topics.

But others believed Red did plan to destroy the master tapes. "I think he actually really wanted to do that," said Ken Shapiro, who worked as a page for *The Red Skelton Hour* in the 1960s.

The combination of Red's haphazard television appearances, Marx's biography, and his writers' lawsuit to protect their handiwork no doubt formed a prejudice within the industry about using Red for any television work. His eccentricities now were public knowledge and damaging to him. Who needed to work with someone so crazy that he would try to destroy his own hard work as well as that of hundreds of other people? Why would anyone trust that person to be reliable and compliant in doing a television show?

Although it's conjecture at best, the fact that hardly any other television jobs for Red outside of awards shows came in the wake of the lawsuit basically indicate that entertainment producers in Hollywood and network executives in New York City no longer deemed him dependable or worthy to do any shows for them. And so he did not.

Luckily for Red, there was cable to serve as a refuge. But only temporarily.

The HBO Specials

In 1981, having had his fill of network television, Red gave cable television a shot when he did the first of several specials for the Home Box Office (HBO) pay cable channel. *Red Skelton's Christmas Dinner* debuted Dec. 13, 1981, with Red as Freddie the Freeloader, Vincent Price as Professor von Humperdoo, Imogene Coca, and a mostly otherwise Canadian cast and crew. The production took place north of the United States to save costs. It was repeated by HBO a year later under the title *Red Skelton Presents Freddy* [sic] *the Freeloader's Christmas Dinner.*

Though no reviewer seemed particularly wild about the special, and there were no blockbuster ratings for it, HBO apparently thought there was enough appeal in Red doing a special that they brought him back to do three more specials over the next year and a half. The first, titled *Funny Faces*, debuted on April 6, 1982, with Red doing Clem Kadiddlehopper, seagulls Gertrude and Heathcliff and plenty of mime.

Red Skelton's More Funny Faces made its bow on March 5, 1983, with Marcel Marceau once again as his special guest. Unfortunately, both men did little pantomime together, although they did some fine solo work, including a great one by Red as a slice of bacon popping and curling up as it is being fried. Again he did the seagulls, Kadiddlehopper, this time narrating a cute poem called "Frogs," standup and pantomime. At the end, he painted himself up somewhat messily as Freddie the Freeloader, complete with silver makeup on his eyelids, but he did not do any comedy as the beloved hobo, just sang a goodbye song, and without bringing Marceau on stage with him too at the end. Nevertheless, the audience at the Centre in the Square, Kitchener, Canada, where *Red Skelton's More Funny Faces* was taped, gave Red a standing ovation.

Funny Faces III debuted May 29, 1983, and featured Red in a solo act with, you guessed it, Kadiddlehopper, the seagulls and pantomimes, the latter ranging from a grandfather teaching his grandson how to play baseball to a veterinarian giving a whale a flu shot. They stood out in a set that had some moments that Red joked about but make one wince a little in retrospect. He told how people in Hamilton, Ontario, Canada, where this special was taped, had told him they thought he was dead or, as one woman asked him, "Are you real or a rerun?" There was a lot of truth in that statement, showing just how people had thought he had disappeared along with his television series.

Red still laughed at his jokes enthusiastically, even though many seemed old and laden with puns. And skeptics will note how hypocritical it was for the man behind the "Dirty Hour" to end his show by telling the audience: "It's a lot of fun to hear laughs without the use of four-letter words." Hearing this statement just before or after HBO ran an unedited movie with profanities intact was odd enough, not to mention the fact that Red had used "hell" in the special and "jackass" in the previous one. For those who knew about his "Dirty Hour," though, it was phony and pandering to his audience.

One person who saw the HBO specials was Red's ex-monologue writer Robert Orben, and he was far from impressed by them. "The pantomimes were fine," he said. "The others were rather pathetic. There was a Christmas show that made me cringe." Having seen the last two specials, I would concur with Orben's comments. Red's material and approach looked old fashioned and out of place on HBO, and without him being allowed to play his old characters except Kadiddlehopper, it made him appear a more limited talent than he was.

Indeed, it was this image from the specials that actor Christopher Guest parodied on NBC's late night comedy series *Saturday Night Live* during the 1984–85 season. In one sketch that year, Guest played Red as a panelist on the legendary New York City talk show *The Joe Franklin Show*, with Billy Crystal playing a dead-on plodding Joe Franklin as host. Guest told jokes, including one involving the seagulls, in Red's silly, childlike voice while drowning out the supposed punch lines under a fit of giggles about his own material. It was not as rough a treatment as *Saturday Night Live* has given other celebrities over the year, yet the point was clear—one of the hippest comedy shows on television found itself laughing at, not with, the Red Skelton being seen on television.

Red did no other HBO shows by 1984. Ironically, that same year it appeared the "old Red" would be returning to television. But it turned out to be naught.

The Plan to Rerun Red

The effort to sell local stations repeats of *The Red Skelton Show* came in the wake of more comedy variety shows being edited into half-hour snippets for reruns for local stations in the mid–1980s, including *Rowan and Martin's Laugh-In* and *The Tonight Show Starring Johnny Carson*. How it happened in Red's case is nearly forgotten by all of his surviving co-workers and pals.

Here's one recollection by former Red writer Robert Orben: "There was, as I understand it, something of an effort 10 years before Red died to syndicate them. Bill [Red's former director and producer Bill Hobin] volunteered to edit them down." Hobin, however, made no mention of the task, if in fact he did so, in his 1986 autobiography.

The most distinct memory about the situation came from Chanin Hale. "I was in Honolulu in 1984, and Red was signing copies of his paintings. I came by with my fiancé and he said, 'Chanin!' and talked with me.

"He told me, 'We just finished editing the tapes.' I thought he meant the CBS tapes. But they never made it into syndication."

What kept the half-hour edited shows from being sold to local stations? According to Hale, "The story I heard was that the price was too high, and it'd been 15 years since the show was on the air. They never ended up in syndication."

The development was indeed puzzling, given the publicity that the idea received at the time. For example, the daily syndicated Hollywood news program *Entertainment Tonight* included the announcement of *The Red Skelton Show* returning to television at the end of one broadcast and included a clip from one of Red's color shows—perhaps the first time since 1971 one had aired on television. But it turned out to be a premature announcement.

Perhaps disgusted that his old show lacked enough takers to be shown again, or maybe just tired of dealing with television executives, Red really pulled back in the wake of this failed deal and rarely did television from the mid–1980s until his death.

"I'm Not Dead"

On Sept. 20, 1986, Red received an overdue lifetime achievement award for his work on television at the annual Emmy Awards presentation. He was the ninth recipient of the ATAS Governor's Award, and he received it from Lucille Ball, a rather odd choice given they had rarely worked together over the years. Nevertheless, both received standing ovations.

And then Red, given a chance to say something sweet or clever in his acceptance speech, decided instead to say after his ovation, "I want to thank you for sitting down. I thought you were pulling a CBS and walking out on me." The joke was weak; it went over the heads of the younger viewers not familiar with Red's cancellation in 1970, and to those who did know about it, it was out of place and judgmental. Most attendees in the Emmy audience had been involved with at least one series the networks cancelled, so why was Red obsessing about his cancellation from so long ago? With Red bringing up a 16-year-old grudge to start his statements of thanks, he immediately blew any chance of the audience having sympathy for him and wanting to do more work with him.

There were only two other major television appearances I could find for Red during the rest of the 1980s. The public television series *American Masters* on Nov. 25, 1987, aired a profile titled "Buster Keaton: A Hard Act to Follow." In it, Red recalled working with the silent movie comic who had coached him on how to do comedy during Red's MGM days in the 1940s.

Then on a special aired Jan. 9, 1989, Red was inducted into the Television Academy Hall of Fame, with Bob Hope recapping Red's television career prior to Skelton receiving the honor with a handful of other industry notables.

Other than those bits, not much seemed to be going on with Red on television, and it resulted in a joke in questionable taste at Red's expense. In late 1989, *Spy* magazine, a publication in vogue at the time for poking fun at celebrities and politicians, did a national poll to assess people's opinions about well-known personalities. The leadoff question asked the 450 respondents whether 10 celebrities were dead or alive. Red was part of that list, and he garnered the highest number of incorrect responses, with 41 percent of those surveyed claiming he was dead.

Assessing the results in the publication's January 1990 issue, writer Jamie Malanowski concluded that "apparently his invisibility on television—no slot on Nick at Nite, no endorsements for Century Village condominiums, no media-drenched fracases with California police officers—has led some of his fellow Americans to conclude that Red has passed on."

Malanowski added the following nugget: "'He was shocked to hear that,' his secretary stated, before issuing his official, good-sport response (which, for the record, was 'I'm not dead—I just appear that way.')"

It's always nice to know you're considered a good sport to joke about people thinking you are dead in your seventies. In the same survey, Red failed to make the lists of famous people Americans loved or hated, which may have been good and bad news at the same time.

"Is Red dead?" was a cruel bit for *Spy* to use in an attempt at humor.

Red showed uncommonly good grace in deflecting the item. But to a certain extent, it had some truth to it. As far as the television community was concerned now, Red was dead. He barely made a blip on the national scene, much less in the industry.

"I talked to Red a few times before he died," Robert Orben said. "I had one sad conversation with him when he performed at the Kennedy Center, and I called him at his hotel. I said that I do speeches and lectures about humor and mention him, very complimentary stories about him. As audiences became younger and younger, audiences forgot about him." It was Orben's way of trying to nudge him to appear more often in public, but Red would have none of it and avoided going into the subject with Orben.

Instead, Red continued to concentrate on one-man shows. One of the last was his 80th birthday celebration at Reno, Nevada, in 1993. That event was taped to use as part of a tribute to Red in a special titled *The First Annual Comedy Hall of Fame* on NBC Nov. 24, 1993. Selected as initial honorees were Red, Carol Burnett, George Burns, Walter Matthau, Milton Berle and Jonathan Winters. But Red apparently was unwilling to appear in person to accept his award, even among his peers, so instead host John Ritter narrated a speech about him over the months-old birthday footage, giving it an air detached from the rest of the lively award proceedings. For Red's fans, it was an opportunity wasted.

Red's final television appearance was as a guest on *Inside the Dream Factory*, a special about the history of movie studio MGM, which aired Aug. 8, 1995, on the cable channel TCM (Turner Classic Movies). Faye Dunaway—not a former MGM star by any stretch of the matter—hosted the affair, with Red being one of a multitude of old stars recalling the good old days at the company.

Now, think about it. Red went into television as a top star and managed despite several bumps in the road to hold onto that position in the medium for nearly 20 years. And now he was reduced to this—being a minor guest attraction on a documentary airing in the summer months, when audiences are lower than the rest of the year, on a cable channel with a small viewership that emphasized the past. What a sad way to fade out of a longtime partnership with a medium.

RIP, Red

Richard Bernard Skelton passed away on Sept. 17, 1997, dying of pneumonia at age 84. He was buried in the Great Mausoleum section of Forest Lawn Memorial Park in Glendale, Calif., on Sept. 23, 1997. His obituary merited prominent though not overwhelming coverage among the national media. *People* magazine, for example, did a spread on him without promoting it on the issue's cover.

TV Guide, which barely mentioned Red after his series ended in 1971, did mention him on the cover of its Oct. 11–17, 1997, issue, along with a reunion of *Lost in Space*, which of course had been funded by Red's production company. (This was not mentioned in that article, however.) The cover photo featured Ellen Degeneres about her being out as a lesbian and what impact it would have on her series *Ellen*.

As for Red's article, "America's Clown," *TV Guide* had Marcel Marceau reminisce about his fellow pantomime artist. He made mention of their work together on the *More Funny Faces* special in 1983 and three of Red's shows in the 1960s, and how they mimicked Maurice Chevalier's accent when he hosted the 1965 show.

Mostly though, it was a virtual deification of Red by his old pal. Marceau noted near the beginning that "Let us mourn a great star, a wonderful clown and a passionate performer. Red Skelton brought joy, happiness and poetry to millions of children and grownups. In his field he had no peer; he was unique in his way of clowning." The effusive praise continued right up to the end, when Marceau concluded "Red, you are eternal for me and the millions of people you made laugh and cry. May God bless you forever, my great and precious *compagnon*. I will never forget that silent world we created together."

The magazine also included four rather unremarkable portions of previous interviews *TV Guide* had done with Skelton in the 1950s and 1960s, which focused mainly on his private life rather than his place in television history, and as such were rather disappointing. Frankly, more insight on Red's career and talent came from Marceau's piece than the old excerpts.

Red's mentions on the medium have been rare since his death. One of the few exceptions came on Aug. 27, 1999, when CBS aired *Influences: From Yesterday to Today: A Museum of Television and Radio Special*. In the program, comedian/actor Paul Reiser named *The Red Skelton Show* as one of his comedy influences. It was one of the rare times in later years the series had even been mentioned by a person younger than Red's generation. (Another Museum of Television and Radio special, *Classic Stand-Up Comedy on Television*, had aired on NBC Sept. 14, 1996, and included a portion of Red's television jokes, presumably from the NBC years.)

Of course, one reason why Red and his show receive little mention is because no one has been allowed to see much of the CBS years in reruns on cable or home viewing, so it's out of sight, out of mind. It's a situation that could be corrected, but according to my sources, it will take a considerable amount of effort to make it a reality.

Bringing Back The Red Skelton Show

Bets Hobin, widow of Red's director and producer Bill Hobin, told me that Red's last wife Lothian controls the status of the CBS shows. "She's the one holding it up. Evidently CBS owns it with Lothian, and it's all tied up with CBS and Mrs. Skelton." Lothian, a very private person, has never said in public why the CBS shows remain unreleased, although it's generally believed Red gave her the rights to the programs with the condition that she never sell them.

As noted previously, Skelton's estate has approved selling two packages of Red's material, one of the NBC days from 1951 to 1953 and the other of the 1970–71 NBC season. In light of why episodes from these years were allowed to be sold, Red's ex-choreographer Tom Hansen noted that "He didn't have any irritation at NBC. I think it was more 'I'll get back at you' to CBS."

Yet there remains a solid core of Red's fans who recall, or want to recall, his best years on CBS and will gladly pay top dollar to do so. This has led to many bootleg copies of the CBS shows, which irked Hansen when he discovered them because he and his dancers get no residuals for the sales of such materials, unlike authorized copies of other series. "None of us got paid for it," he said. "That was not a very nice thing." (In deference to Hansen's sentiments, and wallet, I've not listed the bootlegs I used in researching this book.)

Hansen is of the opinion that Skelton blew it by not following Carol Burnett's lead in 1977 when she put out half-hour edited versions of her hour-long *Carol Burnett Show* for daily repeats under the title *Carol Burnett and Friends*. "Had he sold his shows as Carol did, I think his memory would've lasted a lot longer," Hansen said. "He did not do a lot of guest shots of shows through that period that are repeated."

Still, that situation could be resolved if all the copyright holders change their minds and release the material. With the right editing and packaging, director Terry Kyne said, "I think you could put something together the younger generation will enjoy."

Hansen is less optimistic, feeling Red's drop in activity since the show went off led to less interest in the performer and his work. "Who's going to buy it?" he asked me. Well, maybe Hansen himself, since his collection of Red's series is lacking a great deal. "I wish I had new tapes," he said. "I basically have the first year in black and white, and a few in color."

Robert Orben said if a deal does occur, it will require some negotiating with the various Hollywood unions for the crews who by law can get money from repeats from the show. "It gets a little sticky due to residuals," he said. "We're all covered by the Writers Guild, and they would have to figure out who gets what."

Chanin Hale is doubtful whether Lothian would reverse the decision, given her devotion to Red. Hale hopes and thinks Red's grandchildren by his daughter Valentina will do it instead. "Maybe they'll say, 'Hey, Pop would really want this' and go around Pop's wishes. He was a big part of television who should be remembered."

And as far as any publicity needed for the event, Hale vowed to me that "If they ever put them out, I'll go out and promote them for free."

Let's hope that happens. With Red dead and the network executives who canned his show either dead or retired, it's stupid to deny future generations Skelton's gifts just for the feeling of getting payback over a cancellation few remember from decades ago.

Closing Words: Friends and Colleagues Remember Red and The Red Skelton Show

"I think he stands up with most comedians of his era. His mime was terrific. I would hope he would be remembered. He was a great comedian."
—Terry Kyne

"One of a kind, absolutely. An extraordinary mime, and a great sketch actor. He was never given enough credit."
—June Lockhart

"He was a part of what real wit and real comedy were about, what I think we don't have any more. It's just not funny. What happened with Red is really funny."
—Patrice Munsel

"I thought he was a brilliant comedian, he did a great job. But if you ask a young person, they wouldn't know about him."
—Herb Schlosser

"I think he is one of the greatest entertainers. I admired him very much. He was a very funny person."
—Stanley Green

"This guy was a dedicated clown. He practically said that every show. He would listen to everyone's suggestions before the show—I made some suggestions on 'The Silent Spot'—and no other star would do that."
—Ray Erlenborn

"He's a legend, and I would hope that future generations would appreciate the art of pantomime that he mastered. He and Marcel

Marceau were the giants. And all his characters were so finely defined and funny. When I think of having that association, I'm awestruck."
—Alan Copeland

"I think he had the longest-running comedy variety show. That in itself is an amazing achievement. He was a good film actor and a good-looking guy. To have him play a lead was absolutely credible. He did pantomimes, monologues, acting…. We're not growing that sort of all-around performer."
—Robert Orben

"I think he'll always be remembered for his great characters—Freddie the Freeloader, Clem Kadiddlehopper. Red, of course, was the greatest character of all. He just didn't care about show business at all."
—James Bacon

"He was a big part of television. You always hear 'Uncle Miltie, Uncle Miltie, Uncle Miltie.' It should be 'Red Skelton, Red Skelton, Red Skelton.'"
—Chanin Hale

Maybe someday it will. I hope this book will aid in that effort.

Appendix A: *The Red Skelton Show* Cast and Crew Credits

Star: Red Skelton

Regulars: The David Rose Orchestra, Lucille Knoch (1950–1952), Jan Arvan (occasional 1954–71), The Redettes (1954–1956), The Skelton Dancers (a/k/a the Jack Boyle Dancers; 1956–1962), The Tom Hansen Dancers (1962–70), The Modernaires (1962–January 1963), The Alan Copeland Singers (a/k/a the Skeltones from 1963–1964; January 1963–1969), The Jimmy Joyce Singers (1969–1970), Chanin Hale (occasional 1963–71)

Producers: Red Skelton and Freeman Keyes (1951–52), Red Skelton (1952–53), Ben Brady (1953–54), Douglas Whitney and Jack Donohue (1954–55), Cecil Barker (1955–64), Seymour Berns (1964–68), Bill Hobin (1968–70), Dee Caruso (1970), Gerald Gardner (1970), Perry Cross (1970–71)

Executive Producers: Cecil Barker (1953–54), Nat Perrin (1954–55), Guy della Cioppa (1962–71)

Writers: John Fenton Murray (1951–53), Benedict Freedman (1951–53), Will Fowler (1951–53), Jack Douglas (1951–53), Arthur Stander (1953–54), Howard Leeds (1953–54), Arthur Julian (1953–54), Arthur Ross (1953–54), David Ross (1954), Bob Ross (1954), Hal Goodman (1954–55), Larry Klein (1954–55), Al Gordon (1954–55), Martin Ragaway (1954–55 and 1960–68), Joe Bigelow (1955), Lou Meltzer (1955), Sherwood Schwartz (1955–61), Dave O'Brien (1955–69), Jesse Goldstein (1955–59), Mort Green (1955–56 and 1962–71), Al Schwartz (1960–61), Arthur Phillips (1961–70, 1971), Ed Simmons (1961–64), Hugh Wedlock (1962–64), Rick Mittleman (1962–63), Bruce Howard (1962–63), Larry Rhine (1963–68, 1971), Robert Orben (1964–70), Bob Weiskopf (1964–67), Bob Schiller (1964–67), Fred Fox (1967–70), Seaman Jacobs (1967–70), Charles Isaacs (1967–70), Tony Webster (1968–70), Robert L. Mott (1969–70), George Balzer (1970), Pat McCormick (1970–71), Lionel Burt (1970), Jeffrey Barron (1970)

Directors: John Gaunt (1951–52), Marty Rackin (1952–53), Seymour Berns (1953–54 and 1955–64), Jack Donohue (1954–55), Bill Hobin (1964–68), Howard Quinn (1968–70), Terry Kyne (1970–71)

Appendix B:
The Red Skelton Show Guests by Season

Note: This list is by nature incomplete, given sketchy records for the show and lack of copies for all series against which to check the credits. I have relied primarily on listings in *TV Guide* and *The New York Times* for the guests, but both publications did not start listing guests on the show regularly until the summer of 1954, so the list basically starts then, with a few exceptions that I've found in my research. I have included in the listings those occasions when the series was pre-empted by specials or had a repeat shown prior to its summer hiatus in an attempt to be as complete as possible.

In that same vein, for some of the more obscure acts, I've listed the primary vocation next to their names. For musical acts on the hour shows, I've listed their hit songs they performed on the show as well, but keep in mind that they most likely performed other numbers as well that I didn't include because they didn't make the music charts.

Please realize that most shows in the following list do not have all guests in the minor roles given, unless I was able to find an episode on videotape with the credits at the end. Based on the videotapes for sale of these shows, Benny Rubin, Jane Darwell and Gil Perkins made several guest appearances, though I could not locate exact air dates. For the shows designated as "No one listed," it does not necessarily mean there were no guest stars on it, only none that I could find.

1951-1952
May 4: Kam Tong; show aired from San Francisco

1953-1954
Sept. 22: Marjorie Bennett, Phyllis Coates, James Flavin, Nelson Barclift, Wilda Taylor, Mickie Burton, Yvette Vickers, Mary Lynn

Feb. 9: Ed Sullivan, the King Sisters

Summer 1954

July 21: Liberace, George Liberace, Tony Curtis, the Amin Brothers, the Sahara Hotel chorus line
July 28: Burt Lancaster, Anna Marie Alberghetti, Los Chavales de España (a vocal and instrumental group)
Aug. 4: Rosemary Clooney, the Hi Los
Aug. 11: Gloria De Haven, the New York City Ballet, the Mary Kaye Trio
Aug. 18: Frank Sinatra, Cab Calloway, Georgie Tapps (dancer)
Aug. 25: Helen Traubel, Los Chavales de Espana
Sept. 1: Ed Wynn, Betty Jones (singer)
Sept. 8: Peggy Lee

1954-1955

Oct. 5: Ella Logan
Oct. 12: Helen Traubel
Oct. 19: Anna Marie Alberghetti
Oct. 26: No one listed
Nov. 2: Xavier Cugat, Abbe Lane
Nov. 9: Martha Stewart (not the homemaker!)
Nov. 16: Gloria De Haven
Nov. 23: Dorothy Shay
Nov. 30: Lillian Roth
Dec. 7: No one listed
Dec. 14: Vivian Blaine
Dec. 21: Red's family, as he reads a Christmas story to them
Dec. 28: John Calvert
Jan. 11: George Raft, Reginald Denny, Vicki Raaf
Jan. 18: Peter Lorre, Vampira
Jan. 25: Mary McCarty, Reginald Denny
Feb. 1: Ruth Roman, Reginald Denny
Feb. 8: Charles Coburn, Reginald Denny
Feb. 15: Mary McCarty
Feb. 22: Edmond O'Brien
March 1: Barbara Ruick, Hans Conreid

March 8: Presentation of the *Look* magazine movie awards
March 15: Helen Grayco
March 22: Mary McCarty
March 29: Margaret Whiting
April 5: Mary Meade French (singer)
April 12: No one listed
April 19: Abbe Lane, Xavier Cugat
April 26: Margaret Whiting
May 3: Mary McCarty
May 10: Virginia Field
May 17: Abbe Lane, Xavier Cugat
May 24: No one listed
May 31: Shirley Yamaguchi (Japanese film star)
June 7: Rose Marie, Helen Kleeb
June 14: No one listed

1955-1956

Sept. 26: Ed Sullivan, David Burns
Oct. 4: Jackie Gleason, Mel Allen
Oct. 11: Nancy Walker
Oct. 18: George Raft
Oct. 25: Ed Wynn
Nov. 1: Virginia Grey
Nov. 8: Connie Russell, Jamie Farr
Nov. 15: Lucille Norman (singer)
Nov. 22: Nancy Walker
Nov. 29: Peter Lorre
Dec. 6: Bill Williams (playing his TV character Kit Carson)
Dec. 13: Pre-empted by a special *See It Now*
Dec. 20: "The Cop and the Anthem," with Sara Berner, Eddie Parker and the Mitchell Boys Choir
Dec. 27: Zsa Zsa Gabor
Jan. 3: Billy Gilbert, John Carradine, Jackie Coogan
Jan. 10: No one listed
Jan. 17: Basil Rathbone
Jan. 24: Melville Cooper, Reginald Denny
Jan. 31: Jeanne Cagney
Feb. 7: Cesar Romero
Feb. 14: Marvin Kaplan, Sally Forrest
Feb. 21: Vincent Price

Feb. 28: Marshall Lyou (Korean war orphan)
March 6: No one listed
March 13: Pre-empted by a special *See It Now*
March 20: Charles Coburn, Allen Jenkins
March 27: Judy Canova
April 3: Keefe Brasselle
April 10: Dick Foran, the Warner twins (Sandra and Sonia)
April 17: Paul Coates
April 24: "Robin Hood," with Red as Robin, Kem Dibbs as the Sheriff, Penny Edwards as Maid Marian, Sterling Holloway as Will Scarlet, John Carradine as Little John and Billy Gilbert as Friar Tuck
May 1: Elena Verdugo, Fritz Feld
May 8: Anne Jeffreys
May 15: Buster Crabbe, Jamie Farr, Jimmy Cross
May 22: Allen Jenkins
May 29: ZaSu Pitts
June 5: Billy Gilbert, John Carradine, and Sterling Holloway in a "Captain Kidd" parody
June 12: Marie Windsor
June 19: Anna Sten, Roland Winters

1956-1957

Oct. 2: Rocky Marciano
Oct. 9: Corinne Calvet
Oct. 16: Peter Potter, Gale Robbins
Oct. 23: Johnny Carson, Allen Jenkins
Oct. 30: Sally Forrest, Roland Winters, Nancy Kulp
Nov. 6: Pre-empted by election coverage
Nov. 13: Virginia Grey
Nov. 20: Lola Albright
Nov. 27: Boris Karloff, Eva Gabor
Dec. 4: Marilyn Maxwell, Fritz Feld
Dec. 11: Pre-empted by a Victor Borge special
Dec. 18: Ruth Hussey
Dec. 25: Repeat of "The Cop and the Anthem" from Dec. 20, 1955
Jan. 1: Audrey Totter
Jan. 8: Cesar Romero
Jan. 15: Mickey Rooney
Jan. 22: Vincent Price
Jan. 29: James Dunn
Feb. 5: Eddie "Rochester" Anderson, Allen Jenkins
Feb. 12: John Ireland
Feb. 19: Elena Verdugo
Feb. 26: Charles Ruggles, Marie Windsor
March 5: Carol Channing
March 12: Edward Everett Horton
March 19: Virginia Grey
March 26: Chester Morris, Robert Armstrong, Veda Ann Borg
April 2: Arnold Stang, Jackie Coogan
April 9: Alan Mowbray, Reginald Denny
April 16: Evelyn Rudie, Mary Beth Hughes (actress), Lyle Talbot
April 23: Virginia Grey, Gerald Mohr
April 30: Arnold Stang, Lina Romay
May 7: Una Merkel
May 14: Vincent Price, Jayne Meadows
May 21: Mickey Rooney, Lina Romay
May 28: Pat O'Brien, Amanda Blake
June 4: Rex Allen, Allen Jenkins
June 11: Forrest Tucker
June 18: Jean Parker
June 25: Gregory Ratoff, Allen Jenkins, Douglas Fowley

1957-1958

Oct. 1: Marie Wilson, Marilyn Maxwell, Lyle Talbot, Tom Harmon, Brooklyn Dodgers players Gino Cimola and Don Drysdale
Oct. 8: Hans Conreid, Paul Coates
Oct. 15: Virginia Grey
Oct. 22: Cesar Romero
Oct. 29: Bob Sweeney, Jackie Coogan
Nov. 5: Peter Lorre
Nov. 12: Vincent Price
Nov. 19: Lola Albright

Nov. 26: Edward Everett Horton
Dec. 3: Pre-empted by *Lucille Ball-Desi Arnaz Show*
Dec. 10: Hans Conreid, Benny Baker
Dec. 17: Mickey Rooney, Jack Kirkwood
Dec. 24: James Dunn, Richard Eyer, the Mitchell Boys Choir
Dec. 31: Mercedes McCambridge, Charles Ruggles
Jan. 7: Andy Devine, John Carradine, Sterling Holloway, Franklin Pangborn
Jan. 14: Leo Carrillo
Jan. 21: Pre-empted by special *DuPont Show of the Month*
Jan. 28: No one listed
Feb. 4: Nancy Walker, Hope Emerson
Feb. 11: Rita Moreno
Feb. 18: Mary Beth Hughes, Jackie Coogan, Franklin Pangborn
Feb. 25: Vincent Price
March 4: Reed Hadley, Amanda Blake, Benny Baker
March 11: Sir Cedric Hardwicke
March 18: Marie Wilson
March 25: Billy Gilbert
April 1: Ruth Hussey
April 8: Barbara Nichols, Lynn Bari
April 15: Dick Foran, Craig Stevens
April 22: John Carradine, Franklin Pangborn
April 29: Audrey Totter
May 6: Mona Freeman, Randy Sparks
May 13: Milton Berle as guest host as Red mourns his son Richie's death
May 20: Pre-empted by President Dwight D. Eisenhower's press conference
May 27: Marilyn Maxwell, Steve Dunne
June 3: Charles Ruggles, Marie Windsor
June 10: Repeat of April 8 show
June 17: Jayne Meadows
June 24: Sessue Hayakawa, Lon Chaney, Jr.

1958-1959

Sept. 30: Liberace, Sandra Giles, Robert Eyer, Hector Torres
Oct. 7: John Carradine, Gene Raymond
Oct. 14: Ralph Story, Barbara Nichols
Oct. 21: Ann Rutherford, "Slapsie" Maxie Rosenbloom
Oct. 28: Rudy Vallee, Reed Hadley
Nov. 4: Pre-empted by election coverage
Nov. 18: Vanessa Brown, Jack Kirkwood
Nov. 25: William Frawley, Henry Kulky, Dick Elliot, Dick Crockett, Ray Kellogg, Ann Dore
Dec. 2: Joanne Dru, Marvin Kaplan
Dec. 9: Pre-empted by special *Gift of the Magi*
Dec. 16: Virginia Grey
Dec. 23: Repeat of Dec. 24, 1957, show
Dec. 30: Elena Verdugo, Fritz Feld, Frank Wilcox, Gil Stuart, Jack Boyle
Jan. 6: Edie Adams, Raymond Hatton
Jan. 13: Edward Everett Horton
Jan. 20: Janis Paige, Kathryn Card
Jan. 27: Marilyn Maxwell, Lon Chaney, Jr.
Feb. 3: Lee Aaker
Feb. 10: Gerald Mohr, Mary Beth Hughes
Feb. 17: Mona Freeman
Feb. 24: Pre-empted by special *DuPont Show of the Month*
March 3: Arthur Godfrey, Keefe Brasselle, the Henry Vee Aqua Frolics water show
March 10: Cesar Romero, Terry Moore
March 17: Garry Moore
March 24: Frank Lovejoy
March 31: Mickey Rooney, Mary Beth Hughes
April 7: Jackie Coogan, Gil Stratton, Nobu McCarthy
April 14: John Carradine
April 21: Marilyn Maxwell

April 28: Repeat of June 12, 1956, show
May 5: Dick Foran, Don Wilson
May 12: Peter Lorre
May 19: Wanda Hendrix
May 26: Audrey Totter
June 2: Frank McHugh
[Aired in repeats June 9, 16 and 23]

1959-1960

Sept. 29: Errol Flynn, Scott Engel
Oct. 6: Jayne Mansfield
Oct. 13: Eve Arden
Oct. 20: Jane Russell
Oct. 27: Pre-empted by special *The Bells of St. Mary's*
Nov. 3: Guy Madison, Amanda Blake
Nov. 10: Fabian
Nov. 17: Mercedes McCambridge, Peter Lorre
Nov. 24: Jayne Meadows
Dec. 1: Tuesday Weld, Mary Beth Hughes
Dec. 8: Barbara Nichols, Bobby Rydell
Dec. 15: Marie McDonald
Dec. 22: Repeat of Dec. 25, 1956, show
Dec. 29: Terry Moore, Charles Ruggles, Jack Kirkwood, Ray Kellogg
Jan. 5: Julie London, Jackie Coogan, George Neise
Jan. 12: Al Capp, Peter Palmer, Leslie Parrish and Stubby Kaye in "Clem in Dogpatch," a story involving and promoting the movie version of *Li'l Abner*
Jan. 19: Virginia Grey, Buster Crabbe, "Slapsie" Maxie Rosenbloom
Jan. 26: George Raft
Feb. 2: Fabian
Feb. 9: Pre-empted by special *Playhouse 90*
Feb. 16: Marilyn Maxwell
Feb. 23: Barbara Nichols, Gerald Mohr
March 1: Mae West, William Schallert, Reg Lewis
March 8: Brian Donlevy

March 15: Vincent Price, Jackie Coogan
March 22: Keefe Brasselle, George O'Hanlon, Maxine Gates, Frank Mitchell
March 29: Amanda Blake, Billy Gilbert
April 5: Jay North
April 12: Audrey Meadows, Arte Johnson
April 19: Basil Rathbone, Elena Verdugo
April 26: Repeat of March 31, 1959, show
May 3: Cesar Romero, Arte Johnson, Ray Kellogg
May 10: Edward Everett Horton, Dick Foran
May 17: Repeat of Feb. 16, 1960, show
May 24: Mamie Van Doren, Peter Lorre
May 31: Repeat of June 2, 1959, show
June 7: Vivian Vance
June 14: Marilyn Maxwell, Monty Margetts
June 21: Repeat of May 26, 1959, show

1960-1961

Sept. 27: Live one-man pantomime show from New York City
Oct. 4: Vivian Vance
Oct. 11: William Demarest
Oct. 18: Vincent Price, Marie Windsor
Oct. 25: Jackie Coogan
Nov. 1: Jayne Meadows
Nov. 8: Pre-empted by election coverage
Nov. 15: Virginia Grey
Nov. 22: Repeat of Nov. 25, 1958, show
Nov. 29: Terry Moore
Dec. 6: Keenan Wynn, Adele Mara
Dec. 13: Pre-empted by *DuPont Show of the Month*
Dec. 20: Repeat of Dec. 22, 1959, show

Dec. 27: Sir Cedric Hardwicke
Jan. 3: Mary Beth Hughes
Jan. 10: Guest hosts start as Red recuperates from surgery; Danny Thomas, Rusty Hamer, Angela Cartwright
Jan. 17: Garry Moore, Marilyn Maxwell, Bobby Rydell, Durward Kirby
Jan. 24: Jackie Gleason-Arthur Godfrey interview
Jan. 31: Marcel Marceau, live from New York City, introduced by Desi Arnaz (Red appears in taped segment)
Feb. 7: Ed Sullivan, Wayne and Shuster; last guest host show [Aired in repeats Feb. 14 through March 7]
March 14: Ed Wynn
March 21: Pre-empted by *DuPont Show of the Month*
March 28: Cesar Romero, Adele Mara
April 4: Hans Conreid, Leslie Parrish
April 11: Diana Dors
April 18: Allen Jenkins, Steve Dunne, Emmaline Henry
April 25: Billy Gilbert, Roland Winters
May 2: Marilyn Maxwell
May 9: Mary Beth Hughes, Henry Kulky
May 16: Sebastian Cabot
May 23: Don Knotts, Amanda Blake
May 30: Phyllis Avery
June 6: Vivian Vance
June 13: Jack Kirkwood, Jackie Coogan
June 20: Stanley Adams, Jimmy Cross
June 27: Cara Williams

1961-1962

Sept. 26: Jayne Mansfield, Linda Loftis (Miss Texas), Carol Lassater (Miss Utah)
Oct. 3: Eve Arden
Oct. 10: Jay North, Jackie Coogan, Eve Brent
Oct. 17: Don Knotts
Oct. 24: Bobby Rydell
Oct. 31: Rhonda Fleming
Nov. 7: Audrey Meadows, George Neise, Isabel Randolph
Nov. 14: Hans Conreid, Rosemary DeCamp, Charlie Smith, Gil Stuart
Nov. 21: Ed Wynn
Nov. 28: Marie Windsor, John Carradine
Dec. 5: Ernest Truex, Ronnie Burns
Dec. 12: Amanda Blake, Maurice Gosfield, Arthur Lyman musical group
Dec. 19: Cara Williams, Ross Ford, Emmaline Henry, Bob Duggan, Ray Kellogg, Roberta Lubell (ballerina), the Mitchell Boys Choir
Dec. 26: Marilyn Maxwell, Frank Wilcox
Jan. 2: Phyllis Avery, Dick Foran
Jan. 9: Edward Everett Horton, Jackie Cooper
Jan. 16: Virginia Grey, Gil Stuart
Jan. 23: Leslie Parrish
Jan. 30: One-man show by Red
Feb. 6: Pre-empted by special *Henry Fonda and the Family*
Feb. 13: Joey Faye
Feb. 20: Vivian Vance, Isabel Randolph
Feb. 27: Charlie Ruggles
March 6: John Carradine, Marie Windsor (repeat?)
March 13: Warner Anderson
March 20: Dorothy Provine
March 27: Marilyn Maxwell
April 3: Vincent Price
April 10: Jayne Meadows
April 17: No one listed; an all-pantomime show
April 24: Keenan Wynn
May 1: Repeat of March 15, 1960, show
May 8: Helen O'Connell, Roland Winters
May 15: Pat Carroll
May 22: Dick Foran
May 29: Sebastian Cabot
June 5: Repeat of April 11, 1961, show
June 12: Mickey Rooney

June 19: Repeat of Oct. 17, 1961, show
June 26: Vincent Price, Stanley Adams, Emmaline Henry, Maudie Prickett

1962-1963

Sept. 25: Harpo Marx, Mahalia Jackson, Virginia Grey, Dyan Cannon
Oct. 2: Juliet Prowse, Phil Harris
Oct. 9: Ray Bolger, Brenda Lee
Oct. 16: Kay Starr, Jackie Coogan
Oct. 23: George Gobel, Karen Morrow (network TV debut), Benny Rubin
Oct. 30: Jane Powell, Charlie Ruggles, Jules Munchin
Nov. 6: Pre-empted by election coverage
Nov. 13: Cesar Romero, Jo Stafford
Nov. 20: Janis Paige, Stubby Kaye
Nov. 27: Cyril Ritchard, Joannie Sommers
Dec. 4: Audrey Meadows, Bobby Rydell
Dec. 11: Rosemary Clooney
Dec. 18: Gordon and Sheila MacRae
Dec. 25: Repeat of Dec. 19, 1961, show
Jan. 1: Martha Raye, Tommy Noonan
Jan. 8: Eve Arden
Jan. 15: Miyoshi Umeki, Jules Munshin
Jan. 22: Phil Harris, Alice Faye
Jan. 29: Mickey Rooney, the Paris Sisters, Robert Strauss
Feb. 5: George Gobel, Jana Lund, Frankie Darro
Feb. 12: Cesar Romero, the Kessler Twins (Alice and Ellen; a German song-and-dance duo making its U.S. debut)
Feb. 19: Jayne Mansfield, Virginia Grey, the Lettermen
Feb. 26: Stubby Kaye, Robert Strauss
March 5: Sebastian Cabot, Jerry Lanning (singer; son of Roberta Sherwood)
March 12: Marilyn Maxwell, Jackie Coogan
March 19: Pre-empted by special *Judy Garland and Her Guests*, Phil Silvers and Robert Goulet
March 26: Amanda Blake, Bobby Rydell
April 2: Ginger Rogers, Robert Strauss
April 9: Janet Blair
April 16: Robert Horton, Frankie Darro
April 23: Repeat of Oct. 30, 1962, show
April 30: Forrest Tucker, Pat Carroll
May 7: Keely Smith
May 14: Mamie Van Doren
May 21: Rhonda Fleming, Hank Henry
May 28: Don Knotts, Helen O'Connell
[Aired in repeats from June 4 through June 25]

1963-1964

Sept. 24: Shirley Temple, the Beach Boys
Oct. 1: Steve Allen, Jayne Meadows, Joannie Sommers
Oct. 8: Ginger Rogers, Jackie Coogan
Oct. 15: Rosemary Clooney
Oct. 22: Jane Powell
Oct. 29: Ethel Merman
Nov. 5: Audrey Meadows, Richard Deacon, the Lettermen
Nov. 12: Jack E. Leonard, Roland Winters, Jane Dulo, Beverley Wright (singer)
Nov. 19: Bobby Rydell
Nov. 26: Unknown; this was the first day of regular entertainment on network TV following the assassination of President John F. Kennedy on Nov. 22, and the lineup on the Jan. 7, 1964, show was listed in both *TV Guide* and *The New York Times*, but both publications listed the same guests for the Jan. 7 show without indicating it was

a repeat, as they typically do, suggesting a possible pre-emption or last-minute repeat on this date.
Dec. 3: Raymond Burr, the Kessler Twins
Dec. 10: Cesar Romero
Dec. 17: Joannie Sommers, Jackie Coogan
Dec. 24: Repeat of Dec. 19, 1961, show
Dec. 31: Jane Russell, Beryl Davis, Connie Hines
Jan. 7: George Gobel, Jules Munshin, Vi Velasco (female singer)
Jan. 14: Stubby Kaye, the Paris Sisters
Jan. 21: Merv Griffin
Jan. 28: Pat Suzuki, Jack Soo
Feb. 4: Vincent Price, Helen O'Connell
Feb. 11: Douglas Fairbanks, Jr.
Feb. 18: Pat Carroll, Jean-Paul Vignon (French singer)
Feb. 25: Don Knotts, the Youngfolk
March 3: Liberace
March 10: Jackie Coogan, Vivian Vance, the Womenfolk
March 17: Mickey Rooney, Jo Stafford
March 24: Rhonda Fleming, Hank Henry (comedian)
March 31: Janet Blair
April 7: Connie Stevens
April 14: Vincent Price, Bobby Rydell
April 21: Cesar Romero, Poncie Ponce
April 28: Tony Bennett, Virginia Grey, Jules Munshin
May 5: Mickey Rooney, Jackie Coogan, the Snobs (a British quartet dressed in powdered wigs—their American TV debut)
May 12: Raymond Burr, the Beach Boys ("In My Room," "I Get Around")
May 19: Repeat of Feb. 19, 1963, show
May 26: Repeat of March 26, 1963, show
June 2: Robert Horton
June 9: Eve Arden

1964-1965

Sept. 22: Audrey Meadows, Johnny Rivers
Sept. 29: The Rolling Stones (according to the *Variety* review of the Sept. 22 show, indicating the rock group would be on the next week; no one listed here by both *TV Guide* and *The New York Times*, and despite what several Rolling Stone biographies and the book *Total Television* claim, the Stones did NOT appear on the Sept. 22 show; see also Nov. 10.)
Oct. 6: Robert Merrill
Oct. 13: Ed Wynn, Mary Wickes, Vikki Carr
Oct. 20: Bobby Rydell
Oct. 27: Martha Raye
Nov. 3: Pre-empted by election coverage
Nov. 10: "Red Skelton in London," with Sebastian Cabot and the Rolling Stones
Nov. 17: Vic Damone, Gale Garnett
Nov. 24: Ginger Rogers
Dec. 1: Pat Boone, Will Jordan, Joyce Jameson
Dec. 8: Fernando Lamas
Dec. 15: George Gobel, the Youngfolk, Shirley Mitchell
Dec. 22: Greer Garson, the Hillcrest Elementary School Choir of Los Angeles
Dec. 29: Shirley Mitchell, Milton Frome, the McGuire Sisters
Jan. 5: Al Hirt
Jan. 12: Eve Arden
Jan. 19: Archie Moore, Shani Wallis (British singer)
Jan 26: Don Knotts, the Searchers
Feb. 2: "Concert in Pantomime" with Marcel Marceau and host Maurice Chevalier
Feb. 9: Vincent Price, Anita Bryant
Feb. 16: Robert Goulet
Feb. 23: Hugh O'Brian, Piccola Pupa (Italian singer)
March 2: Janis Paige, Sheilah Rogers
March 9: Ed Wynn

March 16: Paul Anka, Jimmy Cross, Frankie Darro
March 23: George C. Scott, the Honeycombs ("Have I the Right?")
March 30: Raymond Burr, the Kinks ("Got Love If You Want It")
April 6: Patrice Munsel
April 13: Paul Ford, Jan and Dean
April 20: Connie Stevens
April 27: Fred Gwynne, Billy J. Kramer and the Dakotas
May 4: Martha Raye
[Aired in repeats from May 11 through June 15]

1965-1966

Sept. 14: Paul Ford, Freddie and the Dreamers
Sept. 21: Bobby Darin, Jackie and Gayle (singers)
Sept. 28: Mickey Rooney, the U.S. Drum and Bugle Team of Pacific Fleet Force
Oct. 5: Patrice Munsel, Peter and Gordon, Cliff Osmond
Oct. 12: Bobby Rydell, the New Christy Minstrels
Oct. 19: Harv Presnell, Reta Shaw
Oct. 26: Johnny Mathis
Nov. 2: Audrey Meadows, Douglas Fowley, the Lettermen
Nov. 9: Bill Dana, Vic Dana, Mary Wickes, Sandra Gould
Nov. 16: Stanley Holloway, the Youngfolk
Nov. 23: Pre-empted by special *Tribute to Stan Laurel*
Nov. 30: Robert Morse, the Animals ("We Gotta Get Out of This Place," "Don't Let Me Be Misunderstood"), Doris Singleton
Dec. 7: Robert Vaughn, the Doodletown Pipers, Carol Byron
Dec. 14: Tallulah Bankhead, Horst Jankowski
Dec. 21: Repeat of Dec. 22, 1964, show
Dec. 28: Cesar Romero, the Silkie, Emmaline Henry, Barbara Morrison, Helen Kleeb

Jan. 4: Milton Berle, Linda Bennett (singer)
Jan. 11: Buddy Ebsen, Jackie and Gayle
Jan. 18: "Concert in Pantomime" with Marcel Marceau
Jan. 25: Vincent Price, Shirley Mitchell, the Supremes
Feb. 1: George Gobel, the Hollies ("I'm Alive," "Look Through Any Window")
Feb. 8: Tina Louise, Roland Winters, Herb Alpert and the Tijuana Brass ("Zorba the Greek," "Mexican Shuffle," "Tijuana Taxi")
Feb. 15: Ed Wynn, Donna Loren
Feb. 22: Stubby Kaye, Muriel Landers, David Sharpe
March 1: John Wayne, Melanie Alexander
March 8: Repeat of Nov. 9, 1965, show
March 15: Repeat of Nov. 16, 1965, show
March 22: Pre-empted by special *Carol + 2*
March 29: Phyllis Diller, the Rockin' Berries (English singing group)
April 5: Jackie Coogan, the Doodletown Pipers
April 12: Nancy Wilson, Jack Kruschen
April 19: Fernando Lamas, Ike Cole (Nat "King" Cole's singer/pianist brother)
April 26: Abbe Lane
May 3: Robert Merrill
May 10: Jack Jones, Virginia Grey, Hal Smith
May 17: Petula Clark, Romo Vincent
[Aired in repeats from May 24 through June 28]

1966-1967

Sept. 13: Gig Young, Johnny Rivers ("Secret Agent Man," "Poor Side of Town")
Sept. 20: Mickey Rooney, Simon

and Garfunkel ("I Am a Rock," "The Dangling Conversation")
Sept. 27: Nancy Ames, Jackie Coogan
Oct. 4: Godfrey Cambridge, Jackie and Gayle
Oct. 11: Audrey Meadows, Shirley Bassey
Oct. 18: Robert Vaughn, Joyce Jameson, Jay and the Americans
Oct. 25: Polly Bergen
Nov. 1: Frank Gorshin, the Baja Marimba Band
Nov. 8: Pre-empted by election coverage
Nov. 15: Tim Conway, Jane Marsh (classical singer)
Nov. 22: Jack Jones
Nov. 29: Janet Leigh, Dionne Warwick ("Walk On By")
Dec. 6: Allen Funt, Abbe Lane
Dec. 13: Robert Goulet
Dec. 20: Greer Garson, the Recruit Bluejacket Choir from the U.S. Naval Training Center in San Diego
Dec. 27: Tony Randall, Barbara Hewitt (1966 Tournament of Roses Queen)
Jan. 3: Peter Falk, Jane Morgan
Jan. 10: Bob Crane, John Banner
Jan. 17: Ozzie and Harriet Nelson, Barbara McNair
Jan. 24: Eve Arden, Marilyn Michaels
Jan. 31: Merv Griffin, the Youngfolk
Feb. 7: Edie Adams
Feb. 14: George Gobel, Chad and Jeremy
Feb. 21: Pre-empted by an Andy Griffith special
Feb. 28: Terry-Thomas, Joannie Sommers
March 7: Mickey Rooney, Martha Raye
March 14: Cesar Romero, the Serenaders (band of 14 Los Angeles children)
March 21: Richard Chamberlain
March 28: Cliff Robertson, Tony Sandler and Ralph Young
April 4: Tennessee Ernie Ford

April 11: Pre-empted by a Dick Van Dyke special
April 18: Fernando Lamas, Senator Everett McKinley Dirksen
April 25: Vincent Price, June Lockhart, Matt Monro (singer)
May 2: Patrice Munsel
May 9: Nipsey Russell, Lana Cantrell
[Aired in repeats from May 16 through June 27]

1967-1968

Sept. 12: Eve Arden, Robert Stack, Johnny Rivers ("Tracks of My Tears")
Sept. 19: Stanley Holloway, Sergio Mendes and Brasil 66
Sept. 26: Godfrey Cambridge, Janis Paige
Oct. 3: Bert Lahr, Fran Jeffries
Oct. 10: Fernando Lamas, the Fifth Dimension
Oct. 17: Terry-Thomas, Nancy Wilson
Oct. 24: John Forsythe, Michele Lee
Oct. 31: Tim Conway, Jackie Coogan, Nancy Ames
Nov. 7: Wally Cox
Nov. 14: Vincent Price, Dionne Warwick ("I Say a Little Prayer")
Nov. 21: Polly Bergen, Pat Carroll, Reta Shaw, Billy Barty
Nov. 28: Arthur Godfrey, Harpers Bizarre ("Chattanooga Choo Choo")
Dec. 5: George Gobel, the Four Seasons ("Sherry," "Can't Take My Eyes Off of You")
Dec. 12: Milton Berle, Emmaline Henry, Dusty Springfield ("The Look of Love," "Sunny")
Dec. 19: Howard Keel, Joan Freeman, Linda Sue Risk, Jillana (ballerina)
Dec. 26: Maurice Evans
Jan. 2: Repeat of Jan. 4, 1966, show
Jan. 9: Roy Rogers and Dale Evans, Gilbert Price (singer)
Jan. 16: One-man show
Jan. 23: Phyllis Diller, Lou Rawls
Jan. 30: Cyril Ritchard, Jane Powell

Feb. 6: Herschel Bernardi (sang "Sunrise Sunset" from *Fiddler on the Roof*), Diane Linkletter
Feb. 13: Burl Ives, Lulu ("To Sir with Love")
Feb. 20: Terry-Thomas, Shani Wallis
Feb. 27: Vice President Hubert Humphrey introduces Red doing pantomime before the United Nations in "Laughter the Universal Language"
March 5: Liberace, the Youngfolk
March 12: Mike Connors, Tom Jones, Emmaline Henry
March 19: Eddy Arnold, Reta Shaw, Pat Priest
March 26: Pat Carroll, Joe E. Ross, the Doodletown Pipers
April 2: Jack Jones, Jackie Russell
April 9: Repeat of Nov. 28, 1967, show
April 16: Repeat of Nov. 21, 1967, show
April 23: Mickey Rooney, Lana Cantrell
April 30: Nipsey Russell, the Association ("Windy," "Birthday Morning")
[Aired in repeats from May 7 through June 4]

1968-1969

Sept. 24: Vincent Price, Boris Karloff, Ed Sullivan, Spanky Wilson (jazz singer)
Oct. 1: Van Johnson, the Lettermen ("Going Out of My Head," "Can't Take My Eyes Off You")
Oct. 8: Maurice Evans, Shirley Bassey
Oct. 15: Martha Raye, Jimmy Cross, the First Edition
Oct. 22: Pat Carroll
Oct. 29: George Gobel, Jan Davis, the Mills Brothers, Barbara Bostock, Beverly Powers, Bob Duggan, Fred Villani
Nov. 5: Pre-empted by election coverage
Nov. 12: Tony Sandler and Ralph Young (singing duo making their TV acting debuts)
Nov. 19: Jackie Coogan, Sue Raney (singer)
Nov. 26: Jane Wyman, the Vogues ("Five O'Clock World," "Turn Around, Look at Me"), Art Gilmore, Ida Mae McKenzie, Beverly Powers
Dec. 3: Jane Powell
Dec. 10: Ozzie and Harriet Nelson
Dec. 17: Dale Robertson
Dec. 24: "A Christmas Story—1777," with Senator Everett McKinley Dirksen, Georgia (Mrs. Red) Skelton (cameo), Jillana (ballerina)
Dec. 31: Dionne Warwick
Jan. 7: Lana Cantrell
Jan. 14: Audrey Meadows, Ted Mack, the Lettermen
Jan. 21: Carol Lawrence, Lou Rawls, Ross Ford, Tim Herbert, Ida Mae McKenzie
Jan. 28: Phyllis Diller, Grace Markay (singer)
Feb. 4: Jack Soo
Feb. 11: Bobby Rydell
Feb. 18: Mickey Rooney, Hal Frazier (singer)
Feb. 25: Vikki Carr, Florence Lake
March 4: Sergio Franchi (acting as well as singing), Jimmy Cross
March 11: Roy Rogers, Dale Evans, Art Gilmore
March 18: Merv Griffin, Bern Hoffman (actor)
March 25: Arthur Godfrey, the Young Americans
April 1: Jack Jones
April 8: June Lockhart, Gloria Loring, Reta Shaw
April 15: Patrice Munsel, Elaine Joyce, Jimmy Cross
April 22: Sergio Franchi
April 29: Robert Merrill, Arthur Fiedler and the Boston Pops
[Aired in repeats May 6 through July 8]

1969-1970

Sept. 23: Peter Graves, Iron Butterfly ("In-a-Gadda-Da-Vida"), Walker Edmiston, Bill Shannon

Sept. 30: Walter Brennan, The Lettermen ("Hurt So Bad"), Peggy Rea, Bern Hoffman
Oct. 7: Jack Albertson, Gary Puckett and the Union Gap ("This Girl is a Woman Now")
Oct. 14: Martha Raye, the Vogues
Oct. 21: Kaye Ballard, Paul Revere and the Raiders ("Good Thing"), Ed Sullivan (cameo)
Oct. 28: John Wayne, Julius Wechter and the Baja Marimba Band
Nov. 4: Audrey Meadows, Edgar Bergen and his dummy Charlie McCarthy, Three Dog Night ("Easy to Be Hard"), Beverly Powers
Nov. 11: Maurice Evans, Beverly Powers, Oliver ("Jean")
Nov. 18: George Gobel, Lou Rawls, Peggy Rea, Walker Edmiston
Nov. 25: Walter Brennan, Smith ("Baby, It's You"), Peggy Rea, Bern Hoffman (UFO dance number here earned Tom Hansen an Emmy nomination for Best Choreography.)
Dec. 2: Janet Leigh, the Mills Brothers
Dec. 9: Agnes Moorehead, Shirley Bassey
Dec. 16: Jack Wild (as the Artful Dodger), Cyril Ritchard; Red played Oliver Twist Junior
Dec. 23: Repeat of "A Christmas Urchin" from Dec. 19, 1967
Dec. 30: Barbara Bain, Sweetwater (rock group—"Two Worlds")
Jan. 6: Vincent Price, Frank Sinatra, Jr., Bill Shannon
Jan. 13: Pat Carroll, Duke Ellington and His Orchestra
Jan. 20: Robert Merrill
Jan. 27: Jane Powell
Feb. 3: Mike Connors, Danny Davis and the Nashville Brass
Feb. 10: Carol Lawrence
Feb. 17: Barbara Feldon, The Lettermen ("Traces," "Memories")
Feb. 24: Mickey Rooney, Tiny Tim, Audrey Meadows, Jackie Coogan, Jimmy Cross
March 3: Godfrey Cambridge, Pat Carroll, Jackie DeShannon, Ida Mae McKenzie
March 10: Vincent Price, Kenny Rogers and the First Edition ("Something's Burning")
March 17: Fess Parker, Mac Davis
March 24: Tony Sandler and Ralph Young, Billy Barty, Beverly Powers
March 31: George Gobel, the Original Caste ("One Tin Soldier"), Barbara Bostock
April 7: Cesar Romero, Clint Howard
[Aired in repeats April 14 through June 23]

1970-1971 (on NBC)

Sept. 14: Spiro Agnew (introduction only), Jerry Lewis, singer Robin Wilson, Jim Carroll
Sept. 21: Dean Martin (introduction only), Raymond Burr, Barbara Anderson
Sept. 28: Jack Benny (introduction only), Robert Wagner, Emmaline Henry, Brad Logan
Oct. 5: Johnny Carson (introduction only), Mike Connors, Robin Wilson
Oct. 12: Walter Brennan
Oct. 19: Gene Barry
Oct. 26: Van Johnson
Nov. 2: Barbara Feldon
Nov. 9: Dan Blocker, Emmaline Henry
Nov. 16: Godfrey Cambridge, Ida Mae McKenzie
Nov. 23: Mickey Rooney
Nov. 30: Pre-empted by *Winnie the Pooh and the Blustery Day* special
Dec. 7: Michael Landon, Bob Duggan, Adam Kaufman, Billy Barty, Linda Sue Risk
Dec. 14: Telly Savalas, Linda Sue Risk
Dec. 21: Leslie Nielsen; Christmas story written by Red
Dec. 28: Repeat of Oct. 12, 1970, show
Jan. 4: Audrey Meadows

Jan. 11: Jill St. John
Jan. 18: Cass Elliott, Chad Everett
Jan. 25: James Drury
Feb. 1: Eva Gabor, Wally Cox
Feb. 8: Vincent Price, Peggy Rea
Feb. 15: Martha Raye, Peggy Rea, Ida Mae McKenzie
Feb. 22: George Gobel
March 1: Phyllis Diller
March 8: Tony Randall
March 15: Sebastian Cabot
[Aired in repeats June 6 through Aug. 29]

Appendix C: Whatever Happened to...? A Select List of *The Red Skelton Show* Principals

Jan Arvan: Died May 24, 1979, at age 66.

James Bacon: The longtime Hollywood columnist first met Red in 1950 when Bacon was working for the Associated Press. More than 50 years later, in 2002, he was still writing a column, now for the local publication *Beverly Hills (213)*. "I'm only working once a week," he modestly noted, without pointing out the fact that he remained as colorful as the town he covered still at the age of 88. He considers *The Red Skelton Show* a great show. Given his extensive involvement covering entertainment, future TV historians should keep his opinion in mind.

Cecil Barker: Died Nov. 12, 1966, at age 48.

Seymour Berns: Died May 16, 1982, at age 62.

Alan Copeland: He was working on his autobiography in 2002 and also was a staff member at the Jazz School in Berkeley, Calif.

Guy della Cioppa: Died Jan. 17, 2000, at age 86.

Jack Donohue: Died March 27, 1984, at age 76.

Jack Douglas: Died Jan. 31, 1989, at age 80.

Ray Erlenborn: Though officially retired in California, the octogenarian still occasionally participates in radio nostalgia shows in the early 21st century.

John Gaunt: Died Sept. 23, 1958, at age 46.

Jesse Goldstein: Died May 14, 1959, at age 43.

Hal Goodman: Died Sept. 3, 1997, at age 82.

Chanin Hale: Red's favorite leading lady of the 1960s is happily married in California and not pursuing acting with the same vigor she did a few decades ago, doing only a few auditions. But, she told me, "I wouldn't say no to a job now. I have the same clothes and am the same size. I still kind of look like I did." She added that as far as *The Red Skelton Show* goes, "I have only fond memories of the whole thing."

Tom Hansen: He choreographed Jim Nabors' annual Hawaiian stage show, "Merry Christmas with Friends and Nabors," in the late 1990s. He moved to Fallbrook, Calif., near San

Diego in 1980, and 10 years later became a faculty member of Palomar College, where he remained at the time of our interview.

Bill Hobin: Died Feb. 15, 1998, at age 74. He wrote a two-volume autobiography covering his long TV career with Steve Koundakjian (Red's attorney in the 1980 legal suit from his writers) in 1986 that has yet to be published.

Jimmy Joyce: After doing Red's show, his singing group was on *The Tim Conway Comedy Hour* in 1970. He died on May 17, 1974, at the age of 54.

Robert L. Mott: Retired and living in Arroyo Grande, Calif.

John Fenton Murray: Died July 24, 1996, at age 79.

Dave O'Brien: Died Nov. 8, 1969, at age 57.

Robert Orben: The longtime comedy writer lives in the suburbs of Washington, D.C. After his stint with the Ford administration, he worked with many corporations on using comedy in their jobs. "I'm the one who popularized humor consultants to businesses," he said. He remains well regarded as a top comedy writer and often is interviewed about his beliefs in the field. "I'm mostly retired," he said of his work schedule in 2002. "I turn out a book occasionally."

Nat Perrin: Died May 9, 1998, at age 93.

Marty Rackin: Died April 15, 1976, at age 58.

Martin Ragaway: Died April 20, 1989, at age 66.

Larry Rhine: Died Oct. 27, 2000, at age 90.

David Rose: Died Aug. 23, 1990, at age 80.

Bob Schiller: Retired and living in southern California.

Herb Schlosser: A longtime NBC employee who joined the network in 1957, he rose through the ranks to be network president in the mid–1970s and helped in the development of *Saturday Night Live* and other hits. He now works with a law firm in New York City, among other activities.

Al Schwartz: Died March 26, 1988, at age 77.

Sherwood Schwartz: In an interview in the Jan. 11–17, 2003, issue of *TV Guide*, the 86-year-old veteran scribe mentioned there were plans to convert his (in)famous TV series creation *Gilligan's Island* into a Broadway musical—an idea almost as outlandish as most of the scripts he wrote for *The Red Skelton Show*.

Ed Simmons: Died May 18, 1998, at age 78.

Red Skelton: Died Sept. 17, 1997, at age 84. Survived by his third wife Lothian and daughter Valentina. Edits of his 1951–53 and 1970–71 shows are available via his estate's official website, www.redskelton.com, as are his extensive artwork and related memorabilia.

Arthur Stander: Died July 20, 1963, at age 46.

Hugh Wedlock: Died Dec. 13, 1993, at age 85.

Bob Weiskopf: Died Feb. 20, 2001, at age 86.

Bibliography

Books

Allen, Steve. *More Funny People*. New York: Stein, 1982.
Bedell Smith, Sally. *In All His Glory*. New York: Simon & Schuster, 1990.
Brooks, Tim, and Earle Marsh. *The Complete Directory of Prime Time Network and Cable Shows, 1946–Present*, 7th ed. New York: Ballantine, 1999.
Broughton, Irv. *Producers on Producing: The Making of Film and Television*. Jefferson, N.C.: McFarland, 1986.
Douglas, Mike, with Thomas Kelly and Michael Heaton. *I'll Be Right Back*. New York: Simon & Schuster, 2000.
Farr, Jamie, with Robert Blair Kaiser. *Just Farr Fun*. Clearwater, Fla.: Eubanks/Donizetti, 1994.
Fidelman, Geoffrey Mark. *The Lucy Book*. Los Angeles: Renaissance, 1999.
Fireman, Judy, ed. *TV Book*. New York: Workham, 1977.
Frank, Sam. *Buyer's Guide to Fifty Years of TV on Video*. Amherst, N.Y.: Prometheus, 1999.
Gehring, Wes D. *Seeing Red ... The Skelton in Hollywood's Closet: An Analytical Biography*. Davenport, Iowa: Robin Vincent, 2001.
Goldberg, Lee. *Unsold Television Pilots 1955 through 1989*. Jefferson, N.C.: McFarland, 1990.
Greenfield, Jeff. *Television: The First 50 Years*. New York: Crown, 1981.
Hobin, Bill, with Stephen J. Koundakjian. *Window on the Stars: 35 Years of Television from a Director's P.O.V.* unpublished manuscript, 1986.
Hyatt, Wesley. *Short-Lived Television Series 1948–1978*. Jefferson, N.C.: McFarland, 2003.
Kaplan, Mike, ed. *Variety Presents the Complete Book of Major U.S. Show Business Awards*. New York: Garland, 1985.
Keaton, Buster, with Charles Samuels. *My Wonderful World of Slapstick*. New York: Doubleday, 1960.
Lamparski, Richard. *Whatever Became Of...? Tenth Series*. New York: Crown, 1986.
Marx, Arthur. *Red Skelton*. New York: E.P. Dutton, 1979.
McNeil, Alex. *Total Television: A Comprehensive Guide to Programming from 1948 to the Present*. 4th ed. New York: Penguin, 1996.
Mott, Robert L. *Radio Live! Television Live!* Jefferson, N.C: McFarland, 2000.
Norback, Craig T., and Peter G. Norback, eds. *TV Guide Almanac*. New York: Ballantine, 1980.

Paley, William S. *As It Happened: A Memoir.* New York: Doubleday, 1979.
Paper, Lewis J. *Empire: William S. Paley and the Making of CBS.* New York: St. Martin's, 1987.
Rubin, Benny. *Come Backstage with Me.* Bowling Green, Ohio: Popular Press, 1973.
Stempel, Tom. *Storytellers to the Nation: A History of American Television Writing.* Syracuse, N.Y.: Syracuse University Press, 1996.
Wilk, Max. *The Golden Age of Television.* New York: Dell, 1976.
Young, Jordan R. *The Laugh Crafters: Comedy Writing in Radio and TV's Golden Age.* Beverly Hills, Calif.: Past Times, 1999.

Magazine and Newspaper Articles

Albert, Dora. "The Tragi-Comic World of TV." *TV Radio Mirror*, May 1959, pp. 43, 76–77.
"Another Comedy Star Is Heading for Television." *TV Digest*, Sept. 29, 1951, pp. 8–9.
Busch, Noel. "Television Clown Prince." *Television Age*, Jan. 18, 1965, pp. 28–29, 56–60.
"Clown of the Year." *Newsweek*, March 17, 1952, pp. 56–57.
Davidson, Bill. "Red Skelton: 'I'm Nuts and I Know It.'" *Saturday Evening Post*, June 17, 1967, pp. 66–76.
De Roos, Robert. "Television's Greatest Clown." *TV Guide*, Oct. 14–20, 1961 and Oct. 21–27, 1961.
"The Giddy Heights." *Newsweek*, Dec. 28, 1959, p. 58.
Glatzer, Hal. *People*, April 28, 1980, pp. 90–95.
Jennings, Dean. "Sad and Lonely Clown." *Saturday Evening Post*, June 2, 1962, pp. 50–54.
Oliver, Myrna. "Red Skelton Agrees to Preserve Tapes." *Los Angeles Times*, Sept. 5, 1980, pp. II-4.
"Red Skelton a Top Click in TV." *TV Digest*, March 15, 1952, pp. 8–9.
"Right Up There." *TV Guide*, April 28–May 4, 1956, pp. 4–6.
"Skelton Tries Again." *TV Guide*, Oct. 2–8, 1953, pp. 5–7.
"TV Guide's 1951 Awards." *TV Guide*, Dec. 21, 1951, pp. 6–7.
"The Unflappable Miss Morrison." *TV Guide*, July 11–17, 1964, pp. 25–27.
Whitney, Dwight. "What Makes a Clown?" *TV Guide*, Jan. 24, 1959, pp. 17–19.
_____. "The Weekly Ordeal of Red Skelton." *TV Guide*, April 20–26, 1963, pp. 15–18 and April 27–May 3, 1963, pp. 15–17.
In addition to those listed, multiple issues of *The New York Times*, *TV Guide* and *Variety* were consulted for reviews and program details.

Websites

www.idoodit.com
www.imdb.com (Internet Movie Database)

Videos

Red Skelton Collector's Series Vols. 1–3. (1950–52 shows)
The Best of the Red Skelton Show Vols. 1–4 (1970–71 shows)

Index

Unless otherwise noted, entries in italics are television series

Aaker, Lee 64, 165
Abbott, Bud 86
Abbott and Costello Meet the Killer, Boris Karloff (movie) 86
The Abbott and Costello Show (radio) 38
Ace, Goodman 124
Adams, Edie 95, 165, 171
Adams, Stanley 167, 168
The Adventures of Ozzie and Harriet 13
The Adventures of Rin Tin Tin 64
The Adventures of Superman 35
Advise and Consent (movie) 97
The Affairs of Susan (movie) 24
Agnew, Vice Pres. Spiro 115, 129, 148, 173
The Alan Young Show 27
Alberghetti, Anna Maria 163
Albert, Dora 29, 64, 66
Albertson, Jack 80, 173
Albright, Lola 164
The Alcoa Hour 48
Alda, Alan 146
Alexander, Melanie 170
Alfred Hitchcock Presents 123
Alias Jesse James (movie) 42
All in the Family 142, 147
All Star Revue 40, 87, 106
Allen, Gracie 52
Allen, Mel 163
Allen, Rex 164
Allen, Steve 4, 168

Alpert, Herb, and the Tijuana Brass 170
American Masters 10, 155
Ames, Nancy 171
The Amin Brothers 163
Amos 'n' Andy (radio) 38
Anderson, Barbara 173
Anderson, Eddie "Rochester" 164
Anderson, Warner 27, 167
The Andrews Sisters 40
The Andy Griffith Show 38, 92, 93, 95, 106, 123
The Andy Williams Show 91, 107, 136, 137
The Animals 84, 170
Anka, Paul 170
Ann-Margret 132, 147
The Ann Sothern Show 87
Appleby, George *see* George Appleby
"Aquarius/Let the Sunshine In" (song) 114
Arden, Eve 166–169, 171
Armstrong, Robert 164
Armstrong Circle Theater 46, 67
Arnaz, Desi 87, 88, 167
Arness, James 54, 143
Arnie 86
Arnold, Eddy 172
Arquette, Cliff 9
Arthur, Bea 142
Arthur Godfrey and His Friends 35
The Arthur Godfrey Show 68
Arthur Godfrey's Talent Scouts 84
The Arthur Murray Party 68

Arvan, Jan 79, 80, 132, 161, 175
As It Happened (book) 117
The Association 172
Avalon Time (radio show) 9, 11, 12
Avery, Phyllis 167

B.B. and the Oscars 113
Bacon, James 56, 57, 60, 83, 84, 119, 137, 142, 150, 159, 175
The Bad and the Beautiful (movie) 24
Bailey, Pearl 147
Bain, Barbara 173
The Baja Marimba Band 171, 173
Baker, Benny 165
Ball, Lucille 26, 27, 42, 53, 54, 87, 93, 143, 146, 147, 154
Ballard, Kaye 173
Balzer, George 107, 161
Bankhead, Tallulah 170
Banner, John 171
Barclift, Nelson 162
The Bards 113
Bari, Lynn 165
Barker, Cecil 39, 44, 45, 64, 85, 161, 175
Barron, Jeffrey 125, 126, 161
Barry, Gene 133, 173
Barty, Billy 171, 173
Basie, Count 78
Basie Swingin', Voices Singin' (album) 78
Bass, Jules 144
Bassey, Shirley 171–173
The Beach Boys 84, 168, 169

179

Index

Bearde, Chris 126
The Beatles 84
The Bell Telephone Hour 32
The Bells of St. Mary's (special) 166
Benaderet, Bea 119
Bennett, Linda 170
Bennett, Marjorie 162
Bennett, Tony 169
Benny, Jack 4, 40, 107, 131, 132, 140, 173
The Benny Rubin Show 25
Bergen, Edgar 40, 106, 173
Bergen, Polly 95, 171
Bergman, Ingrid 51
Berle, Milton 4, 8, 12, 26, 35, 36, 38, 52, 64, 83, 140, 141, 143, 156, 165, 170, 171
Berman, Pancho 9
Bernard, Victor Van *see* Victor Van Bernard
Bernardi, Herschel 172
Berner, Sara 163
Berns, Seymour 39, 57, 66, 77, 84, 85, 89, 106, 161, 175
The Best of Broadway 48
"The Best of Red Skelton" (compilation) 132, 133
Beulah 105
The Beulah Show (radio) 38
The Beverly Hillbillies 81, 87, 136
Bewitched 13, 86
The Big Clock (movie) 24
Big Town (radio) 55
Bigelow, Joe 43, 44, 161
The Bill Cosby Show 124, 137
Billboard (periodical) 69, 113
Bing Crosby and His Friends (special) 53
Black Shield of Falworth (movie) 36
Blaine, Vivian 163
Blair, Janet 43, 168, 169
Blake, Amanda 14, 93, 164–168
Blocker, Dan 131, 173
Blondie (radio) 55
The Blue Dahlia (movie) 24
Blue Hawaii (movie) 97
Blue Skies (movie)
Blum, Daniel 2

The Bob Crosby Show 77
The Bob Cummings Show 67, 87
Bob Hope Show (radio) 11, 44
Bob Hope's Overseas Christmas Tours (special) 147
The Bob Newhart Show (1961–62 version) 69
The Bob Newhart Show (1972–78 version) 133
Bolger, Ray 168
Bolivar Shagnasty 14, 61, 65
Bonanza 1, 2, 15, 16, 85, 97, 102, 131
The Book of Lists (book) 2
Boone, Pat 169
Borg, Veda Ann 164
Borge, Victor 164
Bostock, Barbara 172, 173
Bouche, Rene 114
The Box (book) 3
Boyle, Jack 161, 165
Brady, Ben 39, 161
The Brady Brides 148
The Brady Bunch 44, 148
The Brady Bunch Hour 148
The Bradys 148
Brasselle, Keefe 49, 164–166
Break the Bank 19
Breakfast at Tiffany's (movie) 97
Brennan, Walter 99, 102, 135, 173
Brent, Eve 167
Bridge on the River Kwai (movie) 96
Bridges, Lloyd 48
Brigadoon (special) 99
Brooks, Tim 3, 132
Broughton, Irv 18, 33
Brown, Les 15
Brown, Vanessa 165
Bryant, Anita 169
The Buick Circus Hour 116
The Bullwinkle Show 11
Burger King 114
Burgundy Street Singers 129, 132, 134
Burnett, Carol 81, 103, 132, 150, 156, 158
Burns, David 163
Burns, George 140, 156
Burns, Ronnie 167
Burr, Raymond 131, 169, 170, 173
Burt, Lionel 125, 126, 161

Burton, Mickie 162
Bus Stop (movie) 96
Busch, Noel 19, 76
Bye Bye Birdie (movie) 97
Byron, Carol 170

C and the Shells 113
Cabot, Sebastian 137, 167–169, 174
Cade's County 139
Caesar, Sid 4, 26, 66
Caesar's Hour 48, 134
Cagney, Jeanne 49, 163
Calhern, Louis 24
Calloway, Cab 163
Calvert, John 163
Calvet, Corinne 164
Cambridge, Godfrey 171, 173
Campbell, Glen 110
Can Can (movie) 96
Cannon, Dyan 90, 168
Canova, Judy 164
Cantor, Eddie 26
Cantrell, Lana 82, 83, 171, 172
Capp, Al 166
Captain Kangaroo 107
Car 54, Where Are You? 106
Card, Kathryn 165
Carney, Art 43
Carol Burnett and Friends 150, 158
The Carol Burnett Show 38, 39, 56, 87, 103, 141, 158
Carol + 2 (special) 170
Carr, Vikki 169, 172
Carradine, John 48, 163–165, 167
Carrillo, Leo 165
Carroll, Diahann 105
Carroll, Jim 173
Carroll, Pat 65, 167–169, 171–173
Carson, Johnny 34, 106, 131, 134, 142, 144–147, 164, 173
Carson's Cellar 34
Carter, Jimmy 148
Cartwright, Angela 167
Caruso, Dee 126–129, 134, 135, 161
Cassavetes, John 132
Cauliflower McPugg 14, 21, 23, 28, 37, 44, 70
Cavalcade of America 46
CBS on the Air: A Celebration of 50 Years (special) 146

Index

Celebrity Time 26
Chad and Jeremy 171
Chamberlain, Richard 83, 95, 171
Chandler, Bob 66
Chandler, George 68
Chaney, Lon, Jr. 165
Channing, Carol 164
Charlie the Swinger 101
Charlie's Angels 147
Chavales de España, Los 163
Chevalier, Maurice 90, 169
The Chicago Tribune (periodical) 68
Cimola, Gino 164
Cioppa, Guy della *see* della Cioppa, Guy
Citizen Kane (movie) 141
Clark, Alice 113
Clark, Petula 170
Classic Stand-Up Comedy on Television (special) 157
Clem Kadiddlehopper 11, 13, 23, 44, 65, 67, 73, 80, 128, 133, 134, 152, 153, 160
Climax! 41, 42
Clooney, Rosemary 36, 163, 168
The Clown (movie) 24
Clown Alley (special) 93
Coates, Paul 164
Coates, Phyllis 36, 162
Cobb, Lee J. 131
Coburn, Charles 163, 164
Coca, Imogene 26, 152
Cole, Ike 170
Cole, Nat "King" 41, 170
The Colgate Comedy Hour 18, 26, 40, 86
Combat! 92
Come Backstage with Me (book) 25
The Comedy Spot 70
Complete Directory to Prime Time Network TV Shows: 1946–Present (book) 3, 132
Complete Encyclopedia of Television Series: 1947–1976 (book) 2
Conducts Music from the Heart (album) 113
Conniff, Ray 78
Connors, Mike 128, 129, 172, 173

Conreid, Hans 163–165, 167
Conway, Tim 83, 103, 171
Coogan, Jackie 82, 93, 163–173
Cook, Fielder 99
Cookie 45, 46
Cooper, Jackie 167
Cooper, Melville 163
Copeland, Alan 72, 76–78, 108–110, 160, 161, 175
The Cosby Show 124
Costello, Lou 86
The Courtship of Eddie's Father 124
Cox, Wally 171, 174
Crabbe, Buster 164, 166
Crane, Bob 171
Crane, Les 113
Crockett, Dick 165
Cronkite, Walter 114
Crosby, Bing 16
Cross, Jimmy 164, 167, 170, 172, 173
Cross, Perry 134, 135, 137–139, 161
Cross My Heart (movie) 24
Crystal, Billy 153
Cugat, Xavier 163
Curtis, Tony 36, 139, 163

Dailey, Dan
Daily Variety (periodical) 36, 43
Damone, Vic 169
Dana, Bill 83, 170
Dana, Vic 170
Danger 35
Dann, Mike 116, 117
The Danny Kaye Show 125
The Danny Thomas Show 51, 87, 123, 130
Darin, Bobby 170
Darro, Frankie 168, 170
Darwell, Jane 162
Davidson, Bill 57, 98
Davis, Andy 104
Davis, Beryl 169
Davis, Danny and the Nashville Brass 173
Davis, Georgia *see* Skelton, Georgia Davis
Davis, Jan 172
Davis, Mac 110, 173
Davis, Sammy, Jr. 147
Deacon, Richard 168
Deadeye 14, 21–23, 37, 44, 82, 110, 134

The Dean Martin Show 131
DeCamp, Rosemary 167
December Bride 31
Degeneres, Ellen 157
De Haven, Gloria 163
della Cioppa, Guy 94, 108, 118, 120, 121, 125, 127–129, 134, 161, 175
Demarest, William 166
Denny, Reginald 36, 163, 164
Denver, Bob 51
DeShannon, Jackie 173
"Desiderata" (recitation) 113
The Detectives 122
Devine, Andy 165
Dibbs, Kem 164
The Dick Van Dyke Show 81, 91, 93
Diller, Phyllis 170–172, 174
Dino (movie) 48
Dirksen, Sen. Everett McKinley 111, 112, 171, 172
Disneyland *see* Walt Disney
Dixon, Ivan 104
The Doctor 27
Dr. Christian (radio) 55
Dr. Kildare 83, 93, 95, 123
The Don Knotts Show 107
The Don Rickles Show 125
The Donald O'Connor Show 109
Donlevy, Brian 166
Donny and Marie 141
Donohue, Jack 39, 44, 161, 175
Donovan's Reef (movie) 96
Doodletown Pipers 84, 170, 172
The Doors 104
Dore, Ann 165
Dors, Diana 61, 167
Douglas, Jack 9, 12, 22, 161, 175
Douglas, Mike 145
Down Beat (periodical) 54
Downtoan Collection 113
Dragnet 116
Dru, Joanne 165
Drury, James 131, 174
Drysdale, Don 164
Duffy's Tavern (radio) 43, 86, 87
Duggan, Bob 167, 172, 173
The Duke 106
Dulo, Jane 168

182   Index

Dunaway, Faye 156
Dunn, James 164, 165
Dunne, Steve 165, 167
DuPont Cavalcade Theater 46, 67
DuPont Show of the Month 165–167
Durante, Jimmy 12, 26, 42, 106
Dusty's Trail 86

Ebsen, Buddy 170
The Ed Sullivan Show 1, 2, 18, 40, 52, 104, 123, 136, 137, 146
The Ed Wynn Show (1949–50 version) 26
The Ed Wynn Show (1958–59 version) 52
The Eddie Cantor Show (radio) 47, 87
Eden, Barbara 104
Edmiston, Walker 172, 173
Edwards, Penny 164
Eheart, Richard Bernard (Red's birth name) 6
Eisenhower, President Dwight D. 112, 165
Ellen 157
Ellington, Duke 173
Elliot, Dick 165
Elliott, Cass 133, 174
Ellison, Harlan 130
Emerson, Hope 165
Emmy awards and nominations 2, 3, 26, 27, 30, 38, 39, 46, 48, 57, 66, 71, 86, 91, 99, 106, 125, 126, 147, 148, 154, 155
Empire 92
Empire: William S. Paley and the Making of CBS (book) 117
Encyclopedia of Television Series, Pilots and Specials (1937–1984) (book) 3
Engel, Scott 166
Entertainment Tonight 154
Erlenborn, Ray 30, 55, 56, 63, 82, 142, 159, 175
Evans, Dale 171, 172
Evans, Maurice 171–173
An Evening with Fred Astaire (TV special) 15
Everett, Chad 133, 174
Executive Suite (movie) 24
Eyer, Richard 165
Eyer, Robert 165

F Troop 93
Fabian 166
The Fabulous Fordies (special) 148
Fair Exchange 123
Fairbanks, Douglas, Jr. 169
Falk, Peter 132, 171
Family Affair 95, 136, 137
Farah, Jameel *see* Farr, Jamie
Farr, Jamie 45, 46, 163, 164
Father Murphy 16
Faye, Alice 168
Faye, Joey 167
Feld, Fritz 164, 165
Feldon, Barbara 173
Felony Squad 95
Felton, Verna 13
Female Animal (movie) 115
Fenton Murray, John *see* Murray, John Fenton
Fidelman, Geoffrey Mark 56, 88
Fiedler, Arthur, and the Boston Pops 110, 172
Field, Virginia 163
Fields, W.C. 14
The Fifth Dimension 114, 171
Fio Rito, Ted 15
Fireman, Judy 149
Fireside Theatre 47
The First Annual Comedy Hall of Fame (special) 156
The First Edition 172, 173
Fisher, Eddie 41
Flavin, James 162
Fleming, Rhonda 167–169
Flight Command (movie) 10
The Flip Wilson Show 38, 39
Flynn, Errol 166
"The Foggy, Foggy Dew" (song) 112
Foley, Red 9
Fonda, Henry 147
Foran, Dick 164–167
Ford, Gerald R. 89, 148
Ford, Glenn 139
Ford, Paul 170
Ford, Ross 167, 172
Ford, Tennessee Ernie 148, 171
Ford Star Jubilee 41
Ford Theatre 47

Forrest, Sally 163, 164
Forrester, David 15
Forsythe, John 171
The Four Seasons 171
Four Star Revue see *All Star Revue*
Fowler, Will 22, 161
Fowley, Douglas 164, 170
Fox, Fred 106, 161
Franchi, Sergio 172
Frawley, William 53, 61–63, 165
Frazier, Hal 172
The Fred Allen Show (radio) 87
The Fred Waring Show 19
Freddie and the Dreamers 84, 170
Freddie the Freeloader 3, 29, 30, 53, 56, 61, 62, 65, 73, 110, 111, 133, 138, 145, 152, 160
Freedman, Benedict 12, 22, 57–59, 161
Freedman, Nancy 58, 59
Freeman, Devery 41–43
Freeman, Joan 111, 171
Freeman, Mona 165
French, Mary Meade 163
From a Bird's Eye View 137
From Here to Eternity (movie) 66
Frome, Milton 169
The Fugitive 96
The Fuller Brush Man (movie) 10, 41
Funny Faces (special) 152
Funny Faces III (special) 153
The Funny Side 139
Funt, Allen 171

Gabor, Eva 164, 174
Gabor, Zsa Zsa 163
The Gale Storm Show 86
Gangbusters 116
Gardner, Ed 43
Gardner, Gerald 126–129, 134, 135, 161
Garnett, Gale 169
The Garry Moore Show 66–68, 79, 132
Garson, Greer 169, 171
Gates, Maxine 166
Gaunt, John 32, 161, 175
Gazzara, Ben 132
G.E. Theater 47
Gehring, Wes D. 6
The Gene Autry Show 31, 35, 149

Index

The Gene Autry Show (radio) 55
The General Electric All-Star Anniversary (special) 147
General Hospital 81
George Appleby 20, 65, 73, 90
The George Burns and Gracie Allen Show 26
The George Burns Show 52
The George Gobel Show 38, 52, 76
Georgetown University Forum 31
Gertrude and Heathcliff 34, 75, 152, 153
Get Smart! 86, 122, 126
Get Yourself a College Girl (movie) 81
The Ghost and Mrs. Muir 122, 126
Gibbs, Georgia 40
Gift of the Magi (special) 165
Gilbert, Billy 48, 163–167
Giles, Sandra 165
Gilligan's Island 44, 57, 86, 176
Gilmore, Art 61, 62, 70, 75, 172
Glass, Ned 29
Glatzer, Hal 142, 150
Gleason, Jackie 43, 47, 52, 56, 65, 67, 117, 163, 167
Gobel, George 53, 83, 102, 135, 168–174
Godfrey, Arthur 85, 165, 167, 171, 172
The Golden Age of Television (book) 149
The Golden Girls 142
Goldman, Ben F., Jr. 151
Goldstein, Jesse 47, 56, 63, 161, 175
Gomer Pyle, U.S.M.C. 96
Goodman, Benny 15
Goodman, Hal 38, 161, 175
Goodyear Television Playhouse 18
Gordon, Al 38, 161
Gorshin, Frank 95, 171
Gosfield, Maurice 167
Gould, Jack 116, 130
Gould, Sandra 170
Goulet, Robert 113, 169, 171
Grable, Betty 40

Grade, Sir Lew 84, 85, 121
Graham, Billy 25
Grammy awards and nominations 69, 78, 110, 114
Granet, Bert 53
Graves, Peter 172
Grayco, Helen 163
"The Great White Hope" (recitation) 114
Greeley, Bill 136
Green, Mort 47, 86, 107, 125, 133, 161
Green, Stanley 107, 108, 118, 159
Green Acres 117, 136
Greenfield, Jeff 149
Grey, Virginia 49, 65, 90, 163–170
Griffin, Merv 85, 88, 169, 171, 172
Griffith, Andy 171
Guest, Christopher 153
Guestward Ho! 87, 88
Gun Shy 125
Gunsmoke 1, 2, 14, 51, 92, 131
Gunsmoke (radio) 60
Gussow, Mel 115
Gwynne, Fred 170

Hadley, Reed 165
Hale, Chanin 20, 74, 79–83, 109, 110, 115, 120, 132, 133, 138, 142, 146, 154, 159, 160, 161, 175
Hamer, Rusty 167
Hampton, Lionel 54
Hansen, Tom 3, 72, 78, 79, 99, 112, 142, 148, 158, 161, 173, 175
Happy Birthday, Bob: A Salute to Bob Hope's 75th Birthday (special) 147
Hardwicke, Sir Cedric 165, 167
Harkins, "Uncle Jim" 8
Harmon, Tom 164
Harpers Bizarre 129, 171
Harris, Jonathan 93, 94
Harris, Phil 168
Hatton, Raymond 165
Have Gun Will Travel 51
Having Wonderful Time (movie) 9
Hawaii Five-O 142, 143
Hawaiian Eye 83, 92
Hawn, Goldie 103
Hayakawa, Sessue 165

Hayes, Peter Lind 40
Hazel 122
Healy, Mary 40
Hee Haw 136, 137
Hendrix, Wanda 166
Henning, Paul 87
Henry, Emmaline 167, 168, 170–173
Henry, Hank 168, 169
Henry Fonda and the Family (special) 167
The Henry Vee Aqua Frolics 165
The Herb Shriner Show 26, 53
Herbert, Tim 172
Hewitt, Barbara 171
Hey Jeannie 106
Hey Mulligan see *The Mickey Rooney Show*
The Hi Los 163
High Adventure with Lowell Thomas 85
High Society (movie) 96
Highway to Heaven 16
Hillcrest Elementary School Choir of Los Angeles 169
Hines, Connie 169
Hippodrome 85, 121
Hirt, Al 169
Hobin, Bets 158
Hobin, Bill 76, 79, 80, 82–85, 99, 102, 106–108, 116, 118, 119, 127, 154, 158, 161, 176
Hoffman, Bern 172, 173
Hogan's Heroes 96, 104, 136
"Holiday for Strings" (song) 15, 69, 73
The Hollies 84, 170
Holloway, Stanley 170, 171
Holloway, Sterling 164, 165
Hollywood Is a Four-Letter Town (book) 150
The Hollywood Squares 141
Hollywood Talent Scouts 85
Home Improvement 1, 2
"Home to the Sea" (recitation) 114
The Honeycombs 84, 170
The Honeymooners 43, 65
Hope, Bob 15, 106, 114, 140, 141, 143, 147, 149, 155
Hopper, Carl 11
Horton, Edward Everett 29, 164–167

Index

Horton, Robert 168, 169
The Hour of Decision 25
House of Windsor cigar commercials 147
How Sweet It Was! (book) 2
How to Marry a Millionaire 106
Howard, Bruce 86, 161
Howard, Clint 173
Howdy Doody 60
Hudson, Rock 139
Hughes, Mary Beth 164–167
Hullabaloo 123
Humphrey, Hal 97
Humphrey, Vice Pres. Hubert 110, 172
Hussey, Ruth 164, 165

I Dood It! (movie) 11
I Dream of Jeannie 104
I Love Lucy 26–28, 47, 53, 63, 87, 97
I Married Joan 44, 86
I Spy 86
Ichabod and Me 68
I'll Be Right Back (book) 145
In All His Glory (book) 118
In Society (movie) 86
Incendiary Blonde (movie) 24
Influences: From Yesterday to Today: A Museum of Television and Radio Special 157
Inman, David 122
Inside the Dream Factory (special) 156
The Invaders 96, 104
Ireland, John 164
Iron Butterfly 102, 172
The Iron Horse 95
Ironside 131, 137
Isaacs, Charlie 99, 106, 161
It Takes a Thief 104
It's About Time 86
It's Always Jan 87
Ives, Burl 54, 172

The Jack Benny Program 38, 39, 52, 53, 86, 91, 122
The Jack Benny Program (radio) 31
Jack Benny's 20th TV Anniversary Special 86, 131

The Jack Paar Show see *The Tonight Show*
Jackie and Gayle 170, 171
The Jackie Gleason Show 59, 116
Jackson, Mahalia 90, 168
Jacobs, Seaman 106, 161
James, Harry 40
Jameson, Joyce 169, 171
Jan and Dean 170
Jankowski, Horst 170
Janssen, David 146
Jay and the Americans 84, 171
Jeffreys, Anne 164
Jeffries, Fran 171
Jencks, Richard A. 117
Jenkins, Allen 164, 167
Jenkins, Dan 39, 51, 54
The Jerry Lewis Show (1963 version) 134
The Jerry Lewis Show (1967–69 version) 105
Jillana 111, 171, 172
The Jim Nabors Hour 1, 148
The Jimmie Rodgers Show 129
The Joe Franklin Show 153
The Joey Bishop Show 122
The John Gary Show 110
The Johnny Cash Show 137
Johnson, Arte 166
Johnson, Van 172, 173
The Joker Is Wild (movie) 96
The Jonathan Winters Show 104
Jones, Betty 163
Jones, Jack 95, 170–172
Jones, James Earl 114
Jones, Tom 172
Jordan, Will 169
Joyce, Elaine 172
Joyce, Jimmy 108, 110, 161, 176
Judy Garland and Her Guests, Phil Silvers and Robert Goulet (special) 168
The Judy Garland Show 85
Julia 105, 136, 137
Julian, Arthur 38, 161
Jumbo (movie) 42
Junior, the "mean widdle kid" 11, 22, 91, 133

Kadiddlehopper, Clem see Clem Kadiddlehopper
Kaplan, Marvin 163, 165
Karloff, Boris 164, 172
Kaufman, Adam 173
Kaye, Mary, Trio 163
Kaye, Stubby 166, 168–170
Kean, Betty and Jane 40
Keaton, Buster 10, 155
Keel, Howard 111, 171
Kellogg, Ray 165–167
Kelly, Gene 139
Kelly, Paula 76
Kennedy, George 139
Kennedy, John F. 168
Kennedy, Tom 8, 9
The Kessler Twins 168, 169
Keyes, Freeman 9, 161
The King Family Show 123
King Sisters 37, 163
King Soloman's Mines (movie) 96
The Kingston Trio 64
The Kinks 84, 170
Kirkwood, Jack 12, 165–167
Kisseloff, Jeff 3
Kleeb, Helen 44, 163, 170
Klein, Larry 38, 161
Knoch, Lucille (Lucy) 3, 21, 23, 161
Knotts, Don 83, 167–169
Korman, Harvey 103
Koundakjian, Stephen J. 151, 176
Kovacs, Ernie 62, 66, 134
The Kraft Music Hall 136
Kramer, Billy J. and the Dakotas 84, 170
Kruschen, Jack 170
Kulky, Henry 62, 165, 167
Kulp, Nancy 164
Kyne, Terry 126–129, 135, 139, 142, 145, 158, 159, 161

Lafferty, Perry 104
Lahr, Bert 171
Laine, Frankie 40
Lake, Florence 172
Lamarr, Hedy 12
Lamas, Fernando 72, 169–171
Lamparski, Richard 25
Lancaster, Burt 36, 163
Lancer 121

Index

Landers, Muriel 170
Landon, Michael 16, 131, 146, 173
Lane, Abbe 163, 170, 171
Lang, Harold 40
Lanning, Jerry 168
Lassater, Carol 167
Lassie 32, 94, 119, 136, 137, 146
The Laugh Crafters (book) 13, 88, 98, 106
Lawrence, Carol 172, 173
Lawrence, Vicki 103
The Lawrence Welk Show 137
Lee, Brenda 168
Lee, Michele 171
Lee, Peggy 163
Leeds, Howard 38, 161
Leigh, Janet 95, 171, 173
Leonard, Jack E. 168
Lester, Jerry 26
Let's Make a Deal 137
The Lettermen 102, 168, 170, 172, 173
Lewis, Jerry 26, 106, 129–131, 173
Lewis, Reg 166
Liberace 36, 163, 165, 169, 172
Liberace, George 163
The Liberace Show 121
Library Journal (periodical) 59
The Life and Legend of Wyatt Earp 47
Life with Father 35
Like Young (album) 15
Li'l Abner (movie) 166
Lilies of the Field (movie) 97
Linkletter, Art 85, 114, 115
Linkletter, Diane 114, 115, 172
"Little Babe" (song) 112
Little House on the Prairie 16, 141
Lockhart, Gene 94
Lockhart, June 93, 94, 119, 159, 171, 172
Loftis, Linda 167
Logan, Brad 173
Logan, Ella 36, 163
London, Julie 61, 166
The Lone Ranger 31
Lonely Are the Brave 96
Lootville (book) 58, 59
Lord, Jack 142
Loren, Donna 170
Loring, Gloria 172

Lorre, Peter 43, 163, 164, 166
Los Angeles Free Press (periodical) 130
The Los Angeles Times (periodical) 97, 151
Los Chavales de España *see* Chavales de España, Los
Lost in Space 93, 94, 104, 119, 157
Louise, Tina 170
Love, American Style 124
Love That Bob see *The Bob Cummings Show*
Lovejoy, Frank 165
Lovely to Look At (movie) 10
Lubell, Roberta 167
The Lucille Ball–Desi Arnaz Show 53, 165
The Lucy Book (book) 56, 88
The Lucy Show 54, 88, 92, 95, 123
Ludwig von Humperdoo 133, 144
Lulu 172
Lump Lump, Willie *see* Willie Lump Lump
Lund, Jana 168
Lundberg, Victor 114
The Lux Show Starring Rosemary Clooney 76
Lyman, Arthur 167
Lynn, Mary 162
Lyou, Marshall 164

MacGyver 86
Mack, Ted 172
MacKenzie, Gisele 53
MacLaine, Shirley 139
MacMurray, Fred 147
MacRae, Gordon 168
MacRae, Sheila 168
Mad (magazine) 126
Madison, Guy 166
Maen, Norman 99
Make Room for Daddy see *The Danny Thomas Show*
Malanowski, Jamie 155
The Man and the City 139
The Man from U.N.C.L.E. 83, 93
"Man on the Moon" (recitation) 114
The Man Who Knew Too Much (movie) 96
Mancini, Ginny 77

Mancini, Henry 77
Mannix 128
Mansfield, Jayne 61, 166–168
The Many Loves of Dobie Gillis 51
Mara, Adele 166, 167
Marceau, Marcel 90, 115, 152, 157, 159, 160, 167, 169, 170
March, Frederic 48
Marciano, Rocky 164
Margetts, Monty 166
Marie, Rose *see* Rose Marie
Markay, Grace 172
Marsh, Earle 3, 132
Marsh, Jane 171
Marshall Dillon see *Gunsmoke*
Martin, Dean 26, 51, 106, 131, 139, 173
Martin, Mary 146
Martin, Tony 40
Marx, Arthur 6, 59, 149, 150
Marx, Groucho 149
Marx, Harpo 89, 90, 168
The Mary Tyler Moore Show 86, 142
*M*A*S*H* 1, 2, 45, 146
Massey, Curt 9
Mathis, Johnny 170
Matthau, Walter 156
Maude 142, 143
Maverick 52
Maxwell, Marilyn 40, 61, 164–168
Mayberry R.F.D. 136
Mayer, Louis B. 9, 14
McCambridge, Mercedes 165, 166
McCarthy, Nobu 165
McCarty, Mary 36, 163
McCormick, Pat 125, 161
McDonald, Marie 166
McGonigle, Strike-Out *see* Strike-Out McGonigle
The McGuire Sisters 169
McHale's Navy 83, 92, 93
McHugh, Frank 166
McKenzie, Ida Mae 172–174
McLeod, Norman Z. 42
McMillan and Wife 139
McNair, Barbara 171
McNeil, Alex 3
McNeill, Don 9
McPugg, Cauliflower 14

Meadows, Audrey 65, 82, 93, 102, 133, 135, 166–173
Meadows, Jayne 164–68
Meet Millie 46, 47
Meltzer, Lou 43, 44, 161
The Men from Shiloh see *The Virginian*
Mendes, Sergio, and Brasil 66 171
Merkel, Una 164
Merman, Ethel 40, 168
Merrill, Robert 93, 169, 170, 172, 173
The Merv Griffin Show 144
Michaels, Marilyn 171
The Mickey Rooney Show 59
The Mighty O (series pilot) 45, 46
The Mike Douglas Show 145
The Millionaire 47
The Mills Brothers 172, 173
Milton Berle Starring in the Kraft Music Hall 64
The Milton Berle Show see *Texaco Star Theater*
Mineo, Sal 48
Minow, Newton 66
Mission: Impossible 78, 93, 95
Mr. Ed 86
Mr. Novak 92
Mitchell, Frank 166
Mitchell, Shirley 169, 170
Mitchell Boys Choir 163, 165, 167
Mittleman, Rick 86, 161
The Mod Squad 131
Modern Screen (periodical) 132
The Modernaires 76, 77, 161
Mohr, Gerald 164–166
Mona McCluskey 106
Monday Night Football 1, 2
The Monkees 95, 126
Monroe, Marilyn 61, 80
Moore, Archie 76, 169
Moore, Garry 67, 79, 81, 165, 167
Moore, Terry 165, 166
Moorehead, Agnes 173
Moreno, Rita 165
Morgan, Jane 171
Morris, Chester 164

Morrison, Barbara 66, 170
Morrow, Karen 168
Morse, Robert 20, 170
Mott, Robert L. 3, 105, 107, 161, 176
Movie of the Week 105
Mowbray, Alan 164
Munro, Matt 171
Munsel, Patrice 82, 159, 170–172
Munshin, Jules 168, 169
Murray, John Fenton 12, 22, 161, 176
The Music Man (movie) 97
My Favorite Martian 86, 123
My Little Margie 28
My Six Loves (movie) 97
My Three Sons 123
"My Way" (song) 114
My World ... and Welcome to It 124

Nabors, Jim 175
Nagel, Conrad 26
Naked City 67
The Name of the Game 136
The National Enquirer (periodical) 142, 150
Neise, George 166, 167
Nelson, Harriet 11, 13, 95, 171, 172
Nelson, Ozzie 11, 13, 95, 171, 172
The New Bill Cosby Show 125
New Christy Minstrels 170
The New Red Skelton Show 44
New York City Ballet 163
The New York Times (periodical) 115, 116, 130, 161, 168, 169
Newdow, Michael 115
The Newlywed Game 137
Newsweek (periodical) 14, 22, 27, 44, 51, 57
Nichols, Barbara 64, 165, 166
Nielsen, Leslie 133, 173
Nightcap 126
Nixon, Pres. Richard M. 115, 129, 148
Noonan, Tommy 168
Norback, Craig T. and Peter G. 149
Norman, Lucille 163
North, Jay 166, 167

"Norwegian Wood" (song) 78

O'Brian, Hugh 169
O'Brien, Dave 47, 56, 63, 86, 107, 161, 176
O'Brien, Edmond 163
O'Brien, Pat 164
Occasional Wife 96
Ocean's Eleven (movie) 41
O'Connell, Helen 167–169
O'Connor, Donald 109, 110
O'Hanlon, George 166
Oliver 173
Oliver, Myrna 151
Omar Khayyam (movie) 97
"An Open Letter to My Teenage Son" (recitation) 113, 114
Oppenheimer, Jess 87
Orben, Robert 60, 88, 89, 99, 106, 107, 112, 117–119, 148, 151, 153, 154, 156, 158, 160, 161, 176
The Original Caste 173
The Oscars 145
Osmond, Cliff 170

Paar, Jack 56, 125, 134
Paige, Janis 82, 87, 165, 168, 169, 171
Pal Joey (movie) 24
Palance, Jack 48
Paley, William S. 16, 116–118
Palmer, Peter 166
Panama Hattie (movie) 10
Pangborn, Franklin 165
Pantomime Quiz 67
Paper, Lewis J. 117
The Paris Sisters 168, 169
Parker, Eddie 163
Parker, Fess 173
Parker, Jean 164
Parrish, Leslie 166, 167
Pasternak, Joe 42
The Paul Winchell–Jerry Mahoney Show 32
Pearson, GeGe 13
Pearson, Jesse 114
People (periodical) 6, 142, 150, 157
Perkins, Gil 162
Perrin, Nat 39, 161, 176
Perry Presents 76
Person to Person 54
The Persuaders 139

Index

Pete and Gladys 86, 88
Peter and Gordon 170
Peter Gunn 122
Peters, Kelly Jean 104
Petrulis, Kenneth G. 151
Petticoat Junction 1, 91, 117, 119
Peyton Place 123
The Phil Baker Show (radio) 57
The Phil Silvers Show see You'll Never Get Rich
Philco Television Playhouse 18
Philip Marlowe 67
Phillips, Arthur 57, 86, 126, 161
The Phyllis Diller Show see The Pruitts of Southampton
A Pictorial History of Television (book) 2
Pitts, ZaSu 164
Playhouse 90 48, 166
"The Pledge of Allegiance" (recitation) 112–115
Ponce, Poncie 169
Potter, Peter 164
Powell, Jane 168, 171–173
Powers, Beverly 172, 173
Presley, Elvis 97, 110, 114
Presnell, Harv 170
Previn, Andre 15
Price, Gilbert 171
Price, Vincent 70, 82, 93, 102, 135, 141, 152, 163–174
The Price Is Right 122
Prickett, Maudie 168
Priest, Pat 172
The Princess and the Pirate (movie) 15
Producers on Producing (book) 18
Producers Showcase 48
Professional Father 87
Proudly They Came (album) 114
Provine, Dorothy 167
Prowse, Juliet 168
The Pruitts of Southampton 96
Psycho (movie) 97
Public Pigeon Number One 41–43
Puckett, Gary, and the Union Gap 173
Pupa, Piccola 169

Quinn, Anthony 139
Quinn, Howard 107, 108, 126, 161

Raaf, Vicki 163
Rackin, Marty 32, 39, 161, 176
Radio Live! Television Live! (book) 107
Raft, George 43, 163, 166
Ragaway, Martin 38, 57, 106, 161, 176
A Raisin in the Sun (movie) 97
The Raleigh Cigarette Program (radio show) 11, 13
Randall, Tony 171, 174
Randolph, Isabel 167
Raney, Sue 172
Rankin, Arthur, Jr. 144
The Rat Patrol 95
Rathbone, Basil 163, 166
Ratoff, Gregory 164
Rawls, Lou 171–173
Ray, Johnnie 23
Raye, Martha 15, 60, 83, 93, 135, 168–174
Raymond, Gene 165
Rea, Peggy 173, 174
Rear Window (movie) 96
Recruit Bluejacket Choir from the U.S. Naval Training Center in San Diego 171
Red, San Fernando see San Fernando Red
The Red Buttons Show 87
Red Skelton (book) 149
The Red Skelton Chevy Special 54
Red Skelton Conducts (album) 113
The Red Skelton Hour 71–122, 137
Red Skelton Presents Freddie the Freeloader's Christmas Dinner see Red Skelton's Christmas Dinner
The Red Skelton Revue 35
The Red Skelton Scrapbook 30
The Red Skelton Timex Special 54
Red Skelton's Christmas Dinner (special) 152
Red Skelton's More Funny Faces (special) 152
The Redettes 161

Redigo 92
Reiner, Carl 48, 91
Reiser, Paul 157
Remington Steele 86
The Restless Gun 31
Revere, Paul, and the Raiders 102, 173
Reynolds, Burt 125
Reynolds, Debbie 41
Rhine, Larry 86, 87, 106, 126, 148, 161, 176
Rich, John 91
The Rifleman 68
Riley, Jack 133
Risk, Linda Sue 110, 171, 173
Ritchard, Cyril 168, 171, 173
Ritchard, Jack 151
Ritter, John 156
Rivers, Johnny 84, 169–171
Robbins, Gale 164
Robert F. Kennedy: A Memorial (album) 114
Robertson, Cliff 95, 171
Robertson, Dale 172
Robinson, Hubbell 39, 52
The Rockin' Berries 170
Rocky and His Friends 11
Rogers, Ginger 168, 169
Rogers, Kenny 173
Rogers, Roy 171, 172
Rogers, Sheilah 169
The Rolling Stones 84, 169
Roman, Ruth 163
Roman Holiday (movie) 96
Romay, Lina 164
Romero, Cesar 61, 82, 93, 163–171, 173
Room 222 124
Rooney, Mickey 9, 59, 82, 135, 141, 144, 164, 165, 167–173
Roos, Bo 24, 32
Roosevelt, President Franklin D. 9
Rose, David 15, 16, 22, 40, 63, 69, 71, 72, 77, 112, 132, 134, 135, 161, 176
Rose Marie 44, 163
Rosenbloom, "Slapsie" Maxie 165, 166
Ross, Arthur 38, 161
Ross, Bob 38, 161
Ross, David 38, 161
Ross, Joe E. 172

Roth, Lillian 163
The Rounders 96
Rowan and Martin's Laugh-In 86, 95, 103, 110, 120, 121, 126, 154
Rubin, Benny 24, 25, 162, 168
Rudie, Evelyn 164
Rudolph the Red-Nosed Reindeer 144
Rudolph's Shiny New Year (special) 144
The Rudy Vallee Show (radio show) 8
Ruggles, Charles 164–168
Ruick, Barbara 36, 163
Russell, Connie 163
Russell, Jackie 172
Russell, Jane 61, 166, 169
Russell, Nipsey 171, 172
Rutherford, Ann 41, 43, 165
Rydell, Bobby 84, 93, 166–170, 172

Sabre Jet (movie) 24
Sabrina (movie) 96
Sahara Hotel chorus line 163
St. John, Jill 174
Saks, Sol 13
A Salute to Television's 25th Anniversary (special) 143
San Fernando Red 14, 22, 23, 45, 65, 73, 94, 133
Sandler, Tony, and Ralph Young 171–173
Santa Barbara 81
Sarge 139
Sarnoff, Tom 125
Saturday Evening Post (periodical) 57, 98, 100
Saturday Night at the Movies 96
Saturday Night Live 153, 176
Saturday Review (periodical) 59, 124, 139
Savalas, Telly 173
Schallert, William 166
Schiller, Bob 54, 87, 88, 97–99, 106, 147, 148, 161, 176
Schlitz Playhouse of Stars 46
Schlosser, Herb 105, 120, 121, 124–126, 136, 140, 159, 176
Schneider, Jack 117

Schwartz, Al 57, 161, 176
Schwartz, Sherwood 44, 45, 47, 49, 56, 57, 63, 65, 66, 86, 98, 107, 148, 161, 176
Scott, George C. 170
SCTV Network 126
The Searchers 84, 169
See It Now 163, 164
The Serenaders 171
Serling, Rod 48, 49
Sesame Street 60
77 Sunset Strip 92
Shagnasty, Bolivar *see* Bolivar Shagnasty
Shannon, Bill 172, 173
Shapiro, Ken 75, 76, 151
Sharpe, David 110, 170
Shaw, Reta 170–172
Shay, Dorothy 163
Shermet, Hazel 86
Sherwood, Roberta 62
Shindig 123
Shirley's World 139
Shoestring Safari (pilot) 104
Shore, Dinah 54, 114, 146
Shower of Stars 39, 40, 41, 48, 69
Showtime 121
Shriner, Herb 26
Shulman, Arthur 2
Sick (magazine) 126
The Sid Caesar, Imogene Coca, Carl Reiner, Howard Morris Special 99
The Silent Show (special) 62
The Silkie 170
Silverman, Fred 116
Silvers, Phil 146
Simmons, Ed 57, 86, 87, 98, 161, 176
Simon and Garfunkel 170, 171
The Simpsons 13
Sinatra, Frank 36, 54, 114, 144, 147, 163
Sinatra, Frank, Jr. 173
Sinatra: The First 40 Years (special) 147
Singleton, Doris 170
60 Minutes 1, 2
The $64,000 Question 47, 49, 66, 122
Skelton, Chris (Red's brother) 7
Skelton, Edna Stilwell (Red's first wife) 7–9

Skelton, Georgia Davis (Red's second wife) 12, 142, 144, 172
Skelton, Joseph (Red's father) 6, 7
Skelton, Joseph Ishmal (Red's brother) 7
Skelton, Lothian Toland (Red's third wife) 141, 142, 158, 159, 176
Skelton, Red: birth name (Richard Bernard Eheart) 6; birthday 6; characters *see* Bolivar Shagnasty; Cauliflower McPugg; Charlie the Swinger; Clem Kadiddlehopper; Cookie; Deadeye; Freddie the Freeloader; George Appleby; Gertrude and Heathcliff; Junior; Ludwig von Humperdoo; San Fernando Red; Strike-Out McGonigle; Willie Lump Lump; childhood 6, 7; children *see* Skelton, Richard and Skelton, Valentina; death 140, 156, 157; father 6, 7; wives *see* Skelton, Edna Stilwell; Skelton, Georgia Davis; and Skelton, Lothian Toland
Skelton, Richard (Red's son) 22, 63–65, 144
Skelton, Valentina (Red's daughter) 64, 65, 132, 176
The Skelton Dancers 161
The Skeltones 77, 161
The Skylarks 21, 22
Smith 173
Smith, Charlie 167
Smith, Hal 170
Smith, Keely 168
Smith, Sally Bedell 118
Smokey and the Bandit (movie) 125
Smothers, Tom and Dick 103
The Smothers Brothers Comedy Hour 39, 97, 102, 103, 110
The Snobs 169
Snorkel 45, 46
"So in Love" (song) 15
Somers, Suzanne 147

Index 189

"Somewhere, My Love" (song) 78
Sommers, Joanie 84, 168, 169, 171
The Sonny and Cher Comedy Hour 137, 138, 141
Soo, Jack 169, 172
A Southern Yankee (movie) 10
Sparks, Randy 165
Spellman, Larry 126
Spotlight 85, 121
Spotlight Playhouse 46, 70
Springfield, Dusty 171
Spy (periodical) 155
Stack, Robert 171
Stafford, Jo 168, 169
Stagecoach West 67
Stalag 17 (movie) 96
Stander, Arthur 38, 161, 176
Stang, Arnold 164
Stanton, Frank 117
Star Trek 93, 95
Starr, Kay 168
Startime 51, 52, 68
Stempel, Tom 86
Sten, Anna 164
Sterling, Robert 68
The Steve Allen Show (1956–61 version) 38, 52, 130
The Steve Allen Show (1968–72 version) 126
The Steve Lawrence Show 85
Stevens, Connie 83, 169, 170
Stevens, Craig 45, 46, 165
Stewart, Jimmy 51, 147
Stewart, Martha 163
Stilwell, Edna *see* Skelton, Edna Stilwell
Stop Me If You've Heard This One 24, 25
Story, Ralph 165
Storytellers to the Nation (book) 86
Stout, Clarence 7
Stratton, Gil 165
Strauss, Robert 168
Strike-Out McGonigle 19
The "Stripper (song) 69
Stuart, Connie 115
Stuart, Gil 165, 167
Studio One 48, 80
Sullivan, Ed 37, 47, 143, 163, 167, 172, 173
The Summer Smothers Brothers Show 110

The Supremes 84, 170
"Suspicious Minds" (song) 114
Suzuki, Pat 169
Sweeney, Bob 164
Sweetwater 173
Swing Out, Sweet Land (special) 131
Synanon (movie) 81

Talbot, Lyle 164
Talent Scouts 85
Tapps, Georgie 163
Tarzan 95
Taylor, Elizabeth 147
Taylor, Robert 10
Taylor, Wilda 162
Telephone Time 67
Television Age (periodical) 19
Television Playhouse see Goodyear Television Playhouse and *Philco Television Playhouse*
Television: The First 50 Years (book) 149
The Television Years (book) 2
Temple, Shirley 91, 168
Terrace, Vincent 2, 3
Terry-Thomas 171, 172
Texaco Star Theater 26, 35, 47, 116, 124
Texaco Star Theater (radio) 55
That Girl 95
That Was the Week That Was 106, 126
That's My Boy 87
They Stand Accused 26
Thinnes, Roy 96
This Is Tom Jones 99, 124
This Is Your Life 10
Thomas, Danny 67, 87, 93, 147, 167
Those Magnificent Men in Their Flying Machines (movie) 42
Three Dog Night 102, 173
Three's Company 147
Thriller 67
Tightrope 68
Tim, Tiny *see* Tiny Tim
The Tim Conway Comedy Hour 148, 176
Time (periodical) 51, 55
Tiny Tim 119, 173
To Each His Own (movie) 24
To Tell the Truth 68

Toast of the Town see *The Ed Sullivan Show*
The Today Show 18
Toland, Gregg 141
Toland, Lothian *see* Skelton, Lothian Toland
The Tom Ewell Show 67, 68
Tong, Kam 162
The Tonight Show 18, 34, 38, 56, 57, 83, 89, 125, 128, 132, 134, 144–146, 154
The Tony Martin Show 15
Tony Orlando and Dawn 141
Torres, Hector 165
Total Television (book) 3, 169
Totter, Audrey 60, 164–166
Traubel, Helen 163
A Tribute to "Mr. Television": Milton Berle (special) 146
Tribute to Stan Laurel (special) 170
Truex, Ernest 167
Tucker, Forrest 164, 168
Tuesday Night at the Movies 96, 97
Tuttle, Gene 54
Tuttle, Lurene 13
TV Book (book) 149
TV Digest (periodical) 19
The TV Encyclopedia (periodical) 122
TV Guide (periodical) 3, 12, 16, 19, 22, 26–28, 31, 39, 46, 48, 49, 51, 54, 60, 63, 64, 81, 100, 101, 126, 127, 157, 161, 168, 169, 176
TV Guide Almanac (book) 149
TV Guide: The First 25 Years (book) 3
TV Radio Mirror (periodical) 30, 64, 66
Twenty-One 122
The Twilight Zone 123
Two Tickets to Broadway (movie) 24
The Tycoon 93, 106

Umeki, Miyoshi 168
The U.S. Drum and Bugle Team of Pacific Fleet Force 170
The U.S. Steel Hour 46

Vallee, Rudy 8, 87, 165
Vampira 163
Van, Bobby 40, 41
Van Bernard, Victor 6
Van Bernard Productions 6, 94, 104
Vance, Vivian 53, 65, 166, 167, 169
Van Doren, Mamie 61, 166, 167
Van Dyke, Dick 171
Van Dyke and Company 86
Variety (periodical) 25, 28, 36, 46, 51, 61, 63, 66, 101, 130, 136, 143, 169
Vaughn, Robert 83, 170, 171
Velasco, Vi 169
Verdugo, Elena 164–166
A Very Brady Christmas (special) 148
Vickers, Yvette 162
Vignon, Jean-Paul 169
Villani, Fred 172
Vincent, Romo 170
The Virginian 122, 123, 131, 136
The Vogues 172, 173
Von Humperdoo, Ludwig *see* Ludwig von Humperdoo

Waggoner, Lyle 103
Wagner, Robert 104, 173
Wagon Train 51, 122
Walker, Nancy 61, 163, 165
Wallis, Shani 76, 169, 172
Walt Disney 1, 2, 47, 123, 144
The Waltons 44, 141
The Warner twins 164
Warwick, Dionne 84, 171, 172
Watch the Birdie (movie) 41
Wayne, Carol 128

Wayne, John 28, 110, 131, 132, 147, 170, 173
Wayne and Shuster 67, 167
"We Love You, Call Collect" (recitation) 114
Weaver, Pat 18, 32
The Web 27
Webster, Tony 106, 161
Wechter, Julius 173
Wedlock, Hugh 86, 161, 176
Weiskopf, Bob 54, 87, 88, 97–99, 106, 147, 148, 161, 176
Weld, Tuesday 166
Welles, Orson 141
West, Mae 61, 166
The Westinghouse Desilu Playhouse 49, 53, 87
Whatever Became Of ...? Tenth Series 25
What's My Line? 40, 53
Where Was I? 47
Which Way to the Front? (movie) 129
Whistling in the Dark (movie) 10
White Christmas (movie) 96
Whiting, Margaret 163
Whitney, Douglas 39, 161
Whitney, Dwight 12, 27, 31, 64, 126–128
Wickes, Mary 169, 170
Wilcox, Frank 165, 167
Wild, Jack 173
Wild Kingdom 136, 137
Wilk, Max 149
Williams, Bill 163
Williams, Cara 167
Williams, Martin 139
Willie Lump Lump 14, 23, 28, 65, 88
Wilson, Don 166
Wilson, Marie 61, 164, 165
Wilson, Nancy 170, 171
Wilson, Robin 128, 173
Wilson, Spanky 172

Winchell, Paul 32
Windsor, Marie 164–167
Winnie the Pooh and the Blustery Day (special) 137, 173
Winters, Jonathan 104, 156
Winters, Roland 164, 167, 168, 170
The Womenfolk 169
Wonder Man (movie) 16
Wonder Woman 126
The Wonderful World of Disney see *Walt Disney*
Wood, Bob 116–118
Wright, Beverley 168
Wyman, Jane 172
Wynn, Ed 7, 26, 48, 49, 67, 73, 83, 163, 167, 169, 170
Wynn, Keenan 73, 166, 167

Yamaguchi, Shirley 163
You Asked for It 31
You Bet Your Life 26
You Came Along (movie) 24
You'll Never Get Rich 47, 52, 106, 146
Youman, Roger 2
Young, Alan 27
Young, Gig 138, 170
Young, Jordan R. 13, 88, 98, 106
Young Americans 172
The Young and the Restless 56
The Young Lawyers 131
Young Man's Lament (album) 15
Youngfolk 169–172
Your Hit Parade 76, 78, 85, 148
Your Show of Shows 26

Zorro 80

www.ingramcontent.com/pod-product-compliance
Ingram Content Group UK Ltd.
Pitfield, Milton Keynes, MK11 3LW, UK
UKHW042010140426
5217IPUK00015B/1090